D0004744

The Mythology of Imperialism

THE Mythology OF IMPERIALISM

Rudyard Kipling · Joseph Conrad
E. M. Forster · D. H. Lawrence
and Joyce Cary

by Jonah Raskin

 Published in the United States by Random House, Inc., New York, and simultaneously in Canada by Random House of Canada Limited, Toronto.

ISBN: 0-394-46837-6

Library of Congress Catalog Card Number: 78-159368

Acknowledgment is gratefully extended to the following for permission to reprint from their works:

The Bodleian Library, Oxford: From unpublished material by Joyce Cary.

Jonathan Cape Ltd.: "Pierre Loti" from *Selected Poems* by Nazim Hikmet, translated by Taner Baybars. Distributed in the United States by Grossman Publishers.

Doubleday & Company, Inc., Mrs. George Bambridge, and A. P. Watt & Son: "The Craftsman" in *The Years Between* by Rudyard Kipling. Copyright 1919 by Rudyard Kipling.

Dufour Editions, Inc. and Jonathan Cape Ltd.: From *The Near and the Far* by L. H. Myers.

Harcourt Brace Jovanovich, Inc. and Faber and Faber Ltd.: From "The Waste Land" in *Collected Poems 1909–1962* by T. S. Eliot. Copyright 1936 by Harcourt Brace Jovanovich, Inc.; Copyright © 1963, 1964 by T. S. Eliot.

Harcourt Brace Jovanovich, Inc. and Edward Arnold (Publishers) Ltd.: From *A Passage to India* by E. M. Forster.

Harcourt Brace Jovanovich, Inc. and Ann Elmo Agency, Inc.: "A Worker Reads History" by Bertolt Brecht from *Selected Poems of Bertolt Brecht*, translated by H. R. Hays. Copyright 1947 by Bertolt Brecht and H. R. Hays.

Harper & Row Publishers, Inc. and Curtis Brown Ltd.: From *The Horse's Mouth* and *Mister Johnson* by Joyce Cary.

The Macmillan Company, W. B. Yeats and Macmillan & Company Ltd.: From "The Circus Animals' Desertion" in *Collected Poems of W. B. Yeats*. Copyright 1940 by Georgie Yeats, renewed 1968 by Bertha Georgie Yeats, Michael Butler Yeats and Anne Yeats.

Manufactured in the United States of America by

Kingsport Press, Kingsport, Tenn.

24689753

FIRST EDITION

This book was written with a little help from my friends. I want to thank them all. Some of my professors and teachers helped too. A long time ago Frank Kermode suggested that I write a book on this subject. Arnold Kettle, C. B. Cox and R. G. Cox read and criticized my work. Maxwell Geismar forced me to write this book. Without his encouragement it would never have been finished. Geismar's stance is exemplary. Because he went before and attacked the cold-war critics I could follow with this book.

J. R.

TO

Ho Chi Minh

If imperialism provides sources of aid to the professions, arts, and publications, it is always well understood that their products must reflect its interests, aims and "nothingness." On the other hand, the novels which attempt to reflect the reality of the world of imperialism's rapacious deeds; the poems aspiring to protest against its enslavement, its interference in life, in thought, in the very bodies of nations and peoples; and the militant arts which in their expression try to capture the forms and content of imperialism's aggression and the constant pressure on every progressive living and breathing thing and on all that is revolutionary, which teaches, which—full of light and conscience, of clarity and beauty—tries to guide men and peoples to better destinies, to the highest summits of life and justice—all these meet imperialism's severest censure. They run into obstacles, condemnation, and McCarthyite persecution. Its presses are closed to them; their names are barred from its columns of print and a campaign of the most atrocious silence is imposed against them—which is another contradiction of imperialism. For it is then that the writer, poet, painter, sculptor, the creator in any material, the scientist, begins truly to live in the tongue of the people, in the hearts of millions of men throughout the world. Imperialism puts everything backward, deforms it, diverts it into its own channels for profit, to multiply its dollars; buying words or paintings or stutterings or turning into silence the expression of revolutionists, of progressive men, of those who struggle for the people and their needs.

—FIDEL CASTRO, *"The Second Declaration of Havana,"* 1962

Contents

A Voice from the Third World

"Opium!
Submission!
Kismet!
Lattice-work, caravanserai
fountains
a sultan dancing on a silver tray!
Maharajah, rajah,
a thousand-year-old shah!
Waving from minarets
clogs made of mother-of-pearl;
women with henna-stained noses
working their looms with their feet.
In the wind, green-turbaned imams
calling people to prayer";

This is the Orient the French poet sees.
This
is
the Orient of those books
that come out from the press
at the rate of a million a minute.
But
yesterday
today
or tomorrow
an Orient like this
never existed
and never will.

Orient!
The soil on which
naked slaves die of hunger.
The common property of everyone
except those born on it.
The land where hunger itself
perishes with famine!

But the silos are full to the brim,
full of grain—
only for Europe.

Asia!
where the young Chinese
hang themselves
with their long hair
like yellow tapers
from the masts of American dreadnoughts.
And on the highest
the steepest
the most snowy
hill of the Himalayas
British officers listen to a jazz band—
down, they dip their soiled feet
into the Ganges
where
pariahs drop corpses with white teeth.
And Anatolia has become
Colonel Armstrong's
training ground.

Orient has had enough!
Orient will swallow
no more—
we're sick of it, sick!
If one of you, Loti,
can give life
to a famishing cow
but if he's a bourgeois
to hell with him!
And especially you,
you Pierre Loti
like a typhus bug
going through
our yellow, oiled skins—
a French officer seems
more sympathetic.

But you, as a French officer, Loti,
how could you forget so quickly,
far quicker
than a prostitute,
the value of a man
who'd just been freed?
You planted his head
on our heart
and taking it for a wooden target
you shot your bullets at it.

Those who do not know
must know now:
you are no better than a charlatan.
A charlatan
who sells in the East
rotten French fabrics
at a profit of five hundred per cent.
Pierre Loti,
oh, what a pig of a bourgeois you are!
If I believed in a soul separate from matter,
on the liberation day of the East
I would crucify your soul
at the head of a bridge
and smoke in front of it.
I give you my hands
We give you our hands
the *sansculottes* of Europe;
let's ride our horses together,
look
the halting-place is near
the day of freedom nearer still.
In front of us
The Year of Liberation of the East
waving a blood-red handkerchief!

Our horses' hoofs
go deep
into the belly of imperialism.

—Nazim Hikmet, "Pierre Loti," 1925

The Mythology of Imperialism

ɫ ɫ ɫ ɫ ɫ ɫ ɫ

Introduction: Bombard the Critics

We, the readers and students of literature, have been hijacked. The literary critics, our teachers, those assassins of culture, have put us up against the wall and held us captive. In classrooms we sat passively and took notes. We were paralyzed, afraid of their power. One hand raised to question might have ended a career, closed the road to success. Confronted with their books, those long, boring reading lists, we were surrounded and taken prisoner. In this helpless position a portion of our lives was extracted, hoarded, invested, transformed.

They have thieved our books, our movies, our hair, our life styles, our words, our passions, our tribal rites. They, the murderers with the pen, have kidnapped our poets, playwrights, novelists, essayists, and demanded ransom—a little piece of our hearts pledged to love the monsters they have manufactured. The writers they held up for us to idolize were either false gods or distorted copies of genuine articles. They wanted their hands on some cold cash, too. We fulfilled our part of the bargain; we have paid to live in bondage to their literary pontifications.

They have conspired for a world-wide cultural coup d'état, plotted to run the world's culture like an industry. Agents were sent to every country. They smuggled literary forgeries in little black bags into libraries and bookstores, planted them on shelves and pawned them off as the real thing. They assassinated revolutionary culture, propped up crumbling academies and bought off young armed poets on the barricades. They banished revolutionary artists, forced them into exile, cut them off from their people, their land, isolated them in foreign cities. They jailed them at home, gagged them to enforce silence and end the words of rage and love. In operating theaters they performed surgery on the artist's work. With their scalpels they hacked away, mutilating and dismembering. At the end the corpse was shipped off to the morgue.

Who are these gangsters, conspirators and terrorists of the literary page? We see their faces on their Wanted posters: T. S. Eliot, E. M. Forster, F. R. Leavis, Lionel Trilling. Nearly all of them are neatly attired men in three-piece suits. They remind us of corporation executives or investment bankers. No Day-Glo paints for them, no long hair, no army fatigues or beards. There is nothing bohemian, or beat, or hippie or freaky about them. They are straights; uptight. Here they are.

The first and most important of them is T. S. Eliot. Eliot comes at us armed with tradition. He stands in the pulpit before the Cross beseeching us to revere the past, preserve the relics of Christianity and come forward to swallow the wafer of empire. His sermon is about anarchy and art. Contemporary history is anarchy, futility, disorder; the cultural atmosphere is polluted, the novel cannot survive. This is what Reverend Eliot preaches. The novel is dead, he says. All art is on the verge of extinction. We look around and see that we are at a funeral for artists. So that art may endure, the writer must resurrect the past, construct a myth, offer a simple diagram for salvation.

Eliot fears civil war. When you off the king, he says, you off art. When Roundheads and Cavaliers cross swords, poets work at cross-purposes. When Northerners and Southerners take up arms, literature is shot full of holes. When in 1914 Europe becomes one battlefield, when in 1917 whites and reds shell one another, culture is bombed. Disturbances in the social world, he laments, are reproduced with grave consequences in the cultural arena. In civil war the ladder of art is chopped into little pieces. The world is leveled. The old authority is toppled. In his royal chambers Eliot is struck with a nightmare. He sees an earthquake: the world split in two, cities sink into the crevice. The writer's head is split too. It comes apart, divides into two parts separated by a chasm. Between the two halves there is no bridge. No longer can the artist simultaneously think and feel as he did in the Middle Ages, before the advent of capitalism, the Protestant ethic, the bourgeois revolution. No longer can he read Jean-Paul Sartre, make love to Jane Fonda and fuse it all together —the intellect and the passion—in a poem. Our minds are blown in two. Our society blown to the winds. In the holocaust Eliot builds an enclave. He wants protection from change and upheaval. Anarchy destroys art: that is his sermon. He spreads the most malicious of modern cultural myths, the myth that art demands order. His solution is totalitarian politics and culture, a close watch, a tight rein on everyone.

Tradition, the dominant idea in the minds of modern critics, is a fraud. What have you got when you possess a Great Tradition? Nothing. F. R. Leavis, the major British critic of the forties and fifties, heard Eliot's sermon, responded to the plea and wrote his own version of the tradition in his study of the English novel. He insists that Jane Austen, George Eliot, Henry James, Joseph Conrad and D. H. Lawrence are the major English novelists. Leavis issues them cards in the Great Tradition Club. He turns down Dickens's application. From the start there is a gaping hole which cannot be filled. The machinery which generates Jane Austen, he says, also generates Joseph Conrad. Leavis does not account for social or cultural changes. He does not illuminate either Jane Austen or D. H. Lawrence by putting them together in the same bag. He is left with an empty bag. It appears that Leavis did not notice sex. It is a cruel joke to have lusty Lawrence embrace frigid Austen. She would run away shrieking. The word "fuck" is not in *Pride and Prejudice,* but it is in *Lady Chatterly's Lover.* Leavis's tradition cannot explain why it—and the act of making love—appears in one and not the other. It puts a clean sheet over the naked man and the naked woman. It covers up the sexual revolution in society and the orgy in the English novel. Lawrence watched Victorian men and women getting into bed with each other. He saw them making love and he knew something was wrong. There was a dead thing between them as they lay together in each other's arms. Englishmen conquered the world, constructed an empire, but between English men and women there was an emptiness. Lawrence began filling the gap with a new, quivering force. We draw a blank from Leavis on that score. Leavis's tradition is silent too when we ask it why Conrad's world is unlike George Eliot's. Leavis has not gotten his fingers into the mud of imperialism and so he cannot feel the extraordinary force of Conrad: his extremes, his terrors, his darkness, his revolutions, his explosions. George Eliot's planet Earth was transformed by Conrad's contemporaries. He mapped the changes; he followed the bulldozer into the jungle. He pried open the future while Eliot excavated the past. He voyaged to the Congo while she sat in London.

Leavis tells us that Austen, Eliot and Conrad share a "reverent openness before life." But *The Great Tradition* blocks the exits to life. It is containment criticism. The three writers Leavis toys with are yanked away from society and hung up to dry on a literary clothesline. Soon enough he has hung them to death. They exist for him only insofar as they converse with each other and plug into his own moral circuit. They are sealed off from their cultures and their nations.

E. M. Forster also divorces art from life. He refuses to see the entanglements of literature and society, culture and politics, writers and history. When we read a poem, Forster says, "common knowledge disappears and uncommon knowledge takes its place. We have entered a universe that only answers to its own laws, supports itself, internally coheres, and has a new standard of truth." But I cannot imagine anyone swallowing a poem in accordance with that prescription. Reading a poem or a novel is not a mystical experience. While we read we think about life, our lives, the life of our times. When society in the novel changes, we evaluate the changes from what we know about social change in this world and in the world our fathers created. When we step into a novel we do not trash the values we live by. If we do not accept tyranny in society, there is no aesthetic reason why we should accept it inside the covers of a book. The things, people and events which exist in a novel are vulnerable to the same standards of truth we exercise when we eat, work, make love and dream. When Forster says of Marcel Proust, "What mattered to him was not life, which he had found unsatisfactory, but art, which alone makes any meaning out of life," he commits three crimes. He vilifies the life-loving Proust, undermines the art which propels us toward action, and collapses before the possibilities of existence. Forster never discovered that life is not a class in grade school for which we receive a satisfactory or unsatisfactory report, depending on our performance at the blackboard.

What matters most for Forster is the pen between the writer's fingers. Everything is in that pen. It is his fetish. Empires fall, revolutions sweep Asia, but the writer simply sits in his soundproof chambers and moves his pen, unaffected. That is the portrait of the artist Forster paints. His writer is immunized to history. When he writes he loses himself. His personality and his past fall away, like a snake shedding its skin. The writer becomes Mr. X. His work is unsigned. He publishes his novel anonymously because who he is, where and when he lives, do not matter. It is pure. It has no sordid ties with the world.

Forster is ashamed that he is a novelist, for he feels that the novel is mediocre. It is in the middle—between the twin peaks of human achievement, history and poetry. He wishes that a novel could be like a poem. But he grieves, for he sees it brought down toward history, toward reality, to touch the prosaic. Forster always wants to push the novel up higher, away from life toward the infinite. He wants fiction to have rhythm; it must aspire to the condition of music. It must not be messy. The world Forster sees is chaotic, contingent. Changes make him unhappy. He turns to the novel for constancy, the permanent, unchanging form, unbroken circles. It is a haven from the wreckers who threaten his security.

The final Wanted poster is for an Amerikan, a cold warrior: Lionel Trilling. He is the prototype of the liberal anticommunist academician. Lionel Trilling poses as a dialectician but he would not be able to recognize the dialectic if it hit him in the street. His dialectic is tame; for him, it means mixing together two dissimilar things in a stew. There is no actual struggle or contradiction. It is abstract; it has nothing to do with the struggles of the world. He makes Matthew Arnold, not Marx or Mao, the supreme dialectician. The dialectical struggle between oppressed and oppressor does not count in his book.

Trilling talks of opposition, opposing selves and opposing cultures, but they are always loyal oppositions. He conceived of no revolutionary culture. He was the pet literary critic of the Amerikan bourgeoisie in the era of the cold war. In his theater he recognized two opponents: the liberal and the conservative. There was no part at all for the revolutionary. We can learn a lot from the conservatives, Trilling says. He did. In the 1950s he tried to gut Marxism and push reality into Freud's tidy patterns. He deadened literature.

His liberal politics and imagination are broadcast clearly in his essay on Dickens's *Little Dorrit*. "The modern self, like Little Dorrit," Trilling writes, "was born in a prison." He goes on to say that the prison in society, and as described in this novel, "is the practical instrument for the negation of man's will which the will of society has contrived." Prisons are necessary because there are evil men. The point of the novel, Trilling says, is that our personal will must find peace in the Will. Finally, men are imprisoned by their own neuroses. On every crucial point Trilling misfires. Dickens's own social vision is blurred as Trilling brings his own ideas into focus. Dickens's prisons have cells, iron bars, rats and vermin, prisoners and guards. Trilling wipes away this reality. For Dickens, release from jail is like being lifted out of the grave. The prisoner is brought back to life. This politics of joy and liberation which bubbles over in Dickens is anathema to Trilling. He diverts us from the real issues by waving placards with the words SELF and WILL. He abstracts and mystifies. And it is not Dickens only who is subjected to these attacks. One writer after the other—Conrad, Lawrence, Tolstoi, Twain—is scarred under Trilling's knife.

Trilling obscures the fact that jails maintain the organized violence of the state, that Bastilles are tools the oppressor uses to dehumanize the oppressed. Not a word does he say about the freedom fighters, the liberation armies, the men executing a jailbreak. Trilling poses as a practical, rational man. He is only tossing a bucket of cold water on the flames of naïve romanticism. But when we tear aside his liberal garments we see the uniform of a prison guard. Trilling is the jailer. He is repressive; he wants to lock us up. He is defeatist, pessimistic—a victim.

Trilling is the mid-twentieth-century Matthew Arnold. He votes for the state. For three decades he acted as a free agent for the Amerikan power elite. Like the State Department officials and the generals in the Pentagon, he designated communism as the "new imperialism." In that way he tried to hide from our eyes the repression in our society; to cover up the fact that our great writers have been held in prison, forced to become outlaws or fugitives because of their resistance to the state. Amerika is the new empire. It inherits the mantle of imperialism. By denying this, Trilling fails to see the rottenness of the old culture, the necessity for liberation. He uses literature to co-opt us, to bring us into the system of oppression. He tries to entice us into accepting the world we have inherited. It is corrupt, but it is the best we can have. Trilling likes that irony. His ironies, ambiguities and paradoxes urge us to lie down passively and die.

He consistently ignored Black culture, the art and literature of Third World people, the literature of liberation. About Malcolm X and Eldridge Cleaver, Franz Fanon and Ho Chi Minh—masters of the word and saints of the revolution—he has nothing to say. Before them he is impotent. He unendingly apologized for the burned-out writers of a moribund imperium: Henry James, E. M. Forster, George Orwell.

Lionel Trilling and his sidekicks took every occasion to say that communism destroys art. They treated us to a thorough brainwashing. But they could never wring the heart of communism out of the works of Richard Wright, Nazim Hikmet, Pablo Neruda, Jean-Paul Sartre, Bertolt Brecht.

Now it is time to parachute out. It is time to snatch back, to grasp in hand the galaxy we designed and executed, forged and cast, painted and carved, printed and shot, illustrated and bound, voyaged and chartered. We have got to drop out, leave behind us tradition, art for art's sake, the values of stability, order, continuity, the politics of liberalism, the feelings of pessimism, boredom, defeatism, egotism, alienation. On the planet we discover beneath our feet we create the cultural revolution. We expose, attack, resist, liberate. What was seized and confiscated is recaptured. On this new planet earth we are, for the first time, outside the capsule of high culture, outside the void of weightless, free-floating things. We communicate. We make connections. We build tribes, come together with our brothers and sisters. There are excavations into the past. There are explorations into the future. They instigate changes. Now we step into history; we bring culture and life together.

This book was a long time coming. It began as a Ph.D. thesis in 1964, which was finished in 1967. The present volume is radically different from the thesis. It was written outside the sterile atmosphere of academia. *The Mythology of Imperialism* was written slowly—between street demonstrations, drafting pamphlets, conspiratorial meetings—from December 1969 to November 1970. It was written in the midst of continual and intense political work. The energy source of this book is the life of the revolution. I wrote with the conviction that life is struggle, conflict, struggle. In that pattern culture is born. I am writing this now with the certainty that the oppressed will triumph over their oppressors. Imperialism, the Amerikan death machine, will surely die.

The book was written from inside the Amerikan Empire. The thesis was assembled in England, in the ruins of the old British Empire. I have been conscious throughout of Amerika inheriting the mantle of British imperialism: standing inside one declining empire writing about the fall of another empire. I decided to write about imperialism because that is the total reality of our time. This book is an attack on the empire, a weapon for the revolution. I feel now, as I have felt every day that I worked on this book, that culture has a crucial part to play in dismantling the Amerikan Empire. Culture means contradiction: out of revolution comes culture; the new culture will flow out of the era of armed struggle; and armed struggle is born out of the cultural revolution. These truths were locked away by the establishment critics. Now we pass them out in the streets to eager hands. Only with the burial of Amerikan imperialism will a genuine and creative life-giving culture exist. The culture of today which has meaning and significance is the culture of the Blacks, the Third World, the white dropouts and rebels. To be a writer and stand inside the establishment means the death of one's art. We are living in a time of intense political struggle and cultural upheaval. The New Man and the New Woman are being born here and now within the old, shattering shell. This book has its place in the context of these changes. It is a chapter in the cultural revolution.

I have written about Kipling, Conrad, Lawrence, Forster and Cary to examine patterns of conflict and struggle, space and time. Kipling and Conrad are posed as antagonists: Conrad the dialectician, Kipling the great compromiser. For Conrad, there is always change, change after change. For Kipling, the status quo is preserved, men and women are locked in place. Forster and Cary are also matched one against the other. Forster has a classic liberal disease. He is paranoid about crisis. He fears the apocalypse. Joyce Cary accepts change. But he too is a liberal. He argues that violent revolution, as in Russia in 1917, China under Mao, Cuba under Fidel, is unnecessary because we live in the revolution of endless change every day. I have also written about Cary because he has been hidden away. He has not received the attention he deserves.

In Lawrence I have located a man who, unlike most of his contemporaries, did not hesitate to destroy. He tore down the crumbling walls and grasped for the new world. He is a pioneer voyager in space and time. He urges us to make a revolution for life.

The Mythology of Imperialism was finished in Algiers in November 1970. With a group of American revolutionaries, I had gone to see Tim Leary and Eldridge Cleaver. From Algiers the fall of the Amerikan Empire seemed more necessary, more imminent. Here we were children of Amerika bound in our struggle for life and love, reaching out to join with the revolutionaries of the Third World, with the exiles from our own land. In Algiers our drive for liberation from the jails of Amerika, and from the mind controls of the state, accelerated. The underlying assumption here is that the principal contradiction in the world is between the revolutionary peoples of Africa, Asia and Latin America and the imperial powers. That is why in this book Ho, Che, Mao, Debray and Fidel are specters haunting Conrad, Lawrence, Cary, Forster and Kipling. They have opened the doors for our own liberation; they have ignited the cultural revolution which will burn away the rags of Amerika and set the stage for a new world-wide commune of free and loving brothers and sisters.

I

Chaos: The Culture of Imperialism

I. THE THIRD WORLD

The world of imperialism came crashing through the walls of the nineteenth-century novel. Old conflicts were terminated, old boundaries were destroyed, old characters were banished. A new universe of fiction was set down in their place. A revolution in the novel was effected. It was Joseph Conrad—the Pole, the outsider—who battered down the old walls. He set the clock on the time bomb of the twentieth-century revolution in the novel. His first blast leveled the old house of nineteenth-century fiction. His second ripped asunder the imperial house of modern fiction: Rudyard Kipling's monument to the empire. Kipling's walls hide the truth of imperialism. Conrad broke them down. He dragged the colonial world onto stage center of English fiction.

In "Autocracy and War" (1905) he described the new world of imperialism:

> Industrialism and commercialism—wearing high-sounding names in many languages (*Welt-politik* may serve for one instance), picking up coins behind the severe and disdainful figure of science whose giant strides have widened for us the horizon of the universe by some few inches—stand ready, almost eager to appeal to the sword as soon as the globe of the earth has shrunk beneath our growing numbers by another ell or so. And democracy, which has

> elected to pin its faith to the supremacy of material interests, will have to fight their battles to the bitter end, on a mere pittance—unless, indeed, some statesman of exceptional ability and overwhelming prestige succeeds in carrying through an international understanding for the delimitation of spheres of trade all over the earth, on the model of the territorial spheres of influence marked in Africa to keep the competitors for the privilege of improving the nigger (as a buying machine) from flying prematurely at each other's throats.

Conrad saw the world-wide extension of capitalism, the antagonism between imperial and colonial lands, the radical upheaval of primitive communities, their introduction into the political and economic context of the twentieth century, the intrusion of machines into the jungles, the exploitation of the peasants, the extraction of wealth and its expropriation by foreigners and colonial rulers. It is a world in which progress drinks nectar from the skulls of the slain, a world of directorates and monopolies, of world wars and revolutions for thc control of wealth and power. It is a time of nationalist, socialist and working-class movements. It is the era of communist revolution. The West collapses, the East rises. The Third World flexes. The peasant, the African chief, the Indian guru, the Hindu monk, the guerrilla fighter, the international financier, the anarchist—all these men become dominant figures in the jungles of Africa and Asia and in the jungles of cities. It is an era of dictatorship, of autocratic democracies. Culture and literature are political weapons, both in the hands of the colonialists and their revolutionary adversaries. Western European culture is increasingly decadent. The cultures of Black, Brown and Latin peoples are the centers of creativity, vitality. Intellectuals join the fight; they become pamphleteers or apologists. It is an era of disintegration and fragmentation; men are acutely conscious of chaos, alienation and loneliness. Racism infests the house of Western thought—divides, corrupts, poisons. Private lives appear dissociated from public existence; history seems to have no meaning.

To date, literary and cultural historians have not reckoned with imperialism. F. R. Leavis, Edmund Wilson, Lionel Trilling, E. M. Forster—they have not performed the necessary task. Raymond Williams's inability to tangle with imperialism distorts modern culture and society. Williams writes that "our moods appear in effect after the war of 1914–18," that "we tend to look at the period 1880–1914 as a kind of interregnum. It is not the period of the masters . . . Nor yet is it the period of our contemporaries, of writers who address themselves, in our kind of language, to the common problems that we recognize." Williams begins *Culture and Society, 1780–1950* by discussing five words which were coined or which gained new meanings at the end of the eighteenth and the beginning of the nineteenth century. These words—industry, democracy, class, art and culture—he says, are the key to "those wider changes in life and thought to which the changes in language evidently refer." They help account for late and middle nineteenth-century history, but in the twentieth century their power to ferret out the truth is sapped. But take these words and phrases which were coined or which acquired new meanings at the end of the nineteenth and the beginning of the twentieth century:

Imperialism
Colonialism
Fascism
Bolshevik
Racism
White Man's Burden
Technology
Freudian
World War

With these words and phrases twentieth-century history comes to life. Then the period 1880–1920 is no interregnum. It is the age of revolution.

No Victorian had Conrad's social vision. He could not have had because the world Conrad saw did not exist in 1830, 1850 or 1880. No Victorian wrote a good novel about the colonial world. Every major modern writer has been preoccupied by the conflict between the metropolis and the hinterlands, the conflict between Europeans and Asians, whites and Blacks, colonizers and the colonized. Third World consciousness transformed their lives. The Victorian novelists breathed the world of class. Modern novelists—from Conrad to Lawrence, from Kipling to Orwell, from Forster to Cary—have been preoccupied with race, with cultural and national conflicts. Twentieth-century novelists have brought the colonial world into the heart of fiction: *Heart of Darkness, Kim, Lord Jim, Nostromo, A Passage to India, The Plumed Serpent, The Heart of the Matter, Mister Johnson, Burmese Days.*

The Victorians were conscious of their empire: their Queen was Empress of India, their sons served in the army in Egypt and Singapore, men invested in overseas companies, ladies wore silks from the East, workers drank tea from China and India. In daily life the fact of empire was difficult to forget. Yet the Victorian novelists imagined that the colonies were peripheral to their domestic concerns, and rarely felt that the colonial world impinged on the metropolis. In Victorian novels the colonies are usually places to transfer burned-out characters, or from which to retrieve characters when they were needed. They are especially convenient for the beginnings, turning points and endings of fiction. The plot began—or flagging interest was revived—when a character returned from abroad, and the action terminated when the characters left for the colonies. For the Victorians existence meant existence in England: it began when they returned to Southampton or Liverpool and it ended when they embarked for Australia, Canada or Nigeria. Going to India was like falling off a cliff. The Englishman coming back to London felt like a fish thrown back into the sea after flopping about on land.

Most nineteenth-century novelists thought solely in terms of England because they were born in and spent their entire lives in England. The Brontës, George Eliot, Mrs. Gaskell and Dickens were all rooted in English communities. Conrad and Kipling, unlike most of the Victorians, were born and lived extensively abroad. They were aliens in England, so they scrambled for roots, created an image of England to suit their foreign appearance. Their contemporaries—James, Pound, Eliot, Joyce, Yeats and Shaw—were all foreigners in England. Modern British literature was created by Irishmen, Americans and a Pole. Outstanding contemporary literature in English is more and more the product of Africans and Indians—Wole Soyinka, R. K. Narayan, V. S. Naipaul. Modern British culture colonized writers from varied cultures and national backgrounds. With the major exception of the Irish writers, the modern British writers—Conrad the Pole, Eliot and James, Americans—were deeply committed to England. They were loyal foreigners. Their dedication to the imperial society binds writers as diverse as Kipling, Conrad, Lawrence, Cary and T. S. Eliot. The only major modern novelist born in England who was nourished by English culture is D. H. Lawrence. He is a lone wolf, an anomaly, but he too, restless with England, seeking an escape from its fettering confines and the confines of traditional English fiction and criticism, went abroad. The harvest was a series of books about the New World, the colonial world, the primitive: *Kangaroo, The Plumed Serpent, Studies in Classic American Literature, Etruscan Places, Mornings in Mexico, The Sea and Sardinia.*

A significant number of late nineteenth and early twentieth century British writers were born abroad. Conrad was born in Poland in 1857, W. H. Hudson in South America in 1841, Hugh Walpole in New Zealand in 1884, Katherine Mansfield in New Zealand in 1888, Christina Stead in Australia in 1902, Angus Wilson in South Africa in 1913, Dan Jacobson in South Africa in 1929, Doris Lessing in Persia in 1919 and, of special importance, Kipling in Bombay in 1865, R. H. Tawney in Calcutta in 1880, George Orwell in Bengal in 1903, and Lawrence Durrell in India in 1912. By contrast (and with the exception of Thackeray), no important Victorian writer or social critic was born in the colonial world. Among the Victorians, only Trollope and Samuel Butler—as compared with the moderns Conrad, Forster, Cary, Kipling, Greene, Orwell and Lawrence—traveled and worked in the hinterlands. Thackeray's birth in Calcutta makes him unusual in the company of Dickens, George Eliot, Mrs. Gaskell and Emily Brontë.

The modern classics that present the colonial world reverberate with contradictions and extreme situations, which are missing from most Victorian novels. The colonial experience, the colonial theme, altered the sense of time and space in the modern British novel. The colonial world brought a sense of urgency and crisis into European society. It shattered the familiar patterns in English fiction. The prevailing contemporary critical view, articulated best by Richard Chase in *The American Novel and Its Tradition,* is that "the English novel has followed a middle way," that the "American novel tends to rest in contradictions and among extreme ranges of experience . . . The English novel has been a kind of imperial enterprise, an appropriation of reality with the high purpose of bringing order to disorder. By contrast . . . the American novel has usually seemed content to explore, rather than appropriate and civilize, the remarkable and in some ways unexampled territories of life in the New World and to reflect its anomalies and dilemmas. It has not wanted to build an imperium but merely to discover a new place and a new state of mind."

Chase is on fairly solid ground when he compares the nineteenth-century American novel with the Victorian novel, but his thesis cracks when one compares the modern British novel with the American classics. The British novel in the age of imperialism has explored unmapped territories in its own new worlds. It has dropped a bucket down into wells of extreme consciousness. By shifting from drawing room to jungles, from city to plains and mountains, the novelist went beyond the familiar sense of well-defined space into what seemed to be an undefined, endlessly moving world. In the colonial world there was a sense that time was speeded up, compressed: the primitive past clashed with the industrial present, which was already shattering into a communist future. In the Victorian novel man is surrounded by comfortable society. In the modern British novel the white man is isolated, thrown back into himself. He finds little middle ground to which he can cling in safety.

II. KIPLING AND CONRAD

The differences between the old and the new novel emerge when James and Conrad are contrasted. *Nostromo* (1904) was published the same year as *The Golden Bowl,* but Conrad describes the present and the future, James describes ancient history. James's New World *nouveaux riches* tangle with Old and New World fortune hunters; his world smacks of perversity, vulgarity, cunning, incarceration and terror. Conrad's Costaguana brings the twentieth century into the realm of fiction: fragmentation, estrangement, dislocation, imperialism, revolution, war. When James thought of revolution an image of the year 1789 flashed across his mind; when he thought of the international scene he engaged an American girl and a European man; and when he thought of culture he re-created the salons of *ancien régime* France and Newport, Rhode Island, in the 1870s.

Terror is a country of the mind and writers who describe it are citizens of the same state. But writers approach terror from different social perspectives. Consider, for example, what Conrad would have done with James's image of the "beast in the jungle," an image which releases a moment of terror. For James the beast is in the self; for Conrad it would have referred to the self, but also literally to real beasts in real African jungles. For James, terror was the feeling that his doomed, wealthy American cousin, Minnie Temple, experienced when at twenty-four she knew she was to die, just when all the possibilities of travel and luxury were made available to her. It is the moment when the young French aristocrats jailed by the revolution knew that they were shortly to be guillotined by their class enemies. For Conrad, terror was the moment in the Congo when, surrounded by the jungle and hidden Black men, he hears a distant drum and confuses it with the beating of his heart. It is the moment when the interrogated knows that unless he confesses, the concentration-camp inquisitor will give the final turn of the screw. Conradian terror is distinct from but akin to Jamesian terror. It reflects a different society.

James had a perverse social sense. He felt doom, crisis, and intuited the process of change. Knowing of the growing power of the working classes and fearing revolution in the streets of London, he noted in 1886 that "in England the Huns and Vandals will . . . come 'up'—from the black depths of . . . the people." He also felt that the empire was threatened at its frontier, the border country between civilization and savagery which haunted the late nineteenth-century Englishman. In 1899 James told Charles Eliot Norton that the English were living "under the very black shadow of S. Africa," and that the Boer War made him "gloom and brood and have craven questions of 'Finnis Britanniae.' " He saw the crisis of the empire, described it as "the greatest drama in history," but in that social drama he detected no material he could transform into his art. He was receptive to new talents, to writers who introduced new material into the territory of English fiction. In 1893, after reading Robert Louis Stevenson's "The Beach of Falesá," a story about the South Seas, he wrote to its author, "Primitive man doesn't interest me, I confess, as much as civilized—and yet he *does* when you write about him." He hailed Kipling for introducing a new land—India—into English fiction; he greeted Conrad as a fellow craftsman, but also because of the fresh experiences he rendered in his work. "What he gives us, above all," James wrote of Kipling, "is the feeling of the English manner and the English blood in conditions they have made at once so much and so little their own . . . He is wonderful about India, and India has not been 'done.' " After reading *The Mirror of the Sea* he told Conrad, "No one has known—for intellectual use—the things you know." Kipling and Conrad were both exotic figures for James.

Not only James, but the society at large enthusiastically greeted Kipling and Conrad, but greeted them as though they were foreigners wearing odd clothes, speaking a different language. Here at last, readers exclaimed, was something new under the imperial sun. *Plain Tales from the Hills, Life's Handicap, The Phantom Rickshaw*—these works by an obscure Anglo-Indian journalist, a provincial from a remote corner of the empire, took the London literary world by storm, disturbed conventional ideas about society. Kipling was a sensation, sought after by publishers, editors, readers. A find: his name in lights, the artist of the season.

Kipling and Conrad both cultivated an exotic air. Conrad used the pen name Kamudi (a Malay word meaning rudder) when he submitted the manuscript of his first novel to his publisher, and Kipling wrote early stories under the pen name Yussuf. Kipling and Conrad both felt that they were bizarre figures, that they were innovators. They made a romantic identification with the East. In their rebellion they turned away from English fiction to American and Russian literature, and often to the other arts. In Russian and American literature these modern British writers found the extremes which were missing from Victorian fiction. In painting, sculpture and opera they touched on artistic forms which liberated them from the old structures of the novel. "I am *modern,*" Conrad wrote, disdaining any comparison between his work and Thackeray's, Walter Scott's and George Eliot's. "I would rather recall Wagner the musician and Rodin the sculptor, who both had to starve a little in their day—and Whistler the painter, who made Ruskin the critic foam at the mouth with scorn and indignation." Like Lawrence, who in his last years spoke of the novel as a bomb, Conrad noted that "an explosion is the most lasting thing in the universe. It leaves disorder, remembrance, room to move, a clear space"; and he claimed that his works "exploded like stored powder barrels." He cleared a space in English literature, blasting away Thackeray and George Eliot, with the help of the saboteurs James Fenimore Cooper, Flaubert, Maupassant and Dostoevsky.

The image that came to his mind when he summed up his view of the Victorian novel sprang from his experiences in the colonial world. "The national English novelist," Conrad wrote, "does not go about building up his book with a precise intention and a steady mind. It never occurs to him that a book is a deed, that the writing of it is an enterprise as much as the conquest of a colony." Writing as defined in his dictionary means colonizing, appropriating space, taming a wilderness of words, building a society. More important than the conquest-of-a-colony metaphor is the "Author's Note" (1895) to his first novel, *Almayer's Folly*. This preface is a revolutionary literary manifesto. It was intended to clear the ground for the new literature about the colonial world. Look out, London, something radically different is on its way, Conrad says. The critics rejected the "literature which preys on strange people and prowls in far-off countries," but that literature was valid, Conrad claimed, because "the picture of life, there as here, is drawn . . . with the same tints . . . There is a bond," he concludes, "between us and that humanity so far away."

When Kipling wrote about India and reached a perilous crossing, he turned for aid to French and American writers. In Mark Twain he found a novelist who had wrestled with the problems which nagged him. In Zola he discovered how "low life," as he called it, how subjects normally excluded from polite English fiction, could be presented in fiction. The foreign observer could understand India, he suggested, not by going to English fiction, but by reading the "more Zolaistic of Zola's novels." Kipling, with his knowing swagger, struck James as a French rather than an English type, and on the basis of his early work James felt that he "contained the seeds of an English Balzac." When James looked for the contemporary writer who had affinities with Conrad, he lighted, though mistakenly, on Pierre Loti. Conrad's gestures to the exotic East are his most superficial. Unlike Loti, he felt that the Third World was the home of all humanity. When the tradition of the English novel caved in, other traditions were useful. An international network of literary relations came into being. Writers became world citizens.

In kicking out the old and introducing the new, Kipling and Conrad often misread English fiction and the nature of their own art. But they recognized that the English novel had neglected the colonial world, that in order to conquer an English reading public skeptical of their alien vision new techniques had to be mustered. "I hope to bring the three men," Kipling wrote in 1888 of his colonial heroes in *Soldiers Three,* "to the notice of the Englishman. But there is no light in this place, and the people are savages living in black houses and ignorant of everything beyond the Channel." With an air of superiority Kipling affirmed that he—an Anglo-Indian and an imperial spokesman—saw a more significant world than did the domestic variety of Englishman. He felt the presence of the colonial empire everywhere and all the time. Kipling noted that for the novelist as well as for the painter—and he frequently made analogies between words and the pigments on a painter's palette—England was a dark place. The English were unenlightened about the empire, and also, literally—since there was little light in England—the English writer necessarily saw things differently from the colonial writer living under the glare of the bright tropical sun. The sense of the contrast between England and India, the metropolitan center and the frontier, is implicit in nearly everything he wrote. It allows him here to speak of the English as savages, to reverse the normal assumptions about civilization and savagery, sophistication and naïveté. He was dissatisfied with the sense of place in traditional English fiction. He wanted to expand it, to introduce new colors and shapes, to cast a different imaginative light on the material world. In place of gray and tan he wanted violet, aquamarine, scarlet, blazing white and harshest black. "Surely there must be things in this world paintable other and beyond the North Cape . . . and Algiers," he observed. "For the sake of the picture," he proposed, it was important "to venture out a little beyond the regular circle of subjects." He and Conrad thought of themselves as explorers venturing out beyond the regular settlements into new fields and forests.

They wrote most of their major works in the same period. Their careers were long: Conrad's lasted from 1895 to 1924, Kipling's from 1884 to 1936. But their most profound and original works—*Heart of Darkness, Lord Jim, Nostromo, Kim, The Just So Stories*—were written between 1899 and 1904. Their other major works, *Plain Tales from the Hills* (1888) and *Under Western Eyes* (1911) are outside these limits, but *Plain Tales* is the seed which yielded *Kim,* and *Under Western Eyes* is the last flowering of the imagination which created *Nostromo*. These were times of social upheaval and intellectual ferment. Their work takes us to the midst of the crisis; it indicates the cultural and social antagonisms of the period. The differences between Kipling and Conrad are a reflection of the contradictions within the society as a whole.

The period 1898 to 1905 was defined by the Spanish-American War, the Boer War, the Russo-Japanese War, the first Russian revolution, the Dreyfus affair, the death of Queen Victoria, the assassination of President McKinley. Those seven years saw the publication of J. A. Hobson's *Imperialism,* Max Weber's *The Protestant Ethic and the Birth of Capitalism,* Freud's *Traumdeutung,* Einstein's basic theories, James's *Varieties of Religious Experience,* Moore's *Principia Ethica,* the creation of the new journalism and changes in technology and communications.

Conrad and Kipling are fundamentally disparate, dissimilar. In their work opposing ideas find expression. Kipling writes of contrasts and compromises, Conrad writes of crisis and contradiction. Conrad defined himself as a historian and a magician, writing from the conflicts in himself. Kipling saw himself a tribal bard, a mastersinger. Kipling ventures out into the world. Conrad extracts the world from the depths inside. Kipling wanted literature to incite men to action, to participate in Empire. More than any other English writer in the last one hundred and fifty years he changed the society's image of itself. Conrad asked of the novel that it produce a moral discovery. Kipling offered detail, catalogs, surfaces. Conrad sought the pattern, the hidden, the essential. Kipling was an imperialist. Conrad was an anti-imperialist.

To critics and readers in the late 1890s, Kipling and Conrad seemed to be engaged in similar work. Arthur Symons reviewed *Captains Courageous* and *The Nigger of the Narcissus* together; the review was severely critical and Conrad recoiled in anger. Symons, Conrad wrote, "went out of his way to damn Kipling and me . . . He says that *Captains Courageous* and *The Nigger* have no idea behind them." The fact that they wrote about sailors and soldiers and that they told exciting tales led readers to assume that they had common pursuits. Conrad was widely called the "Kipling of the Seas." This distorted view is still often expressed. John Bayley distinguishes them from E. M. Forster and notes that they were the "last great representatives of the literature of achievement. They celebrated activity." But it is much closer to the truth to say that Kipling thought in terms of action while Conrad thought of creation.

Conrad, like most of the English reading public in the late 1890s, read widely in Kipling's work. In 1897 he wrote to his friend R. B. Cunningham Graham, the wealthy socialist, "Mr. Kipling has the wisdom of the passing generations—and holds it in perfect sincerity. Some of his work is of impeccable form and because of that little thing he shall sojourn in Hell only a very short while . . . In the chaos of printed matter, Kipling *ébauches* appear by contrast finished and impeccable." The next year, 1898, he told a Polish cousin, "Among the people who deserve attention the first is Rudyard Kipling (his last book *The Day's Work*)."

But Conrad was also aware of his differences with Kipling. He told Edward Garnett that his integrity had been compromised by writing for *The Outlook,* a popular magazine edited by Kipling's friend W. E. Henley. "Words. Words. Words." Conrad exclaimed. "Apparently that is what they want. They asked for more. Today I've sent a silly thing about Kipling. It took me one and a half days to write 1500 words." Conrad sent the piece about Kipling to *The Outlook* (it was never published), but he did not like the magazine or its editor. He noted that the policy of the magazine was "imperialism, tempered by expediency," and that Henley was "a horrible bourgeois." As Kipling's popularity waned and as he turned from India to England, from man to animal and then to machine, Conrad became more critical of his work. He told his French translator H. D. Davray in 1908:

> I am a thoroughly English writer, extremely difficult to translate into another language. A national writer like Kipling is easy to translate. People read him for his subject matter, people read me for the effect my work produces. Kipling speaks of his countrymen. I write for them. Foreigners are very much interested in his work. It is very difficult, perhaps impossible, for them to be interested in my work.

Earlier, Conrad had been influenced by Kipling's work. His subject is occasionally also Kipling's, especially in *The Nigger of the Narcissus*. As the tale begins, the white crew assembles; they talk in "masterful tones" while the Asians clamor and babble in feverish Eastern tongues. As the Asians rage and shriek for a few more rupees the white sailors admire the "resplendent and bestarred peace of the East." Kipling would have been sympathetic to Conrad's attack on working-class agitators, on West Indian Blacks, and his eulogy of England. Conrad's concluding description of England is as patriotic and sentimental as anything Kipling ever wrote.

In times of crisis they defended Britain, but politically their positions were antagonistic. In 1898 and 1899 Conrad opposed the wars in South Africa, Cuba and the Philippines, all of which Kipling supported. Kipling moved to South Africa, helped publish a military newspaper, met consistently with Cecil Rhodes and Jameson, and congratulated the United States on becoming an imperial power. For Conrad the Boer War was anguishing; he exploded with anger against Kipling and the English. "If I am to believe Kipling," he wrote, "this is a war undertaken for the cause of democracy. *C'est à crever de rire*." The war, as he saw it, was idiotic. Kipling pumped out story after story, poem after poem, about the war. Conrad noted that "all that's art, thought, idea will have to step back and hide its head before the intolerable war inanities." While he knew that the war was not being fought for democracy but for wealth and power and that English victory would bring "ruthless repression," he hoped that British success would "be crushing from the first—on the same principle that if there's murder being done in the next room and you can't stop it, you wish the head of the victim bashed in forthwith and the whole thing over for the sake of your own feelings." He opposed the war but did not participate in any anti-imperialist movements.

Kipling celebrated the white man's burden. Conrad deflated it. During World War I Conrad described Germany as that "promised land of steel, of chemical dyes, of method, of efficiency," and he called the Germans "that race planted in the middle of Europe, assuming in grotesque vanity the attitude of Europeans amongst effete Asiatics or barbarous niggers; and with a consciousness of superiority freeing their hands from all moral bonds, anxious to take up . . . the 'perfect man's burden.' " Kipling was enthusiastic about efficiency, industrial production, the machine. Conrad was sickened by the financial and industrial power which had precipitated the crisis and the technological advances which had brought death to the battlefields.

Kipling had an official role as defender of the empire. In 1915, when James, in the midst of the imperial holocaust, became a citizen of the empire, Kipling wrote to tell him that his act was of the utmost significance for the British Empire and for all the civilized world. At long last, Kipling sighed, James had won his deepest admiration, not for his literary work, but because James had taken a stand against barbarism. It was a day Kipling would remember proudly for the rest of his life. Conrad was not the establishment spokesman. He loved England, but he was not at the dock to welcome American or French exiles to the English shore.

III. T. S. ELIOT

T. S. Eliot was the first critic to corral Conrad and Kipling. He branded them both as no other critic has yet done, for he saw their importance in British culture. In his essay "Kipling Redivivus" (1919) Eliot noted that Conrad is:

> . . . the antithesis of Kipling. He is, for one thing, the antithesis of Empire, (as well as democracy); his characters are the denial of Empire, of Nation, of Race almost, they are fearfully alone with the Wilderness.

He saw Kipling and Conrad as antagonists springing from hostile camps: one affirming order, empire, race, the other negating order, empire, race. Eliot's perspective on Kipling and Conrad is part of his larger concern with imperialism, with the British Empire. Eliot defended the British Empire. Out of one side of his mouth he attacked imperialism, but with the other side he talked up the empire. Eliot had the prime handicap of modern British writers. He saw no pattern in history, only chaos in the breakup of the imperial order and the development of the forces of revolution. He turned to the British Empire and the Catholic Church to conserve the old order. He looked to myth to contain the forces of change. He ran from communism and the future and hid in the ancient house of imperialism.

"I am all for empires," Eliot told Ford Madox Ford in 1924, "especially the Austro-Hungarian Empire, and I deplore the outburst of artificial nationalities, constituted like artificial genealogies for millionaires all over the world . . . let us not have an indiscriminate mongrel mixture of socialist internationals or of capitalist cosmopolitans, but a harmony of different functions." The idea of different races and cultures preserving their ancient languages and customs and united under a common aegis—the British Empire—

seized his imagination. Like Kipling, he was dizzy with the thought that Egyptians, Indians, Chinese, Australians, South Africans and Canadians all pledged allegiance to Britain. Eliot exposed "the exploitation of the earth . . . for commercial profit," but he did not connect it with capitalism or colonialism. He saw "dearth and desert" brought about by man's profit motive, but he did not favor a socialist revolution which would transform economic relationships. Communism seemed to Eliot "merely an attempt to catch up with Western Capitalism, and to imitate some of . . . its most objectionable habits." His insistence on the necessity of empire sprang from his feeling that revolution was imminent. This feeling pervades *The Waste Land* and it is especially pronounced here:

> What is that sound high in the air
> Murmur of maternal lamentation
> Who are those hooded hordes swarming
> Over endless plains, stumbling in cracked earth
> Ringed by the flat horizon only
> What is the city over the mountains
> Cracks and reforms and bursts in the violet air
> Falling towers
> Jerusalem Athens Alexandria
> Vienna London
> Unreal

"The most important event of the War," Eliot wrote, "was the Russian Revolution. For the Russian Revolution has made men conscious of the position of Western Europe as . . . a small and isolated cape on the western side of the Asiatic continent." He saw Europe at the edge of a precipice, on the verge of falling off into outer space. Eliot wanted a European empire to hold off the Bolsheviks, to convene a new congress of Europe, to forge a holy alliance of reaction. In the age of revolution Britain had a special part to play, for she was "the only member of the European community that has established a genuine empire . . . a world-wide empire as was the Roman Empire." In response to economic imperialism Eliot wanted a Christian imperium. He wanted a European culture in the twentieth century which would continue Roman and medieval culture. To resurrect the Roman and the Holy Roman Empires in a modern shape was his dream. Tradition was his prime value, for it emphasized conservatism, continuities, and sought to smother upheavals, innovations, revolutions. It was through a European culture that Eliot wanted to create a European empire. He created an imperium of writers, an aristocracy of artists. Dante spoke to Shakespeare, Virgil chatted with Goethe, Milton talked with Aeschylus. Virgil stands at the head of Eliot's imperium of artists; he is the link between the ancient and the modern world. "Destiny" for Virgil, Eliot writes, "means the *imperium romanum* . . . He set an ideal for Rome and for empire in general, which was never realized in history." Eliot goes on to say that "We are all, so far as we inherit the civilization of Europe, still citizens of the Roman Empire." Reverence for the past is what he preaches. Eliot distinguishes between Virgil's *Aeneid* and the actualities of Roman history:

> The Roman Empire which Virgil imagined . . . was not exactly the same as the Roman Empire of the legionaries, the pro-consuls and governors, the business men and speculators, the demagogues and generals. It was something greater, but something which exists because Virgil imagined it. It remains an ideal.

So, too, in his own day Eliot created a British Empire which was an ideal. His imaginary empire had nothing to do with soldiers, diplomats, financiers. It was a never-never land. By creating it, Eliot obscured the realities of exploitation and oppression. He led men on a false pilgrimage toward the imperial chalice.

For Eliot the most important modern writer was Rudyard Kipling. Eliot wrote three essays on Kipling. Kipling is as important a figure as Milton or Shakespeare in Eliot's literary cosmography. He invested everything he had in Kipling's stock, for Kipling extends the imperial tradition. He is Virgil's successor. Eliot's attitude toward Kipling changed several times between 1919, the date of the first essay, and 1958, the date of his last essay on Kipling. As he got older, Kipling loomed larger and larger on the horizon, but the figure on the horizon resembled less and less the flesh-and-blood Rudyard Kipling.

In 1941 Eliot argued that Kipling's vision is:

> . . . of the people of the soil. It is not a Christian vision, but it is at least a pagan vision—a contradiction of the materialistic view: it is the insight into a harmony with nature which must be re-established if the truly Christian imagination is to be recovered by Christians. What he is trying to convey is . . . a point of view unintelligible to the industrialized mind.

For these same reasons Eliot had praised Virgil. He was aware of the predicament his admiration for Kipling got him into. Eliot knew that Kipling's critics argued that since the architect of the white man's burden "dwelt upon the glory of empire . . . he helped to conceal its more seamy side: the commercialism, exploitation and neglect." But Eliot's response is that "no attentive reader of Kipling can maintain that he was unaware of the faults of British rule: it is simply that he believed the British Empire to be a good thing." And Eliot, too, condemns the exploitation of the earth but believes that the British Empire is a virtuous institution. He proclaims his hostility toward industrial and commercial society, but he praises Kipling, the chief celebrant of the machine and the industrial state. Eliot also supported the British Empire, knowing its exploitation and commercialism. Below his appeal to Christianity, order, harmony, tradition, is his objective stance—side by side with the masters of empire against the colonized peoples of the earth.

His emphasis on the imperial tradition in literature is in keeping with his preoccupation with the British Empire, his belief in continuities and harmonies. Luckily, no one took Kipling for the great artist Eliot did. Near the end of his life he was a rabid Kipling fan. In 1958 he noted that his and Kipling's "feeling about England springs from causes not wholly dissimilar." Kipling had praised James for becoming a citizen of the empire. Now Eliot joined the imperial order. He became a British subject, and he paid his tribute to the foremost imperialist-artist. He declared that Kipling was the "greatest English man of letters of his generation."

As Kipling loomed larger and larger on the horizon for Eliot, Conrad receded further and further into the background. As is well known, earlier and in his most creative period he had taken *Heart of Darkness* as a holy text. Kurtz's cry, "the horror, the horror," was to have been the epigraph to *The Waste Land*. "Mistah Kurtz—he dead" is, of course, the epigraph to "The Hollow Men." This is the Eliot who distorted Conrad's vision of horror, but who recognized Conrad's revulsion from European civilization. Eliot assumed then that Conrad was the finer of the two artists. In 1924, the year of Conrad's death, Eliot wrote in *The Criterion* that Conrad "was beyond question a great novelist," that his "reputation is as secure as that of any writer of his time." As the years went by Eliot said less and less about Conrad and instead crusaded for Kipling. His hatred for the English revolution and civil war of the seventeenth century governed both his dislike of Milton and his love for the metaphysical poets. His commitment to the British Empire determined his love of Kipling. In celebrating Kipling and neglecting Conrad, Eliot buried the realities of imperialism and accepted the falsehood of empire.

We need to return to Eliot's idea that Conrad and Kipling

are antagonists. We need to explore the remark in *The Sacred Wood* (1920):

> It would be of interest to divagate from literature to politics and inquire to what extent Romanticism is incorporate in Imperialism; to inquire to what extent Romanticism has possessed the imagination of Imperialists.

To do that would also define much of Eliot's own work.

We need to examine the culture of imperialism; we need an aesthetics which allows for change, crisis and chaos, for imperialist criticism shuns dialectical contradiction and struggle. The best place to begin is D. H. Lawrence's essay "Chaos in Poetry." "Man cannot live in chaos," Lawrence writes. In "his terror of chaos he begins by putting up an umbrella between himself and the everlasting whirl. Then he paints the underside of his umbrella like a firmament. Then he parades around, lives and dies under his umbrella." The great writers tear the umbrella; they let chaos in, but men patch it up. "Chaos is all shut out." But "chaos is always there," Lawrence concludes, "and always will be, no matter how we put up umbrellas of vision." Eliot's concern with tradition and order needs to be replaced by Lawrence's sense of chaos. We need to see the contradictions between the ideal imperium and the actualities of imperialism. We need to get away from the ideal imperium of order to the actual imperialism of crisis and change. We need to celebrate the modern writers who were nourished on conflict. The modern titans let chaos in: they brought a new universe under the umbrella. By exploring this world of imperialism, they expanded the possibilities for man. They saw that men live in isolation in society, that men live through crisis as well as stability. They stand to testify that art and culture are bathed in the chaos of war and revolution.

Kipling and Conrad are antagonists. Their work reveals

the broad and deep tensions within the culture of British imperialism. They indicate the conflicting attitudes about race, industrial and commercial society, technology, communications, England. Both were dedicated to the British Empire, but Conrad saw beyond its limits to imperialism, exploitation, racism. Kipling moved with and reflected the dominant social and intellectual currents of his time. He was a spokesman for the empire. He accepted the values and limitations imposed upon him by the establishment. Conrad saw society in conflict. He thought of strife and violence. He thrived on contradictions. Kipling wanted order and a hierarchical society which negated conflicts. These two men indicate how profoundly British culture changed in the age of imperialism, in particular how British fiction took on the extremes of experience, explored a vast and chaotic world and diverged from the Victorian novel. They both saw the extremes, the contrasts, but Conrad immersed himself in them, squeezing his art from the clash of opposites. Kipling retreated from the extremes, from the conflicts. He ensured that they were frozen, separated, that they would never rebound against one another. But together they brought about a literary revolution which altered the course of modern literature. Eliot, Lawrence, Forster, Cary and Orwell have had to respond, to recast their world. Kipling accepted and dominated his culture. The British lived the myth of the white man's burden. Conrad fought against his society. He is most representative of his time because he stands in sharpest opposition to it. He reminds us that the great modern writer is a rebel and a craftsman, that he is both a nihilist and a utopian. He destroys old worlds and builds new ones from the rubble about him.

2

Kipling's Contrasts

In poem after poem, story after story and novel after novel Kipling repeatedly and untiringly carved out sharp, broad areas of contrast. Kipling insists on the distinctions between man and beast, the primitive and the civilized, the insider and the outsider, the patrician and the plebian, East and West, England and India, black and white, heaven and hell. There is the possibility for violent antagonism here but it doesn't develop in Kipling's world, even though his characters are often bloody and scarred. In his earliest work—*Plain Tales from the Hills, Life's Handicap* and *The Phantom Rickshaw*—he contrasts the plain with the extraordinary, phantoms with realities, the handicapped with the potent; he contrasts provincial Anglo-India with England, comfortable society with the anarchic forces beneath its surface and beyond its frontiers. He marshals the forces of order and disorder, stability and fragmentation, onto the Indian stage. In *Captains Courageous* he contrasts Harvey Cheene, the rich boy, with Dan Troop, the poor boy; the novice with the initiate; the life of leisure with the life of work. In *The Naulahka,* "A Story of East and West," written in collaboration with Wolcott Balestier, he compares the American West with the Indian plains; the fair American girl with the dark Indian princess; the aristocratic splendor of India with the simplicity and industriousness of Colorado. In *The Light That Failed* he compares the Egyptian battlefield and Tommy Atkins, the British soldier, with London, the literary world and the artist. He compares the world of respectability, love and marriage with passion, sex and the disreputable. He contrasts the demands of art with the necessities of action. In *The Jungle Book* he compares the tribe with the outsider, the village of man with the confederation of beasts, law with anarchy.

The contrasts are firmly established but the dramatic situations are terminated without rigorous struggle. They do not precipitate dialectical conflicts. Kipling's heroes stand in a world which is divided between East and West, Black and white, rich and poor. They are composed of atomic particles which pull them toward the East and then back toward the West, toward the Brown man and then back to the white man. But there is little pull or push. The particles do not collide to produce new particles or antiparticles. Kipling keeps the opposing impulses in his heroes and the rival armies in society under control. He is the master at the machine, pulling levers and pushing buttons. Kipling's contrasts are immutable; he catalogs and compartmentalizes his characters. He allows his men time to wander on the leash, but demands of them that they remain close to home. They inevitably do. Hell, the East, the Jungle—these worlds are seen and explored by his heroes, but they are seen in concave or convex mirrors and they are scouted rather than explored. The under- and the outer worlds are rejected. Kipling's characters scurry back to heaven, the West and civilization. Early in the game the outcome of the foraging expeditions is clear. In *The Naulahka* we know that Tarvin will not remain in India; he will not marry the Indian princess. He must return to Colorado with the plain American girl. At moments he is terrified and fascinated by the extraordinary horrors and beauties of India, but he goes back to Middle Amerika. In *Captains Courageous* we know that Kipling will lift Harvey Cheene from the fishing schooner *We're Here* as swiftly and decisively as he lets him fall from the luxury liner into the Atlantic Ocean. Work is attractive for a summer but not as a way of life; Cheene returns to his wealthy and powerful family. We don't feel, as the author wants us to feel, that he will be a better capitalist because he has been a worker.

Kipling describes the organization man in isolation, the puritan in Bohemia, the white man among Brown men. His men are defined, their minds made flexible, their muscles made taut, through contact with their opposing types. They watch the moves of their adversaries in a magical mirror and adjust their own selves accordingly. There is rarely open conflict between Kipling's characters. In *Captains Courageous* there is no conflict between workers and bosses. In the tales of Anglo-India there is no dialectical relationship between East and West, Black and white. Kipling creates harmony between classes and cultures. On his ladder there is movement in only one direction: the puritan moves down among the bohemians, but the bohemian cannot move up among the puritans; the white man lives among Brown men, but the Brown man cannot live among whites. The rich boy plays poor boy, but the poor boy cannot play rich boy. Harvey Cheene exchanges his tweeds for a fisherman's garb, he learns the fisherman's slang, but he is always a rich boy mimicking a fisherman.

Mowgli is the prototype of all Kipling's heroes. He defines his own predicament when during a jungle ritual after the hunt he chants:

> I dance on the hide of Shere Khan, but my heart is very heavy. My mouth is cut and wounded with the stones from the village, but my heart is very light because I have come back to the jungle. Why? These two things fight together in me as the snakes fight in the spring. The water comes out of my eyes; yet I laugh while it falls. Why? I am two Mowglis . . .

Mowgli the son of man is an alien in the jungle, and Mowgli a brother of the jungle tribe is an outcast among men. He has parents in both the Indian village and the Indian jungle. He is manchild in the jungle. Kipling creates a contrast between man and beast, but it is diversionary. The vital contrast in *The Jungle Books* is not between man and beast but between law and anarchy, the empire and the Indians. When Mowgli chooses sides he leaves the beasts to join the world of men; but the men are white men, not Brown men. He exchanges the yoke of jungle law for the yoke of empire; he rejects the lawless rabble and embraces the stern officials. Mowgli leaves the beasts' world to become a man, but he mounts a rung at the bottom of the imperial ladder in the Department of Woods, exchanging a tribe for a bureaucracy. Kipling's contrasts give the appearance of objectivity, but no stories are more partisan. Behind the cunningly arranged contrasts lie the values of an authoritarian.

The first story Kipling wrote about Mowgli, "In the Rukh," describes the last incident chronologically in his saga—his coming of age. His hero is married to an Indian woman and appointed to a post in the empire. From the start Mowgli is respectable. In the stories that followed, Kipling retraced his earlier career; he described the boy Mowgli. But Kipling does not reject the British Empire, as one might expect, when he describes Mowgli's youth. He celebrates law, hierarchy and empire in different ways. At the conclusion of *The Jungle Book* Kipling's spokesman says:

> Mule, horse, elephant, or bullock, he obeys his driver, and the driver his sergeant, and the sergeant his lieutenant, and the lieutenant his captain, and the captain his major, and the major his colonel, and the colonel his brigadier commanding three regiments, and the brigadier his general, who obeys the Viceroy, who is the servant of the Empress.

The tales about men and beasts offer a message: the empire. *The Jungle Book* culminates in a vision of the imperial hierarchy. The little world of the jungle forms a small circle within other circles within the circle of empire. Kipling's circle of empire contains all. In *The Naulahka, Captains Courageous* and *Plain Tales from the Hills,* contrasts are sustained and differences are tolerated because all individuals, classes, races and groups are incorporated under the empire or into the imperial hierarchy. In Kipling's model society the bear, the wolf, the snake, accept the law. In the Anglo-Indian society of his day men pledged their allegiance to Victoria, Empress of India. Each species is different from the next, each man is distinct from his fellow-man, but they are all contained in an overarching structure. Divisions in the hero are subsumed under his one patriotic self. The two Mowglis merge in the one Mowgli, who accepts the law in the worlds of both man and beast.

Kipling's theme is simultaneously the separation of races, classes and lands, and the links between two men of opposite places of origin. The societies are opposed, but the individual men are together. Kipling writes of diversity in unity and unity in diversity. Rich and poor are different, but Harvey Cheene and Dan Troop are comrades; man and beast are different, but Mowgli is a friend of the wolf and the bear. The contrast at the core of Kipling's work is between cultures which are at opposite ends of the spectrum and individuals from those cultures who stand side by side. Kipling's classic statement of the theme is from "The Ballad of East and West":

Oh, East is East and West is West, and never the twain shall meet,
Till Earth and Sky stand presently at God's great judgment Seat,
But there is neither East nor West, Border nor Breed nor Birth,
When two strong men stand face to face though they come from the ends of the earth!

Kipling is concerned equally with the irreconcilable hemispheres and the reconciled men. He is the poet of inequality who simultaneously celebrates the friendship between the Brown man and the white man, the rich man and the poor man. The poet of inequality deceives us; he appears in the guise of the poet of democracy and lauds Black men, Brown men, poor men. In Kipling's work the common soldier loves his officer and praises the colonial people. "The finest man I knew," says the cockney soldier in one of Kipling's best-known poems, "was our regimental bhisti Gunga Din." But when two strong men from the ends of the earth come face-to-face and embrace in Kipling's world, it is not a celebration of human fraternity. The friendships between the rich and the poor, Black and white, the tribe and the alien, in *Captains Courageous, The Jungle Book,* "The Ballad of East and West" and "Gunga Din" are unlike the genuine moments of humanity reflected in literature. When Melville describes Ishmael and Queequeg locked in each other's arms, he presents an ideal of human fraternity in a world of violent hatred. When Tolstoi depicts an old Russian peasant sharing bread with Levin, he offers a utopian vision in a world where masters and peasants are in conflict. At first glance Kipling's scenes have the look of these situations in Tolstoi and Melville. But unlike Melville and Tolstoi, Kipling neglects the real conflicts between rich and poor, Black and white. Kipling is out to co-opt us. He wants us to remember the friendship between Kim and the lama, Cheene and Troop, and forget about the exploitation of Black by white, the oppressed by their oppressors. When his heroes, Mowgli and the wolf, Cheene and Troop, join in common aim, they stand in contrast with—but not in defiance of—the divisions between men. Kipling's images of unity define oppositions and contrasts. The exception proves the rule. His characters offer fellowship to each other because they know their places, they accept the social hierarchy. There is only fraternity between unequal partners in Kipling's world, and that is no fraternity at all.

Kipling's earliest coherent expression of this idea is the story "East and West." Two passengers, one of them Kipling and the other an elegant and educated Afghan, sit facing each other on a train. They converse cordially. They never fight, but they never sit arm in arm and they never embrace. They are rigid machines whose jaws open and close, and whose arms move up and down. Kipling, the white machine, tells the Afghan that "God made us different." The oracle has spoken. Differences in this case mean British superiority and Afghan inferiority. Kipling asks us to imagine "parallel straight lines" which, "being continued to all eternity, will never meet." As the train goes onward, carrying an Afghan and Kipling in the same compartment, the railway tracks remain forever apart, a reminder to Kipling of the inevitable and necessary division of Black from white. Apartheid is his law of nature. In *Life's Handicap* he describes a monastery in Northern India which shelters men of different races and religions: "Mohamedan, Sikh, and Hindi mixed equally under the trees. They were old men, and when man has come to the turnstiles of Night all the creeds in the world seem to him wonderfully alike and colourless." It sounds internationalist in spirit, but these men, none of whom are white, come together in weakness rather than in strength, rejecting rather than preserving their individual differences. Here unity is based on the denial of diversity. As a Freemason in India Kipling boasted that he knew Muslims, Hindus, Sikhs and Jews, but he accepted them because the important thing was not that they were Jews or Hindus or Muslims, but because they were Freemasons. His view of empire was of Freemasonry writ large. He would shake any man's hand—Black or white, rich or poor—if he defended the empire. The different nations were incorporated after combat in one body. In the formation of the empire he noted that the

Zulus, the Malays, the Maoris, the Pathans, the Arabs and the Sudanese "played a thoroughly good game. For this we owe them many thanks." It was all good sport.

Kipling's contrasts, his celebrations of individual customs and traits, are incorporated into a world of masters and slaves, rich and poor, victimizers and victims. The fear of miscegenation, rebellion and social upheaval struck deep into the core of his being. In his nightmares he envisioned the overthrow of white by Black, West by East. Those nightmares were warnings to him that the things which he loved, things as they were and as he hoped they would continue to be, were threatened. He believed in the necessity of racial separation, class lines, law, social hierarchy; but he was captivated by the things he feared most. Kipling defended the establishment, the West, the white man, the rich, and was fascinated by the world outside and beyond those limits—by the poor, the East, the Black man. His fascination for the latter does not call into question or negate his commitment to the former. Kipling stands for order, empire and white men, and he stands for them precisely by going beyond them to describe disorder, Black men, loneliness and horror. Kipling creates his contrasts—sits in heaven as opposed to hell, with the white as opposed to the Black, with the philistines as opposed to the bohemians, with the tribe as opposed to the alien—but he descends into the regions he fears. When he describes his expeditions into the world beyond and below, his vision is more significant than when he describes the protected, secure world. When he stops seeing the jungle as the law, as he does in *The Jungle Books,* and begins to see it as a threat, when he describes white men as estranged from white society and fearful of Black men and hostile nature, he reveals himself, the white man, and offers work of importance. His intention was usually to strengthen the law and the imperial hierarchy through making the descent into hell, but apart from his conscious aim the sense of contrast which results from the descent is important. When he writes that "When a man is absolutely alone in a Station he runs a certain risk of falling into evil ways," when he notes that "Few people can afford to play Robinson Crusoe anywhere—least of all in India," there is the sound of truth. This Kipling encircled the core of reality that Conrad probed in *Heart of Darkness*. While he did not confront loneliness as Conrad did, he offers more meaningful and vital material when he presents horrors and terrors than when he hides the facts and retreats into his luxurious, exotic and nostalgic worlds.

3

Portrait of the Artist as Imperialist

I. ORWELL AND KIPLING

"Kipling *is* a jingo imperialist," George Orwell wrote. "He *is* morally insensitive and aesthetically disgusting." He begins by digging a deep trench between himself and Kipling and then fills it in. At the end they're standing beside each other. Orwell dislikes the brazen jingoist, the sadist, the snobbish conservative. But he admires Kipling because he was neither a liberal nor a radical, neither an intellectual nor a humanitarian. Orwell admires Kipling because he advocated action, because he was not a pacifist, because he understood responsibility and state power. He finds Kipling exemplary because he was not a rebel, because he had "no wish to *épater les bourgeois*." This Kipling, Orwell claimed, had a "grip on reality" because he "identified himself with the ruling power and not with the opposition." Kipling wrote about important things, about urgent social issues, and he had a world view. He was not limited by Bloomsbury. Kipling is refreshing to Orwell after Oscar Wilde and Virginia Woolf. And he uses Kipling as a hammer to beat down the liberal left on the anvil of hypocrisy. Orwell, the self-proclaimed radical, joins with Kipling, the conservative, in attacking the left. "All left-wing parties in the highly industrialised countries," Orwell wrote, "are at bottom a sham, because they make it their business to fight against something which they do not really wish to destroy. They have internationalist aims, and at the same time they struggle to keep up a standard of life with which those aims are incompatible. We all live by robbing Asiatic coolies, and those of us who are 'enlightened' all maintain that those coolies ought to be set free."

Orwell exposes the hypocrisy of many left-wing radicals in the imperial nations, the so-called humanitarians, the socialists who do not reject their white-skin privilege. But he fails to see the possibility for a truly internationalist left wing in the heart of the empire. He does not see white radicals whose revolutionary interests coincide with those of Black and Brown peoples in the colonies. And Orwell can see no possibility for a fundamental change between exploiters and exploited, Black and white. "He sees clearly," he wrote of Kipling, "that men can only be highly civilised while other men, inevitably less civilised, are there to guard and feed them." Orwell feels that class inequalities are bred deep into the human tissue, that all societies will be class societies.

Orwell, like Kipling, when faced with a choice, took the British Empire over all other states and empires. Since all societies were racist and bound by class he might just as well have his own British, class-bound, racist society. "It is a great deal better," Orwell wrote of the British Empire in the mid-1930s, "than the younger Empires that are going to supplant it." Looking right to Hitler's Germany, left to Stalin's Russia, over the Atlantic to Roosevelt's America, Orwell rejected them all—these younger empires—and stood beside the British Empire.

That perspective informs *1984*. In that work, the new empires are competing for control of the world, fascism and communism are made to look identical and the ideal world, more than anything else, is the middle-class Victorian past. It is the idyllic English countryside and the comfortable middle-class home, the closeness of family life and middle-class possessions, which appeal to Orwell. Today *1984* is relevant, for it describes something that Orwell had not intended: the brutality of the Amerikan invasion and destruction of Indochina. The helicopters which land in distant battlefields in *1984* are the Amerikan helicopters which are landing in Laos, Cambodia, Vietnam.

Orwell took Kipling to task for not understanding what he knew, that "an empire is primarily a money-making concern." But he finds Kipling and the British more attractive than the fascist and the Stalinist because, as he writes, "the modern totalitarians know what they are doing, and the nineteenth-century English did not know what they were doing." Orwell assumes that the English did not mean to bring injustice, war and oppression to Black and Brown peoples. He feels that they were unconscious of the realities of power and wealth. And he believes that Kipling himself, although a jingo imperialist, was not a sinister character. "The imperialism of the 'eighties and 'nineties," he wrote, "was sentimental, ignorant and dangerous, but it was not entirely despicable . . . It was still possible to be an imperialist and a gentleman, and of Kipling's *personal* decency there can be no doubt." But a reading of *Something of Myself* (1937), Kipling's autobiography, indicates that toward his Indian servants he didn't exhibit personal decency. When his "coolies," as he called them, became mutinous, he cursed them and lashed the headman on the back with a whip. Kipling's racism was apparent not only in his writings but in his day-to-day relations with Indians and Africans. He was no part-time imperialist; it was a twenty-four-hour-a-day job.

Because he too was born in India, had attended a public school in England which prepared boys for the empire (Eton) and had served with the Imperial Police in Burma from 1922 to 1927, Orwell felt he had much in common with Kipling. His own experience in the colonial world, like Kipling's experience, provided material for his fiction. And he especially valued that type of fiction. "Civilised men," he wrote, "do not readily move away from the centres of civilisation, and in most languages there is a dearth of what one might call colonial literature." Orwell's work and travels in Africa and the East resulted in a number of essays, especially "Shooting an Elephant," "Reflections on Gandhi," "Marrakech," and the novel *Burmese Days* (1934). "Shooting an Elephant" reflects his own ambiguous position. Orwell is one of those left-wing intellectuals who speak against imperialism, but who are not ready to sacrifice the rewards of a life as a colonial officer. He is a hypocrite. "Theoretically—and secretly, of course," he writes, "I was all for the Burmese and all against their oppressors, the British." He feels that "imperialism was an evil thing." But in practical circumstances he acts like a sahib. He is "stuck between my hatred of the empire I served and my rage against the evil-spirited little beasts who tried to make my job impossible." The idea of driving a bayonet into a Buddhist priest's guts is one which has a great deal of appeal for him. The story describes how he shoots an elephant because the Burmese expect him, as the English policeman, to shoot it. "A sahib has got to act like a sahib." He describes how he is overpowered by his role, how he can't step out of being a sahib. Orwell fears the Burmese; he makes us feel that he kills the elephant because the Burmese have a power over him. They force him to act against his own will. He presents himself as a trapped man, caught in the web of colonialism, constricted by the colonized people themselves. He is contemptuous of the Burmese. He is not disturbed that the elephant tramples a "coolie" to death. After all, nobody is dead, only a nigger. In "Marrakech" there is the same chauvinistic view of Brown men and women. Orwell tells us that "In a tropical landscape one's eye takes in everything except the human beings," that "people with brown skins are next door to invisible." He is conscious of his own debilitating perspective, but he also indulges it, plays with it, and makes no effort to cleanse it from his mind. He brings it to our attention as a curious fact. In the colonial world the death of a mule upsets us, but the "plight of the human beings does not." Orwell both feebly protests the fact, and sadly laments that it is part of the scheme of things. "Marrakech" ends with a description of a Senegalese French regiment passing by. Here are Black men with guns. Orwell is in fear of them. He assumes that he is more intelligent than they are. The Black boy in the French army "has been taught that the white race are his masters, and he still believes it," he writes. What Orwell and every other white man has on his mind is "how long before they turn their guns in the other direction." He assumes that only the white man is conscious that Black men can turn their guns toward their white officers, the white colonialists. He would have us believe that Black men are children to whom that thought has simply not occurred. Orwell is the white police chief surrounded by Black men. He too fears that his subordinates may pull the trigger on him.

His hero in *Burmese Days* pulls the trigger on himself. He commits suicide. It is the sordid, horrible end of a grubby, seedy life. When the shots of Flory's gun ring out, we see the shattered brain of a dog, which looks like red velvet, and a tiny, gelatin-like lizard. That is what human life amounts to, Orwell says. The book is pervaded by a sense of despair, of pessimism, of man's powerlessness. It is an earthquake in Burma—not the acts of human beings—which settles the destiny of the characters. Flory himself has a birthmark, the sign of his inner decay, his fated corruptibility. There is absolutely no way out for Flory. Nor is there any way out for the Burmese. There is no indication that national liberation is possible. In a long discursive passage in the novel Orwell describes Flory's own thoughts and situation. They also reflect Orwell's own feelings about the colonial situation:

What was at the centre of all his thoughts now, and what poisoned everything, was the ever bitterer hatred of the atmosphere of imperialism in which he lived. For as his brain developed—you cannot stop your brain developing, and it is one of the tragedies of the half-educated that they develop late, when they are already committed to some wrong way of life—he had grasped the truth about the English and their Empire. The Indian Empire is a despotism—benevolent, no doubt, but still a despotism with theft as its final object. And as to the English of the East, the *sahiblog,* Flory had come so to hate them from living in their society, that he was quite incapable of being fair to them . . .

It is a stifling, stultifying world in which to live. It is a world in which every word and every thought is censored . . . even friendship can hardly exist when every white man is a cog in the wheels of despotism . . . In the end the secrecy of your revolt poisons you like a secret disease. Your whole life is a life of lies. Year after year you sit in Kipling-haunted little Clubs . . . You hear your Oriental friends called "greasy little babus," and you admit, dutifully, that they *are* greasy little babus. You see louts fresh from school kicking grey-haired servants. The time comes when you burn with hatred of your own countrymen, when you long for a native rising to drown their Empire in blood. And in this there is nothing honourable, hardly even any sincerity. For, *au fond,* what do you care if the Indian Empire is a despotism, if Indians are bullied and exploited? You only care because the right of free speech is denied you. You are a creature of the despotism, a pukka sahib, tied tighter than a monk or a savage by an unbreakable system of tabus.

Flory and Orwell are both trapped in the house Kipling built. Orwell's blood is boiling. He takes an automatic rifle, and the bullets fly all over the room. Finally, he aims it at himself. The mark of Cain is on his brow. Orwell cannot imagine a world other than that of the "Kipling-haunted little clubs." He shares Kipling's sense of corruption in the East, of grotesque Indians. "Anyone who starts out with a pessimistic, reactionary view of life," Orwell concludes in his essay on Kipling, "tends to be justified by events, for Utopia never arrives." *Burmese Days* and *1984* present that view of life. Orwell is an embittered old man. He admires Kipling's conservatism, his defense of what is.

Orwell escalates the imperial mythology into the idea of totalitarianism. Socialism and fascism are the modern empires in Orwell's eyes—more exploitative and tyrannical than the British Empire of old. In *1984* there is no hope for the future; there is only a world of competing totalitarian societies. Orwell closes the door on revolution. He cannot envision an internationalist politics or an internationalist poetics.

Orwell's own dilemma is his failure to become a rebel. He is a victim. *Burmese Days* is a poor novel because for all the hatred Orwell feels for imperialism, he does not become an anti-imperialist. He lacks the revolutionary's sense of rage or his love for the people. He, unlike Kipling, knows that the empire is "despotism with theft," but he does not commit his life to toppling the despot from the throne.

Orwell was wrong about Kipling. Rudyard Kipling did not derive his power from his identification with the establishment. His work suffers precisely because he was a poet for the power elite. Where his fiction is inventive and challenging, he is a rebel. It is his sense of insecurity and loneliness, of freedom and insurrection—not his allegiance to discipline, hierarchy and order—which energizes his work.

II. HONKY IN NIGHTTOWN

Rudyard Kipling was the propagandist for the masters of war and the prophet for the agents of oppression. He proudly articulated the ideas of Milner, Chamberlain, Cecil

Rhodes and Jameson. He celebrated Queen Victoria, denounced Irish nationalists and the Indian Congress movement. He campaigned for right-wing Tories, slandered trade unions, rallied the West against Czarist and Red Russia. To his contemporaries he was "the great living laureate of imperialism." The currency he handled was stamped in the image of Britannia. Kipling had power. He was "the only person not head of a nation," Mark Twain observed, "whose voice is heard round the world the moment it drops a remark." H. G. Wells noted that Kipling was a "national symbol," that the English ism was Kiplingism. Kipling engineered the entrenchment of the ruling class. He defended autocracy and the white race, industrialism and conservatism. In the marketplace he hawked the white man's burden, the official myth of the British Empire. He maliciously neglected economic exploitation and advertised empire as the heroic endeavor of fraternal white men, enslaving themselves to free Black men and Brown men from poverty and tyranny. The big lie.

No one commissioned Kipling. He understood the house rules and obediently executed his self-imposed task. No subversive papers were issued from his desk. He achieved financial success because he was popular, and he was popular because he told the English people what the elite wanted them to hear. John Lockwood Kipling, Rudyard's father, advised young writers that "the nations that make up the Britain of our love grow year by year stronger in local patriotism and richer in local pride." These elements, he concluded, "should not be neglected by writers who hope for success." For those, like his son, who wrote patriotically about the colonies, there were rewards.

Kipling never conceived of the writer as a revolutionary. He never considered that the writer fulfilled himself or fathomed the nature of society in the act of defying or resisting the bourgeoisie. Kipling argued that no victory could be gained by railing against society. Neither slaves nor writers had the right to rebel. Writers were bound by the law. He thought of the writer only as a servant of the ruling class. His ideal community was a tribe, a gang. Within that gang he envisioned harmony between the artist and his society. The words of the artist brought social cohesion and continuity. Art was inseparable from ritual. Kipling created his own tales of primitive times to justify his view of art. He tells us that after the hunt the assembled tribe would listen to the ancient storyteller:

> His tales wouldn't grow less in the telling. Tales don't. His actual fight was probably a crude affair; but he would act it at home before the family with stately leaps and bounds to represent the death scuffle, and with elaborate wavings of his club and thrustings with his lance to show how he did his man in.

Then the drama followed the tale. While the cave men danced, the entire tribe

> . . . would all sing like children: "this is the way we kill a bison. This is how we stand up to a tiger. This is how we tackle men." The drama would be accepted as the real thing by the women and the juniors, till at last the bison, or the tiger, or the man-killing charade would become a religious ceremonial—a thing to be acted, said, or sung before going up to battle or chase, with invocations to great hunters in the past . . . It would end by being a magic ritual, sure to bring good luck if it was properly performed. And so far as that ritual, with its dances, and chants, and stampings, and marches round, gave the men cohesion and confidence, it would go far towards success in the field. That principle holds good to this day.

Kipling's empire was the modern tribe. He was the tribal bard, arousing men for war, the exploitation of the earth, the oppression of colonial people, the repression of revolutionaries.

Kipling defended the establishment and scorned rebellion, but at the same time he sought out the exiles, the outcasts, the bohemians; he roamed the underground, looked for the forbidden, the hidden, the disreputable. He boxed, exported and sold under the imperialist label folk culture, popular culture, the culture of the colonial people. Kipling wrote half a dozen tales and a novel, *The Light That Failed,* about art and the artist. They are the best place to look to understand his aesthetics.

In "To Be Filed for Reference" (1888), his first portrait of the artist, he depicts the English writer in India. He defines the problem of the European artist in the colonial world. There are three important characters: a narrator, his friend McIntosh Jellaludin, the author of the novel *The Book of Mother Maturin,* and McIntosh's Indian mistress. To the gentlemen and officers of the club, the wives, lovers and spinsters of Simla and Lahore, McIntosh is a splotch on the whiteness of the imperial record. The narrator explains that McIntosh

> . . . was the most interesting loafer that I had the pleasure of knowing for a long time; and later on he became a friend of mine. He was a tall, well-built, fair man, fearfully shaken with drink, and he looked nearer fifty than the thirty-five which, he said, was his real age. When a man begins to sink in India, and is not sent Home by his friends as soon as may be, he falls very low from a respectable point of view. By the time that he changes his creed, as did McIntosh, he is past redemption.
>
> In most big cities, natives will tell you of two or three *Sahibs,* generally low-caste, who have turned Hindu or Mussulman, and who live more or less as such. But it is not often that you can get to know them.

McIntosh rejects Anglo-India; he is friendless, as isolated as "Ovid in exile," and like no other white man in India. McIntosh is the only Englishman with whom the narrator discusses literature. He is a genuine Oxford man who speaks Greek, Latin and German. Unlike the narrator, he has a formal education. But the two men are linked by their dislike of the philistines, their enthusiasm for unfashionable literature and a taste for the pessimistic and the grotesque. McIntosh is a writer in a society which does not honor its writers, an intellectual in a society which is anti-intellectual. The narrator is anti-intellectual too, and wary of college dropouts, but he finds McIntosh attractive because he has escaped from the boredom of middle-class, churchgoing Anglo-India. He has discovered a world of mystery and intrigue and written a novel. The narrator is unwilling to drop out of the straight world, but he knows that McIntosh's world offers more to the writer than the dull Anglo-Indian drawing room. The English have all the power. The Indians have all the imagination. It is the perfect setup for the imperialist.

McIntosh is the bohemian; the narrator, the official journalist. McIntosh experiences and explores, the narrator classifies his experience and sells it on the market. McIntosh lives in Nighttown, cut loose from Anglo-India. The narrator lives with his parents, makes forays into the night and returns home again. He is never far from Papa or the policeman. The narrator visits McIntosh only at night. He does not want Anglo-Indians to see him in broad daylight associating with a white man who is a loafer, an opium-eater, an alcoholic, and whose wife is an ugly Indian. McIntosh is the stereotype of the bohemian artist—the mad, irrational genius, suffering in isolation. His "mind was a perfect ragbag of useless things"; the manuscript of *Mother Maturin* is in "a hopeless muddle," the narrator laments, but he offers to make the useless useful. He will give the manuscript shape and coherence and publish it under his own name. McIntosh's manuscript is lewd. The narrator will expurgate it. Damned and damning, McIntosh writes his masterpiece with help from no one. He sells his body to the devil to feed his head. His "bestial body" is caught "in the garbage," he explains, but his soul is "among the Gods."

Mother Maturin arises from a life of degradation, exile and self-destruction. McIntosh is the narrator's guide. He leads him through the underworld, initiates him into Nighttown. He tells him that he will give him the "materials of a New Inferno," which will make him "greater than Dante." The New Inferno, this book about hell, will depict the Indian underworld, the departure from Anglo-India, the descent, one circle at a time, to the core of hell. McIntosh offers up India to the narrator—a strange, virgin world, unseen and untouched by English writers.

McIntosh is Kipling's own night self. Kipling roamed the streets at night. He looked for and found opium dens, houses of prostitution, dens of iniquity. He considered that walk into the night a rejection of the establishment, proof of his ties with the poor and the outcast and evidence of the authenticity and vitality of his work. He was fascinated by the world of the poor and the outcast. He was driven by his curiosity; he wanted to know, so he went slumming. In foreign cities—and every city was foreign—his instinct was to dive immediately into their seedy quarters, to hug the walls of narrow alleys, to trace the strange odors in the marketplaces. He pokes his nose into the darkened faces of white men lost in the dark maze of Calcutta's streets, or European travelers meditating with Buddhist priests in remote monasteries. Kipling was a junkman with a pushcart picking up loot in the flea markets of the Third World. He wanted his readers to accept him as the world's foremost authority. He presented his credentials; he stands so that we can see him on the deck of a ship, abaft the funnel, swapping yarns with an old salt, or in a dark London street, engaged in conversation with a cockney who knows the city's labyrinths. He seeks out the initiate, he watches for the knowing look. In each city he poses as the friend of the poor and acquires a veneer of information, a handful of facts. He fakes his way, flashing his press credentials. In his autobiography he described how he would roam the streets at night in India:

> Often the night got into my head as it had done in the boarding-house in the Brompton Road, and I would wander till dawn in all manner of odd places—liquor-shops, gambling and opium-dens, which are not a bit mysterious, wayside entertainments such as puppet shows, native dances; or in and about the narrow gullies under the Mosque of Wazir Khan for the sheer sake of looking. Sometimes, the Police would challenge, but I knew most of their officers, and many folk in some quarters knew me for the son of my Father, which in the East more than anywhere else is useful. Otherwise, the word "Newspaper" sufficed; though I did not supply my paper with many accounts of these prowls. One would come home, just as the light broke, in some night-hawk of a hired carriage which stank of hookah-fumes, jasmine flowers, and sandalwood; and if the driver were moved to talk, he told one a good deal. Much of real Indian life goes on in the hot-weather nights. This is why the native staff of the offices are not much use the next morning.

"To Be Filed for Reference" captures Kipling's sense of isolation from England and English culture while in India. He longed for "the lost heritage of London," of the metropolitan center. He missed the "roar of the streets, the lights, the music," the theaters and restaurants. For amusement in India he only had the "dolorous dissipations of gymkhanas, where everyone knows everybody else," and the "chastened intoxication of dances," where men's and women's pasts were "as patent as his or her method of waltzing."

Kipling felt that for the artist transplanted from England to Anglo-India there was very little society to write about. In Anglo-India there were only a few shaky social institutions which shielded the white man from his environment: the club, the barracks, the administrative offices. There was no dense social web, no complicated social structure. The material the English writer instinctively handled was not available in Anglo-India, so the artist had to look elsewhere. The Anglo-Indians had little history. Kipling saw no complexity in the relationship between the individual Anglo-Indian and his society. He felt that in Anglo-India there was no private life, that there was only the public sphere to write about.

White writers in colonial lands have shared Kipling's dilemma. The South African conditions Dan Jacobson describes are very much like those Kipling found in India. In "The Writer in the Commonwealth" Jacobson noted that South Africa lacked local literature, an intellectual tradition, established social forms and a local audience. He suffered from the "condition of exile" and felt the "attractive power of the metropolitan country, of England." Neither Kipling nor Jacobson remained in the colonies. The colonial world seemed the natural place to write about, but England was the place where the artist necessarily had to live and work.

Jacobson omits the key problem for the provincial writer, the white writer in South Africa or India. The white writer in both countries is cut off historically, culturally and racially from the society at large. He is outside the mainstream of a cultural and historical flow. The Anglo-Indians were isolated from the Indians; the South African whites were isolated from the Blacks. The two societies and cultures were at war with each other.

In his search for new material to write about, Kipling turned from Anglo-India to India itself. He felt that the white artist had to write about the Brown world. Of all the Anglo-Indian writers he was especially critical of the poet Henry Derozio (1809–1831), for he had failed to write about India. Kipling described Derozio as "the man who imitated Byron." He wrote that Derozio, "bitten with Keats and Scott and Shelley, overlooked in his search for material things that lay nearest him."

The Anglo-Indian critics of the 1880s and 1890s pleaded with the English to write about India. Edwin Arnold, the author of *The Light of Asia,* an interpreter of Buddhism and also an imperialist, wrote that "a treasure-mine of art, literature and picturesque description lies unworked in the common experience of our life in India." John Lockwood Kipling, Kipling's father, demanded that Anglo-Indian fiction offer "the picture from the inside," that it reveal all of "native life, thought and character." Alfred Lyall, the most perceptive of Anglo-Indian reviewers, leveled these critical charges against Kipling, and in 1899 noted with justice that "the secret of successfully interpreting Indian life and idea to the British public . . . still awaits discovery." He felt that Kipling's *The Naulahka* was an "extravagant improbability," but recognized Kipling's talents and hoped that he would write the great Indian novel. Lyall suggested that Kipling "turn his unique faculty of painting real Indian pictures toward the composition of a novel which shall *not* be about Anglo-Indian society (for the thin soil of that field has already been over-harrowed), but shall give a true and lively picture rendering the thoughts which strike an imaginative Englishman when he surveys the whole moving landscape of our Indian Empire." But these critics had little understanding of the white writer's relationship to his own society, to India, and no sense of the profound changes the European writer would have to undergo to be able to write about India from the inside.

In the middle and late 1880s Kipling was confident that *Mother Maturin,* the novel he was writing, would be the great Indian novel. In "To Be Filed for Reference" it is McIntosh who is writing *The Book of Mother Maturin.* Kipling felt that it was his dark self, his night self, his unconventional, rebel, bohemian self, which was bringing into existence this masterpiece. It was to have been the *Black Like Me* of the 1880s. When he evaluated his own work he evoked a little-known novel by Mirza Murad Ali Beg entitled *Lalun the Bargum* (1884). In his view, *Lalun the Bargum* was a classic, the measure for all other novels about India. "What Mirza Murad Ali Beg's book is to all other books on native life, will my work be to Mirza Murad Ali Beg!" McIntosh says in "To Be Filed for Reference" and Kipling adds, "This, as will be conceded by anyone who knows Mirza Murad Ali Beg's book, was a sweeping statement." *Lalun the Bargum* is a romantic tale of knights and ladies, medieval combat, a conscious imitation of Walter Scott's historical romances. The heroine of the work is a beautiful courtesan, a type Kipling often depicted in his own stories. T. S. Eliot, who especially liked McIntosh among Kipling's characters, said that "What Mirza Murad Ali Beg's book is to all other books of native life, so is Mr. Kipling's to all other works of Anglo-Indian life." Eliot noted that in *Plain Tales from the Hills* Kipling presented "the one perfect picture of a society of English, narrow, snobbish, spiteful, ignorant and vulgar, set down absurdly in a continent of which they are unconscious." But Kipling never finished *Mother Maturin*. He never wrote a perfect, or near-perfect, picture of Indian society.

Kipling began to write *Mother Maturin* in 1885. "It's not one bit nice or proper," he confessed while working on it, but he added that "it carries a grim sort of moral with it and tries to deal with the unutterable horror of lower class Eurasian and native life as they exist outside official reports." Kipling believed that Indian life offered the novelist richer material than Anglo-Indian life. But he had special additional reasons for wanting to write about the Eurasians. "The people of India," he wrote, "are neither Hindus nor Mussulman—Jew, Ethiop, Gueber, or expatriated British. They are the Eurasians." The Indians were "there from the first"; the "Englishman only comes to the country," but the Eurasians "have been made here." Eurasians were the offspring of European/Asian marriages. It was unfortunate, he admitted, that little was known about their life, "which touches so intimately the White on one hand and the black on the other," and he argued that a tale about Eurasians was desperately needed. It would be "more interesting than the colourless Anglo-Indian article." He concluded: "Wanted, therefore, a writer from among the Eurasians, who shall write so that men shall be pleased to read a story of Eurasian life." Kipling believed that by writing about the Eurasians he could connect two worlds normally estranged. His selection of the Eurasians indicates his failure to perceive the conflict between the two worlds, his predilection for combinations and for midpoints and his determination to perform a balancing act. Kipling denied that Muslims and Hindus were genuine and representative Indians because he refused to admit that India was their country or that they could govern it themselves. He was confused by India's diverse sects, religions and castes.

His original notion was that a writer would spring from the Eurasians themselves and describe life as he felt it, from the inside. "One of these days, this people," he predicted in "His Chance in Life," "will turn out a writer or a poet; and then we shall know how they live and what they feel. In the meantime, any stories about them cannot be absolutely correct in fact or inference." That judgment was sound, but it did not stop Kipling from writing lies about the Eurasians—the "Borderline folk," as he called them. He darkened his face, put on Indian clothes and looked in strange places. What we get are remarks like this:

> . . . the Black and the White mix very quaintly in their ways. Sometimes the White shows in spurts of fierce, childish pride—which is Pride of Race run crooked—and sometimes the Black in still fiercer abasement and humility, half-heathenish customs and strange, unaccountable impulses to crime.

Kipling's art was perverted from the start because he dismissed Hindus and Muslims as unfit subjects for the novelist. It was perverted because he secretly admired McIntosh, the bohemian, but knew he was a bad man. In *Kim* neither of his two main characters is Indian, although the novel is avowedly and explicitly about India. Kim is Irish, the Lama is Tibetan. The claims about India that Kipling makes in the novel are misleading because there are no important Indian characters. Kipling's imperialist perspective allows him to write about India without creating one genuine Indian. Kipling's art was also distorted because he thought of India as simultaneously exotic and grotesque. But it was primarily "unutterable horror" that he saw in India, an enigmatic land of evil beauty.

He thought of India as hell, as an inferno. When McIntosh tells the narrator of "To Be Filed for Reference" that he will give him the "materials of a New Inferno," it is his and Kipling's idea that India is a place of evil. In choosing to write about horror and evil, Kipling conceived of himself as a rebel, snubbing the Anglo-Indian civil servants who preferred to be entertained by pleasant tales—tales about courtship, love, marriage—rather than to be shocked by descriptions of corruption and vulgarity. In a series of newspaper articles written in 1888, which he entitled "The City of Dreadful Night" after James Thompson's poem, Kipling describes Nighttown in Calcutta. This is the world McIntosh inhabits. Here Kipling is aroused by the "deep, full-throated boom of life and motion and humanity," repelled and entranced by the smell which "resembles the essence of corruption." On that night he is led by the police through a tangled network of streets, through "mysterious conspiring tenements as Dickens would have loved." Finally he arrives at "the last circle of the Inferno," in which he stares at two Indian women. One of them is Dainty Iniquity, the other one is Fat Vice. Dainty Iniquity's is the "face from which a man could write Lalla Rookhs by the dozen . . . Hers was the beauty that Byron sang of." She is covered with jewels, veils, bangles, and surrounded by gorgeous women and opulence. She is the goddess of sex. By writing about Dainty Iniquity and Fat Vice, Kipling announces to the shocked society matrons that he knows all the dirt. The Indian woman is, for Kipling, the essence of evil. She is at the center of the inferno. His rejection of Hindus and Muslims as fit subjects for fiction blinded him only in one eye. Coupled with this view of Indian women he is totally blind, in need of a seeing-eye dog.

This handicap is not limited to Indian women alone. The beautiful but immoral women in his fiction are often night club performers; sometimes they are dark Jews or animalistic Blacks. In *The Light That Failed* (1890) Dick Heldar, his artist, paints pictures of naked Zanzibari girls, an immoral Cuban-Jewess-Negress and a poor English working-class girl.

Plain Tales from the Hills is dedicated "To the Wittiest Woman in India." She is white. Wit is important for Kipling because it saves the English colonials from drowning in bitterness and cynicism. Mrs. Hauksbee is the single most important character in the Anglo-Indian stories because she holds the society together. She is the witty white woman. She makes and breaks marriages and careers. She is always trying to hold the white race together. White civil servants may fall in love with Eurasians or Indians, but if they marry them their careers will be ruined and a tremor will pass through Anglo-India.

Kipling saw in the beautiful Indian courtesan and the sinful Indian whore alternatives to the dull and proper English maiden and the Anglo-Indian matron. The sisters of light are balanced against the sisters of darkness. Kipling's mother censored his works and edited them when she felt they were immoral. He was dedicated, body and soul, to her and later to his wife, but in his fantasy life he imagined the beautiful, dark, immoral woman as the companion of the artist, the inspiration for his art. The beautiful woman is always shadowed by Fat Vice. Kipling cannot disentangle

Indian beauty and sexuality from ugliness and immorality. The things he admires and desires are repulsive and evil. He was attracted to the Indian woman but unable to possess her; restless with the English matron but unable to reject her. Uptight, and unlike McIntosh, who feels no shame in living with an Indian woman and smoking hash, Kipling accepted the values and judgments of the matron, his mother, but longed for a bohemian literature which would appeal to the prurient, and for romance with an Indian woman of passion.

III. GEORGE WASHINGTON CABLE

Kipling's treatment of the Black man falls into perspective when it is placed beside the work of one of his contemporaries, George Washington Cable. Kipling had read Cable's work, but he did not learn from Cable, as he could have, how the white writer could depict the Black man honestly. Cable's *The Grandissimes* (1880) is set in New Orleans at the beginning of the nineteenth century. The main characters are Creoles. The novel is about racism. Cable describes exotic ladies, brutal men and grotesque deeds, but, unlike Kipling, the horror for him is slavery; what is shocking to Cable is the inequality between the races, not a twisted limb or scarred face. The Grandissimes are an old family: part of the family is white, part of the family Black; one Honoré Grandissime is white, the other Honoré Grandissime is a freeman of color. They are brothers, but because they live in a racist society they live in unequal conditions. But Cable does not offer a dark world in contrast to a respectable white world. He traces the connections between the seemingly respectable white family and its actual involvement with the horrors of the slave system. Kipling never showed the part Anglo-Indians played in creating and perpetuating an unequal society. Cable attacked American society: "I meant to make *The Grandissimes,*" he wrote, "as truly a political novel as it has ever been called." He added that "it was impossible that a novel written by me then should escape being a study in the fierce struggle going on around me, regarded in the light of that past history." *The Grandissimes* is set in 1800 but it is also about the era of Reconstruction. A novelist first, Cable was also a sociologist who studied Southern social structure. He had an eye for historical patterns, for representative situations and characters.

The central chapter in *The Grandissimes* describes Bras-Coupé, a slave from Africa. Nearly all of the Blacks in the book are freemen. Cable was concerned with racism, not slavery. But he knew that it was impossible to understand racism without first explaining slavery. Bras-Coupé's story reveals the atrocities in the Grandissime family's past. Cable tells us that slavery is the burden of Southern history, that present dilemmas grow out of a record of oppression. The conflict between free Blacks and whites, he felt, could be fathomed when it was remembered that the Blacks were former slaves, the whites the slave masters. In Cable's day Bras-Coupé's story was a legend in New Orleans. He heard the tale from the lips of an old porter in his office. Unlike Kipling, Cable did not depict the Black man as a marvelous storyteller, gifted with imagination, socially backward and therefore in need of the white man's law and supervision. Cable used New Orleans Black dialects without parodying the Black men who used them. He was not satisfied with a tale, however exciting it was, from an old porter. He studied the past and discovered the Black Code, laws restricting the rights of Black people. Kipling was a reporter, not an historian. He did not find the details, as Cable did, which revealed the nature of the society. Behind the lifeless details of the Black Code, Cable envisioned and re-created the living histories of New Orleans Black men and women.

Cable follows Bras-Coupé from his capture in Africa to

his death in America, where he dreams of returning home. Bought for a looking-glass, Bras-Coupé becomes a commodity, boards the slave ship *Égalité* and is reborn in chains in the New World. He is destroyed physically by his masters, but he never loses the original dignity he has when he is marched down out of the jungle to the Atlantic shore. Bras-Coupé is a rebel in every fiber of his body. He takes the name Bras-Coupé, the "Arm Cut Off," to express his hatred of slavery. "He made himself a type of all Slavery, turning into flesh and blood the truth that all Slavery is maiming."

Cable knows that slavery maims both the slaves and the masters. Kipling's tales are populated with Indians who are crippled, deformed, but they are simply grotesque shadows for whom he has no sympathy. They are mysterious and repulsive. Bras-Coupé makes no deals, no compromises; he refuses to work or to become a slave driver and force others to work. After his attacks on the white masters his ears are shorn off his head and the tendons behind his knees are severed. Then he is delivered "to the law to suffer only the penalties of the crime he had committed against society by attempting to be a free man." In defeat he maintains his heroic stature. Cable is not pessimistic or defeatist, nor does he feel that moral victory is possible only after material defeat. He shows the destructive, dehumanizing force of slavery. He does it without making his white men devils or his Black men angels. Individual whites and Blacks are good or bad, but slavery as a system is evil. When he describes the reactions of the whites to the torture of Bras-Coupé he has one eye on the liberals of his own time. One New Orleans citizen argues that the Blacks must "be taught their place," while another says, "My dear Sir, they lied to me—said they would not harm him."

Cable's portrait of Southern slavery was controversial. The *Atlantic Monthly* rejected the original story of Bras-Coupé because of the unsentimental, brutal descriptions of slavery. Kipling did not conceive of himself as a writer attacking social institutions. He was incapable of creating a character of Bras-Coupé's dimensions and in no position to offend respectable magazine editors. Cable's own voice, filled with passion, grief and hope, comes through *The Grandissimes:*

> It seems to be one of the self-punitive characteristics of tyranny, whether the tyrant be a man, a community, or a caste, to have a pusillanimous fear of its victim . . . it is barely now, that our South is casting off a certain apprehensive tremor, generally latent, but at the slightest provocation active, and now and then violent, concerning her "blacks." This fear, like others similar elsewhere in the world, has always been met by the same antidote—terrific cruelty to the tyrant's victim.

The tyrannical English feared their Indian victims and lashed out with atrocities. Kipling lashed out with a racist pen.

In "A Conference of the Powers" (1890) Kipling diagramed the relationship between the aesthete, the propagandist and the soldier. Kipling wanted aesthetes to convert to empire. This is the passage of Dick Heldar in *The Light That Failed*. People suffer so that he can paint. He exploits them. Heldar believes that "men and women were only material to work with," and that "what they said or did was of no consequence." He vows to "take toll of the ills of others"; the "poor at least should suffer that he might learn, and the rich should pay for the output of his learning." But Heldar goes blind: he is punished for gaping at the strange and forbidden places. To look beneath is a crime. The light fails. But Heldar escapes purgatory; he is saved because he becomes a soldier. After wandering in Nighttown Heldar feels sinful. The only way to make amends is to commit genocide. Heldar rushes off to the Sudan. He rejects the artist's life in favor of the soldier's death. Better to die a hero than to suffer life as a blind artist, Kipling tells us. "King and

Country," Heldar shouts as he runs off to serve the empire.

In "A Conference of the Powers" Kipling attacked both art for art's sake and the ivory-tower artist. Eustace Cleever, the main character, a "decorator and colourman in words," is the prototype of the effete and genteel isolated artist. The "outer world doesn't trouble us much," he says of his own circle. His crime, in Kipling's eyes, is that he is a "home-staying" Englishman ignorant of the empire. It is every white artist's burden, Kipling argues, to applaud colonial exploits. He himself jumped at the opportunity of recording and celebrating the panorama of the empire. He volunteered to be the encyclopedist of imperialism, to present an "Army and Navy Stores List . . . of the whole sweep and meaning of things and effort and origins throughout the Empire." During his trip to the United States at the end of the 1880s he was convinced that

> . . . there must be born a poet who shall give the English *the* song of their own, own country—which is to say, about half the world. Remains then only to compose the greatest song of all—The Saga of the Anglo-Saxon all round the earth—a paean that shall combine the terrible slow swing of the *Battle Hymn of the Republic* (which if you know not, gets chanted to you) with *Britannia Needs No Bulwarks,* the skirl of the *British Grenadiers,* with that perfect quickstep *Marching Through Georgia,* and at the end the wail of the *Dead March*. For, We, even We who share the earth between us as no gods have ever shared it, we also are mortal in the matter of our single selves. Will anyone take the contract?

Kipling followed along behind the trail of the soldier and the statesman. He offered a parable of ancient times to justify his allegiance to them:

> . . . when a man first achieved a most notable deed he wished to explain to his Tribe what he had done. As soon

> as he began to speak, however, he was smitten with dumbness, he lacked words, and sat down. Then there arose . . . a masterless man, one who had taken no part in the action of his fellow, who had no special virtues, but who was afflicted . . . with the magic of the necesssary word. He saw; he told; he described the merits of the notable deed in such a fashion . . . that the words "became alive and walked up and down in the hearts of all his hearers."

In "A Conference of the Powers" the aesthete learns that the army has its own regimental bards who sing the glories of war with the "true barrack-room twang." He discovers that this artist lives among the ranks rather than caging himself with theorists, sculptors and painters. The regimental bard sings for empire. Cleever's ivory tower crumbles; the aesthete visits London music halls, embraces violent soldiers and never again longs for the ideal realms of pure art. Cleever visits Nighttown in London. Here are the London poor, similar in appearance to the Indians. Kipling paints grotesque features on their faces and registers them in "the chamber of horrors." "The gas-lamps are their sun, and the Covent Garden wains the chariots of the twilight," he wrote of the London lumpen proletariat in "The Record of Badalia Herodsfoot" (1890). They were born into "Death, and Death crowded down by unhappy life." In the music halls Kipling saw the immorality, the vice, the noise and the "good fellowship of relaxed humanity" he hungered for. He thought that the music hall, like the Indian underworld, was not nice or proper, but that it was exciting, boisterous and an inspiration for his art.

"A Conference of the Powers" depicts the artists of the 1880s and 1890s who emerged from their cocoons of art and developed passions for British soldiers and the imperial enterprise. In his introduction to *Mine Own People,* a collection of Kipling's stories, Henry James described his own fascination with military combat and violence. Eustace Cleever observes that "the whole idea of warfare seems so foreign and unnatural, so essentially vulgar," but he discovers that he has a love of militarism. James's initial reaction was identical to Cleever's, and he also revealed his own fascination with imperial violence:

> People who know how peaceful they are themselves and have no bloodshed to reproach themselves with needn't scruple to mention the glamour that Mr. Kipling's intense militarism has for them and how astonishing and contagious they find it, in spite of the unromantic complexion of it—the way it bristles with all sorts of uglinesses and technicalities.

At least Kipling was consistent. In "The Eye of Allah" (1926), a late story, Kipling put the finishing touches on his portrait of the artist. There are a few changes, but the portrait is nearly identical to the original sketch. There are three central characters—an artist, a scientist and an authoritarian. Brother John, a medieval artist in a monastery, uses the microscope—the eye of Allah, an evil eye—to look at beasts which he then copies in his religious paintings. "My shapes," he says, "are to be seen honestly, in nature." He paints "devils . . . with lobes and protuberances—a hint of a fiend's face peering through jelly-like walls. And there was a family of impatient, globular devilings." In his Anglo-Indian tales the devils are Indians, hell is India. In his late stories the devils are microbes under the microscope. Wherever he went he saw devils. He peers into forbidden places, into Indian opium dens and into the microscope. The abbot of the monastery declares the eye of Allah evil and subversive to society, and destroys it. The artist will no longer see the unseen, but he does not protest. He accepts the official decree. Over the entrance to Kipling's monastery these words are written: Artists, heed your abbots. Do not go beyond, do not flaunt authority. Obey.

4

Terror

The very best of Kipling's Anglo-Indian tales plumbed the fears and paranoia of his society. Kipling and the Anglo-Indians were frightened of the Indian masses, of mutiny and rebellion, and haunted by images of the Black Hole of Calcutta. They created the image of the brutal Indian to justify their own brutality. They built a Frankenstein which turned against them. They feared rebellion but tried to live as if no danger existed. "I have always felt the menacing darkness of tropical eventides," Kipling wrote in his autobiography. Blackness was a threat to whiteness. One incident from his childhood stood out: his parents returned unexpectedly early from a dinner party because "the big Lord Sahib" had been assassinated by an Indian. Meeta, his Hindu bearer, explained to him that Lord Mayo had been stabbed with a knife.

Kipling wanted to believe that his servants had a deep affection for him and his family. Every morning before he awoke his face was shaven clean by an Indian. His personal servant was the son of his father's personal servant. Only the comforting illusion that Indians loved the English could free him from continual fear of the barber's razor; it enabled him to forget nightmares of slit throats and mangled bodies. But Kipling wanted both to believe that his servants loved him and to feast his imagination on the sight of gored bodies.

His Anglo-Indians are plagued by unrealities. They are haunted men and women. They must smile and be charming while hatred and cruelty rages beneath the surface. The

Anglo-Indian mind is unbalanced: the "Powers of Darkness" have infiltrated its lines of defense. The ordinary Anglo-Indian has two selves. One self inhabits the material world, the other inhabits a world of appearances. The most common things become ghosts. In "The Phantom Rickshaw" (1885), a rickshaw, with an Englishwoman for a passenger and a retinue of Indian servants, passes back and forth before Jack Pansy. All else seems unreal—England, Anglo-Indians homeward bound and Anglo-India itself. Sometimes India seems illusory and England tangible. At other times remote England seems to drop out of existence like a ship rounding the horizon. Then the Indian nightmare becomes the only firm reality. Provincial life seems unsubstantial, a game among shadows. In the midst of these horrible, fearful, yet pleasurable phantoms there is no exit. At night, as they gaze into strange, distorting mirrors, Kipling's Anglo-Indians watch an image of the self they regularly hide—faces seared, scarred—signifying their inner cynicism and corruption. In dream and fantasy Kipling and his fellow exiles in bondage confront and acknowledge the anguish of Anglo-Indian life.

For Kipling, India was a collection of boxes, one inside the other, mounting to form a pyramid. The slaves are at the bottom, the empress at the top. The boxes are self-contained, yet each one rests on the other, and the bottom of each box opens at irregular intervals and plunges the inhabitants into an underworld of intrigue. In one box the women pursue their social work, serve tea, exchange afternoon vists. The men sit in offices during the day, go to the club in the evening, and on weekends they flee into the jungle to hunt. Below that box in an identical cubicle the same figures, now stripped naked, bite and snarl like caged beasts. Husbands and wives exchange partners, then return to their spouses in an elaborate dance. On one floor the husbands and wives behave in civilized fashion; on another floor they are brutal. The pretense of civilization is broken, the gulf is opened wide; then all is forgotten and the game resumes once more. The boxes are houses; they are prisons. There is no escape for the inmates; visitors are rare. Beyond the windows the inmates see vast plains and mountains—no other cities, no other men.

Sometimes, with an exertion of the will, Kipling squeezes the Indians from the stage of his imagination. They are gone from the face of the earth; only the imprint of a foot remains —a suggestion of their departure and a hint of their reappearance. The white man sees no one, but fears an invasion of dark powers from abroad. He hears strange laughter. From inside temples, in dark streets, on the open plains, the white man in India sees encroaching shadows and senses his nakedness. He is sure that men are laughing at him. His pith helmet, mustache, cane and white shorts seem absurd. The land echoes with laughter, but the laughing Indians are never seen. When they appear they are silent; their expressionless faces give no hint of emotion or thought.

Kipling's Anglo-Indians are haunted by diseased old men in temples, thieves in the market place. But their fears are rarely located or defined precisely. They fear, they experience moments of terror. Since Indians are inferior beings incapable of terrorizing white men, the fears are abstract and undefined. Kipling even hesitates before allowing a native ghost to haunt flesh-and-blood Englishmen. Among supernatural creatures, too, there must be an imperial order. "No native ghost," Kipling writes, "has yet been authentically reported to have frightened an Englishman; but many English ghosts have scared the life out of both white and black." In "Bubbling Well Road" Kipling ventures into a jungle which conceals a one-eyed priest whose forehead has been burnt with the impress of two copper coins. Like this priest, Kipling's Indian characters are often deformed; the scars they carry imply torture and brutality at the hands of the master race. They suggest vengeance, too. They are the open marks of latent fear and hate. These branded creatures are Untouchables, men continually suspected of planning rebellion. They are rounded up, savagely beaten and tortured and held guilty for conspiracy to spread hatred of the white man. In the jungle of the "Bubbling Well Road" Kipling loses his bearings. Everything he says is echoed by an unseen voice; he becomes nervous and self-conscious. At the heart of the jungle, in the center of a pit, he meets a priest who howls with terror and embraces Kipling's boots to prove his obedience to the white man. Kipling wanted to be loved by the man he detested; he wanted the oppressed to genuflect before the oppressor. His closing remark in "Bubbling Well Road" is a malicious jest. Some day soon, he says, he will return and burn the entire jungle down to the ground, revealing its horrors, destroying its inhabitants in one engulfing blaze.

Anglo-Indian bungalows are haunted by dark figures and drifting voices. In "At the End of the Passage" a white man is found dead. His friends, each one living an isolated life on the frontier, photograph the frozen picture on the retina of a dead man's eyes and thereby capture the negative image of the beast which has terrified and killed him. But the nature of the beast is never revealed. Kipling does not tell us what it is. Sometimes these haunted houses contain the bodies of dead Englishmen murdered by their servants. The killers are tracked down, caught and executed. But servants are rarely murderers. They are usually trustworthy, obedient, loving. They are quick to bow. Kipling's perfect servants never need to be spoken to or directed.

The old Indian woman who nurses the Anglo-Indian male child is dressed in glowing raiment. Through her milk the imperialist baby receives the Indian heritage. Because that fluid flows through his veins he is a better ruler than the Englishman raised in England and shipped abroad. Servants arrange everything quietly, unostentatiously. In "A Deal in

Cotton" the white man's servants secretly arrange for slave labor and the sordid commercial deals while he grows cotton for fun and adventure.

No place is safe for the white man, least of all Indian temples and palaces. These gory places, streaked with the blood of ritual sacrifices, become living things whose walls seem to breathe and gather around the Englishman. Things catch at his throat. The hero of *The Naulahka* rides out of an Indian king's courtyard and

> Something sprang out of the darkness where the guard slept, and where the King's fighting apes were tethered; and the horse reared as a grey ape, its chain broken at the waist-band, flung itself on the pommel of the saddle, chattering. Tarvin felt and smelt the beast. It thrust one paw into the horse's mane, and with the other encircled his own throat . . . The creature rolled off to the ground, moaning like a human being.

Kipling's beast is half man, half ape. He is the embodiment of all the forces which threaten the white man in India.

In populous cities, too, fear and terror strike: "the indescribable taint of overcrowded humanity" engulfs and nauseates the European. Sometimes the terror arrives to punish the white man's indiscretion. In "The Mark of the Beast," Fleete, a colonial civil servant, violates the temple of Hanuman, the monkey-god, and in retribution he is transformed into a beast. Fleete is a jolly, inoffensive civil servant who has no knowledge of the Indians. Ignorance of their customs is his crime. The tale begins in a comfortable club where Englishmen have gathered from the ends of the empire, in a "general closing of the ranks." It swings into an Indian temple where Fleete is bitten by a faceless, silver-colored leper. It is important for Kipling's purposes that the attacker be a leper who is faceless and formless, unable to communicate. Kipling wants him to be beyond our range of sympathies. Fleete drops from the ranks of humanity and from the English club; he becomes a beast, carrying on his left breast a black rosette mark which signifies his loss of human intelligence, his possession by the forces of India. Kipling was fixated by the notion of a white man swallowed up by the Indian world and finally transformed from man to beast. In India Dr. Jekyll became Mr. Hyde under the threat of violence from man, beast and nature.

Kipling was compelled to write about estranged men. Like Conrad, he traced the fate of the isolated white man. But Kipling glanced at alienation and then stressed the need for a "general closing of the ranks," for the procedures and decorum of the British army and club. Frank O'Connor, the Irish critic and short-story writer, notes that Kipling "cannot write about the one subject a story teller must write about—human loneliness." Kipling learned from his Indian experience that the colonial Englishman could never be alone. Fearful of colonial uprising, he huddled with his fellow exiles to hide from the "essential loneliness" of Anglo-Indian life.

The scene in "The Man Who Was" is an army hall: a strange creature crawls from the plains of Russian Asia, returning by instinct to his army unit. He is an Englishman who has been a prisoner in a Siberian concentration camp. The tale represents an attack on Russia, a call for defense of the Indian frontier and an assault on the Russian character. Kipling observes that

> . . . the Russian is a delightful person till he tucks in his shirt. As an Oriental he is charming. It is only when he insists upon being treated as the most easterly of western peoples instead of the most westerly of easterns that he becomes a racial anomaly extremely difficult to handle.

Kipling wants us to understand that Russians are Eastern barbarians and that they will destroy the Western civilizers unless the empire is defended. The Russian has the power to transform the Westerner into an Easterner. The central figure in "The Man Who Was" is no longer a man. Kipling reveals the awesome and destructive power of Siberia. He applauds the Englishman's instinct which draws him back to his army barracks. We are supposed to feel that English civilization must be defended against Russian barbarism. The man who was, Number Fourteen, can never again become a soldier. But Fleete is able to return intact to the club. The mark of the beast is removed by Kipling and Strickland, the plain-clothes policeman who is Kipling's ideal colonialist. Kipling tells us that Strickland triumphs over the Indians because he takes in hand their own weapons. In effect, he offers a manual for torture. Here again Kipling reverses the relationship between the Indians and the English: he turns the Brown victims into the Brown victimizers, the white oppressors into the white oppressed. He seems, in his descriptions of torture, to enjoy the spectacle of suffering:

> The leper only mewed. Strickland wrapped a towel round his hand and took the gun-barrels out of the fire. I put the half of the broken walking stick through the loop of the fishing-line and buckled the leper comfortably to Strickland's bedstead. I understood then how men and women and little children can endure to see a witch burnt alive; for the beast was moaning on the floor, and though the Silver Man had no face, you could see horrible feelings passing through the slab that took its place, exactly as waves of heat play across red-hot iron—gun-barrels.

In "The Strange Ride of Morrowbrie Jukes" (1885), one of his earliest and longest stories, Kipling weaves together these different themes. He provokes, badgers and laughs at his readers, who he assumes are skeptical, matter-of-fact businessmen and housewives. He wants them to drop their questions and be prepared to accept a fantastic tale. "The Strange Ride" was originally part of a collection which included two other stories, "The Man Who Would Be King" and "The Phantom Rickshaw," and which was published in Allahabad under the title *The Phantom Rickshaw and Other Tales*. In the preface Kipling spars with his wary readers:

> This is not exactly a book of real ghost-stories, as the cover makes believe, but rather a collection of facts that never quite explain themselves . . . All that the collector can be certain of is that one man insisted upon dying because he believed himself to be haunted; another man either made up a wonderful fiction, or visited a very strange place; while the third man was indubitably crucified by some person or persons unknown, and gave an extraordinary account of himself.

In the first edition he had written: "There, as the conjurors say, is no invention about this tale." But for the later English editions he deleted the phrase "as the conjurors say." Since a wonderful city for rich men exists in the desert, Kipling says he is convinced that there also exists the Village of the Dead, a little world concealed in a deep pit in the desert. Hindus who have been pronounced dead and have then recovered are imprisoned in the pit. The inmates are the living dead. Jukes, the central character and the narrator of "The Strange Ride," once heard a wandering traveler's tale about the Village of the Dead, but laughed at the preposterous yarn. He discovers that the story is true, that the actual place is identical to the fiction about it. Kipling intimates that his readers will find his stories useful in learning how to cope with the natives. Jukes is the only Englishman who has ever been to the Village of the Dead. He is a civil engineer "with a head for plans and distances . . . and he certainly would not take the trouble to invent imaginary traps." Jukes gives precise dates, lists of things, accurate descriptions, mathematical figures:

> Imagine then, as I have said before, a horseshoe shaped crater of sand with steeply-graded sand walls about thirty-

> five feet high. (The slope, I fancy, must have been about 65°.) This crater enclosed a level piece of ground about fifty yards long by thirty at its broadest part, with a rude well in the centre. Round the bottom of the crater, about three feet from the level of the ground proper, ran a series of eighty-three semicircular, ovoid, square, and multilateral holes, all about three feet at the mouth.

When he finds a dead mummified body in one of the holes he gives an inventory of the items beside it. Jukes tells us that he is "not of an imaginative temperament." He is presented to us as the "average Englishman." But the Village of the Dead is not an average place. It is an extraordinary pit in the Indian desert, in existence since "time immemorial." In the extraordinary pit the Indian realities are revealed. It is an amphitheater which heightens ordinary life into a fantastic drama.

"Accuracy," Kipling wrote in 1889, "is surely the touchstone of all art." In the act of writing Kipling tells us he "revelled in profligate abundance of detail . . . for the joy of it." In an 1898 essay on *The Tempest,* Kipling claimed that the first law of literature was that "a story to be truly miraculous must be ballasted with fact." *The Tempest* evoked dream and magic, but it was built on "profligate abundance of detail." Shakespeare's vision was woven from the "most prosaic material." In "The Craftsman" he depicts Shakespeare acquiring material for his plays

> . . . at an alehouse under Cotswold,
> He had made sure of his very Cleopatra
> Drunk with enormous salvation-contemning
> Love for a tinker.
> . . . he hid from Sir Thomas's keepers,
> Crouched in a ditch and drenched by the midnight
> Dews, he had listened to gipsy Juliet
> Rail at the dawning.

In "The Strange Ride" Kipling offers details and exact proportions, but the story is organized by the image of a lone Englishman trapped in a pit with hostile Indians. That image, not the accurate details, gives the story its power. Kipling resorted to accurate details as an indication of his dedication to the West. He wanted his readers to know he was scientific, exacting, not totally fanciful like the Easterners. He felt that accuracy was the white man's value. It accorded with law, order, technology and power. Indians were inaccurate. His father had asserted that Indians habitually evade making "accurate statements, whether in a literary, scientific, or artistic sense." Rudyard Kipling, in a joking spirit, claimed that "if there is one thing the Oriental detests more than another, it is the damnable Western vice of accuracy." Kipling stuck to the West by offering accurate details. They are usually a burden to the stories, unnecessary cargo which his racist ideology demands he transport.

But in "The Strange Ride" they are not an encumbrance. In this story the accurate details impress upon us the horror of the pit. Escape seems impossible. The pit is enclosed by quicksand and guarded by the English. When Jukes stumbles accidentally into the pit, a crowd gathers. "They were all scantily clothed in that salmon-coloured cloth which one associates with Hindu mendicants, and at first sight gave me the impression of a band of loathsome fakirs. The filth and repulsiveness of the assembly were beyond description." Jukes's white skin confers no privilege. "Even in these days," he notes, "when local self-government has destroyed the greater part of a native's respect for a Sahib, I have been accustomed to a certain amount of civility from my inferiors, and on approaching the crowd naturally expected that there would be some recognition of my presence." But the Indians laugh, howl, yell and whistle at him. He discovers that the Indians despise him or, at best, treat him with indifference. Jukes has no power over the Indians. He is overpowered by "nameless terror." "Here was a Sahib," he says of himself, "a representative of the dominant race, helpless as a child and completely at the mercy of his native neighbours."

The story tears aside the illusions of Anglo-India and shows that the whole of the society is based on the white man's violence. Jukes calmly threatens the Indians with murder. In order to survive, he says, one must remember that "there was no law save that of the strongest." The tale points up the discrepancy between English democratic rhetoric and the actualities of English tyranny. While Jukes asserts that might makes right, the Indian Gunga Dass expresses the official democratic view. He tells Jukes that the pit is a republic with procedures for elections, that each citizen of the pit is entitled to his fair share of the goods. The underground republic is governed according to this maxim: "greatest good of greatest number." Kipling shows what would happen if India were really governed along John Stuart Mill's democratic utilitarian lines instead of by bureaucratic utilitarian principles. He wants a return to the past when Indians respected white men. Kipling knew that empire and popular democracy were incompatible, and he opted for empire. In "The Strange Ride" he depicted a nightmarish future, a world in which Indians held sway over the English. He could imagine nothing more terrifying. But the tale, apart from its conscious aim, captures the bitter strife between the two races. It strips aside the myth of the white man's burden.

"The Strange Ride" has two endings. The first is congruous with the body of the tale and therefore acceptable. The second is incongruous: the imperial *deus ex machina* descends. Kipling was incapable of sustaining the anguish of loneliness and isolation. He rescues his Englishman. Even in fiction he cannot leave the white man to be preyed upon by Indians. Ending number one: Gunga Dass offers Jukes help in escaping, but at the crucial moment, just as they reach the top, Dass kicks Jukes back into the pit and escapes alone. Jukes is left trapped with the living dead. The story should rightly stop there. But Kipling continues it. In ending number two Jukes recovers consciousness and hears a voice shout "Sahib, Sahib"; he is rescued by his loving and obedient servant. The bonds between white master and Brown slave are reaffirmed.

In "The Strange Ride" Kipling used the traditional devices of the horror story, especially those used in Edgar Allan Poe's tales, and transformed them to suit Anglo-India. "My own personal debt to Poe is a heavy one," Kipling noted in 1896, and it is especially evident in this tale. Like Poe, Kipling sought the arabesque and the grotesque. The horror stories of the antebellum Virginian and the post-mutiny Anglo-Indian reflect racist mentalities. By presenting marks of the beast, villages of the dead, "men who were," Kipling served the empire. The white man is threatened; his only option, these tales suggest, is to stifle rebellion and pursue law and order. The stories raise the level of white hysteria and fear to the boiling point. Kipling knew about the Indian Congress movement and Indian nationalism. He knew there was exploitation and political repression. But he never described the social and political relationships between the two races. Terror and horror are the emotions which link them. His tales of Indian horrors reveal the minds of the English and distort the bodies of the Indians.

The terrors of Anglo-India were soon replaced by others. Revolutionaries haunt the decent citizens in Kipling's tales. They grunt like cave men; they are reversions to a primitive type, speaking for democracy and communal life. The radicals bring chaos and destruction. In "As Easy As A.B.C.," a tale about Chicago in the year 2065, a city in which "transportation is civilization," the revolutionaries are finally rounded up and sent to a zoo. There they will be on exhibit as an odd and disappearing species. The Serviles, as Kipling calls the radicals, arouse the people, force them to recall "the Planet's inherited memories of horror, panic, fear and cruelty." They bring "riot, pestilence and lunacy." The

Serviles rally the mob before a mysterious concealed statue which is called "The Nigger in Flames." While the Serviles are carted off and put behind bars the statue is destroyed. The barbarism of revolution is destroyed.

In World War I Kipling found new terrors, especially the Germans—the Huns. Kipling became especially interested in the mind and the drama of terror in the human psyche. He had long been interested in dreams and nightmares, but after the war this interest was intensified. In 1925 he told his friend Rider Haggard that he had collected a "whole mass of incredible stuff for war-stories." Kipling was the official historian of the Irish Guards and wrote a two-volume study of them, *The Irish Guards in the Great War*. He was interested in the "Battalion's psychology," and the "psychology of war." He described the troops as "crazed humanity"; war brought about a reversion to neolithic society. Soldiers became "man-hunting savages." He presented the horrors of the war in great detail. The "sufferings of our armies were constant," he observed; the scenes of carnage and destruction were "burnt in on one's brain to the exclusion of all else." The collective memory of the battalion was dislocated by traumatic events. At the second battle of Ypres the soldiers were subjected to "sheer concentrated . . . prolonged, terror, confusion and a growing sense of hopelessness among growing agonies." In the trenches the human mind was tested to its breaking point. "Human nature ceased to take conscious account" of the things of this earth; no man "could recall any connected order of events." Under these horrific conditions the soldier created a rich fantasy life. He constructed mysterious cause-and-effect relationships to explain the horrors of everyday life. Nightmares dominated the soldier's life and became the links between men.

Long after the guns had stopped and he had returned home, the soldier was haunted by memories of the front. Kipling noted that there are "limits . . . of shock and exhaustion beyond which humanity cannot be pressed without paying toll later." In the quiet of peaceful English towns the "hearts of the men who had borne the burden were still pulsing to the thud of the guns; their minds still obsessed in their leisure by the return of horrors seen and heard." It was under these conditions that Kipling envisioned the writer as a doctor whose drugs are words. He wanted his art to bring the war-weary public back to imperial sanity.

Kipling presented the horrors of the war, but he also depicted heroism. His sense of heroism and his optimism outweigh his sense of defeat and pessimism. He noted that the war "tested human virtue" to the hilt and that the "Irish Guards stood to the test without flaw." He claimed that the soldiers became childlike savages in face of their continual fear of death, but concluded that they met events "with even temper and cool heads." Three things in particular preserved the sanity of the Irish Guards: their sense of humor, their concern for the petty details of everyday life and their dedication to the regiment. Laughter, patriotism and coziness were the three values Kipling praised. He claimed that "the housekeeper's instinct . . . of primitive man" aided the soldier in crisis. The Germans were the barbaric primitive men, the Irish the heroic neolithic warriors. He believed that the Irish soldiers were braver than soldiers of other nationalities because of "an elasticity in Celtic psychology that does not often let things reach breaking point." He affirmed the value of toil. The most fortunate people at the end of the war were those who had "their hands full of necessary and obvious work." Kipling concluded with the observation that the Irish Guards "had been a 'happy' Battalion throughout."

Kipling could not face the terror of World War I head-on. He flirts with terror: he draws the curtain aside for a moment, lets his readers gasp at the rotting corpse and pulls the curtain closed. He never faced the destruction and violence of World War I. He never questioned or examined the nature of the catastrophe. He turns from terror and horror to the inane. In his stories about the effect of the war

—"A Madonna of the Trenches," "The Janeites" and "In the Interests of the Brethren"—he offers the rituals and secrets of the Masonic Lodge and meticulous chores as the best therapy for soldiers who have been broken by trench fighting. Kipling has been praised for his compassion, for the art of healing. But he will only heal the British soldier. He has no compassion for the enemy. In "Mary Postgate" (1915) a young Englishman is killed in the war. One night, while Mary, the family servant, is in the backyard burning his belongings, a German pilot crashes in the nearby trees. She does nothing to help. Instead, she pokes at the fire as the German cries out in agony and then dies. Mary Postgate, the Englishwoman, and not the German, is the agent of terror, and Kipling relishes her cruel figure. He wants the reader to smell burning flesh, to imagine the hot iron penetrating the German's skin in the same way it once tortured a leper in India. In "Sea Constables" Kipling's sailors let the captain of a neutral ship die at sea, though they could save him, because he is not fighting the enemy. In "A Friend of the Family" his hero, an English pilot, bombs an English home because the sons of the household have grown rich while most young Englishmen have been fighting in the war. Kipling is as vicious as ever. To the soldiers maddened by the war he says: laugh, join the Masonic Lodge, smoke a pipe, polish brass. His suggestions are feeble. He had no valid alternatives to offer, no vision for a new mankind after the war.

In the early years of the war Kipling had urged young men to enlist. His own son was killed in the war, but even that event did not lead him to question the war, the senseless deaths. Kipling presents the horrors of the war only to bring the survivors back into the palm of empire. In many of Kipling's late stories that are set in the Masonic Lodge (Kipling's ideal community), Doctor Keede cures the shell-shocked soldiers. He is a psychiatrist, and he enables the soldiers to relive the horrifying experiences of the war so that they can live happy lives in the future. Doctor Keede is probably the first Freudian psychiatrist in fiction. In "The Woman in His Life" an English soldier who during the war was trapped underground and who has experienced "the horror, the blackness, the loss of meaning of things" conquers his fears by rescuing his dog who is trapped underground. He overcomes his fears. In "Fairy-Kist" a soldier who was "wounded and gassed and gangrened in the War" is cured by Keede. An old Englishwoman tells the doctor and his friends that they are "a couple of magicians who's broken the spell." Kipling views the psychiatrist as the equivalent of the ancient witch doctor.

Kipling had read Freud, knew his basic ideas and was familiar with the effect of Freud's ideas on literary criticism. Freud had also read Kipling, and confessed that *The Jungle Book* influenced his ideas. But there is very little in common between Doctor Keede and Freud, between Kipling's psychology and Freud's. Freud noted that modern soldiers were "like primitive man, simply a gang of murderers." For Kipling only the Germans were the brutal savages. War, Freud believed, strips man "of the later accretions of civilization, and lays bare the primeval man in each of us." The war did not lead Kipling to question the basic structure of European civilization, nor the relationships between men under that system. He retained his faith in modern capitalism. He did not see the horror of modern war, the horror of commercialism and imperial rivalry which precipitated the war. He didn't see the war as "the catastrophe of modern imperialism," as H. G. Wells described it. Even Freud saw the war in terms of imperial rivalries. In "Thoughts for the Times on War and Death" he noted that man was prepared "to find that wars between the primitive and the civilized peoples, between those races whom a colour-line divided . . . would occupy mankind." He observed that before 1914 all Europe believed that the "great ruling powers among the white nations" would discover "another way of settling misunderstandings and conflicts of interest." But the war shook the values and beliefs of the civilized world; it revealed that the imperial powers were unable to prevent wars because they were engulfed in a situation of their own making. No one had foreseen, Freud claimed, that wars between the civilized and the primitive peoples would eventually lead to wars between the civilized powers. The war did not lead Kipling to question political power or the empire.

Kipling's house of horrors is filled with crippled Indians, bloodthirsty Germans and frenzied revolutionaries. Anyone who challenged the British Empire, anyone who challenged the establishment, anyone who challenged the white race was placed in the house of horrors. His characters are terrified of the dark unknown before them. They need someone to protect them. Horror is the emotion which most often fills their hearts. They recoil from the promise of freedom. They want everything orderly, everything defined. But they will use their sticks and knives to terrify the poor tenant, the white man's servant. Kipling's terrors are diversions from the atrocities of imperialism.

5

Imperia Romana

Kipling left no space outside the imperial boundaries. He measured all time with the clock of empire. He wrote three books about the English past: *Puck of Pook's Hill* (1906), *Rewards and Fairies* (1910) (both collections of stories for children) and, with C.L.R. Fletcher, *A History of England* (1911). Kipling twisted history to sanction colonialism, capitalism, racism. For Kipling history was a succession of empires; the British Empire was the culmination of world history. The Roman Empire was the first imperium. In the biographies of the Caesars he found parables for the present. He was not alone in digging up the relics of the Roman past: the English inhaled and exhaled in the belief that they were the modern Romans. Rome was all things to all men. To Henry James, England was "like the heavy, congested and depraved Roman world upon which the barbarians came down." London, like ancient Rome, was "the city to which the world paid tribute." Both Rome and Britain had "the same vast and multifarious needs, gratified on the same huge scale—in the one case by conquest, in the other by industry; the same immense development of practical and material resources." For Conrad the modern colonialist experienced disease, exile and death in Africa, just as the Roman colonialist had in Britain. In *Heart of Darkness* he asks us to

> . . . think of a decent young citizen in a toga . . . coming out here in the train of some prefect, or tax-gatherer,

> or trader even, to mend his fortunes. Land in a swamp, march through the woods, and in some inland post feel the savagery, the utter savagery, had closed round him,—all that mysterious life of the wilderness that stirs in the forest, in the jungles, in the hearts of wild men.

Lawrence, too, imagined the overcivilized Romans confronted by barbarians, exiled in the wilderness of Northern Europe, "surrounded by the frozen, crackling darkness." For Lawrence there were two Romes. One was the city of "a free, proud people," with a "love of justice," who brought "splendour and peace." The other was imperial Rome, and Lawrence despised the conquering Romans. He concluded that genocide was the "inevitable result of expansion with a big E, which is the sole *raison d'être* of people like the Romans." The colonized and exterminated Etruscans celebrated natural and spontaneous human sexuality, which the Romans denied because they sought "empire and dominion, and above all, riches: social gain." In Lawrence's book the lesson of the Roman Empire was that "you cannot dance gaily to the double flute and at the same time conquer nations or rake in large sums of money."

While in Italy in the 1920s Lawrence noted that the "Fascists, who considered themselves in all things Roman, Roman of the Caesars, heirs of Empire and world power," were restoring Etruscan places. He commented that, ironically, of all the Italians "the Etruscans were surely the least Roman." Their struggle, more noble "than conquering the world," was to "preserve the natural humour of life." When Mussolini's officials saluted him "in the Fascist manner *alla* Romana," he protested and demanded a revival of Etruscan ways. Lawrence wanted an Etruscan empire which liberated men; he wanted citizens who would envision the world "in the human light, the light of the deep, real human intelligence."

In Rome, Lawrence, James and Conrad saw reflected the decadence, commercialism, exile and horror of their own age. Kipling thought that the English could eternally halt the process of decline and fall. Rome died of "too much power, too much prosperity, too much luxury," he observed in *A History of England.* He told the English to reject imperial pride, to shun affluence and ease. For Kipling all of history emanated from Rome. The sacred flame of empire passed from the Romans to the Gauls, then to the Normans and finally to the English. The Romans fixed the pattern of history. Since the Irish were never conquered by the Romans, they "never went to school," so they have been, Kipling asserted, "a spoilt child ever since." The conquered gained their identity through the conquerors. The African countries which were conquered by Rome received "justice and mercy." With the fall of Rome Africa sank back into barbarism, and only the coming of the British, Kipling says, returned to them law, dignity, equality.

Three tales in *Puck of Pook's Hill*—"A Centurion of the Thirtieth," "On the Great Wall" and "The Winged Hats"—are parables about the Roman Empire. Kipling compares civilization with barbarism, the citizen on the frontier with the citizen in the metropolis. The Romans are threatened from without by alien tribes and from within by political crisis. The wall around the boundary of the empire is manned by criminals, derelicts, outlaws, men of all races and creeds, bound together as equals, pledged to the defense of the empire. The troops from Rome are effeminate, the provincial troops hard and brutal. Roman decadence is mocked beside frontier strength. With growing social crisis in Rome (the emblem for London) the situation on the wall (the emblem for the perimeter of the British Empire) becomes increasingly perilous and the danger of barbarian attack increases. "I fear that Roman Britain went to sleep behind the wall," Kipling writes in his history of England. "Recruiting fell off, the strength of the legions became largely a 'paper strength.'" Kipling campaigned for a strong army; he told soldiers their duty was to the empire and the white race, not to a specific prime minister or political party. He wanted to ensure that no matter who was in power the defense of the empire would be primary.

The Roman Empire had incorporated diverse cultures, races and religions. The British Empire bound heterogeneous cultures, and the British themselves were a composite of different races and nationalities. To Kipling English soil had a mystic power. England conquered her conquerors. The successive waves of Celts, Romans and Normans responded to the "spirit of the dear Motherland" and were stripped of their heritage and absorbed into the nation. The first primitive men felt loyalty to and would die for their tribe. From that beginning patriotism and militarism sprouted. Kipling believed that the English had "behind them this continuity of immensely varied . . . race-memory, running equally through all classes back to the very dawn of our dawn." The British imperial historians created a myth about racial mixtures. J. A. Cramb, one of the most notorious apologists for empire, noted that "the Roman ideal moulds every form of imperialism in Europe"; he offered elaborate analogies between England and Rome. He boasted that Britain conquered "less for herself, than for humanity," that Britain set the "foundations of States unborn . . . as Rome in the days of Tacitus was laying the foundations of States and civilizations unknown." Cramb feared that the Germans of the twentieth century would destroy the British Empire, as the Germans of ancient history had sacked Rome. But Cramb and Kipling believed that England had an indestructible strength. "Into England, as into some vast crucible, the valour of the earth pours itself," Cramb said, "till, molten and fused together, it arises at last one, and undivided, the English nation." In *Physics and Politics* (1872) Walter Bagehot proposed that in Rome "the *mixture of races* was often an advantage," that there was "more life in mixed nations." Kipling was sure that England was powerful because the land, salted with mystical powers, had, by a process of evolution and natural selection, combined diverse strains into a hearty species. The cry of the Norman soldier in *Puck of Pook's Hill,* "England hath taken me!" is echoed by each successive invader.

Kipling pretended that in English history there was no class warfare. An unbroken cord stretched from the primitive past to the twentieth century. Kipling's heroes are kings and queens; his villains are the common people, radicals and revolutionaries. He attacked Jack Cade and Oliver Cromwell for abolishing "Law, Order, and the old *natural* constitution," for constructing an *"artificial"* system and for establishing the "worst of all conceivable tyrannies." Kingship was the order of nature; revolution was a monstrous event that was outside the laws of organic growth. "Revolutions," Kipling exclaimed, "are bad things." In his view the French Revolution was an event of the "utmost horror and cruelty"; the people of France, "once the most civilized in Europe, seemed to have gone mad." Revolution is madness, law and order is sanity, in Kipling's history. His is anti-popular history. Kipling addressed himself to the masses and was widely read, but he patronized the public. His view clashes with that of Dickens, who also thought of himself as a popular writer. In *A Child's History of England* (1851–1853), Dickens defended the people. He did not idealize royalty or the establishment, but, instead, criticized the "fatal results" of conquest and world-wide ambitions. Dickens was patriotic but not jingoistic. Mid-nineteenth-century England was not an imperial power. It was possible for a popular writer of that era to describe, as Dickens did, Queen Elizabeth as "coarse, capricious, and treacherous," to praise Oliver Cromwell for ruling wisely and to suggest that the Bloody Assizes in England were more savage than the Reign of Terror in the French Revolution. Wherever he turned, Kipling saw love and good will between kings, queens and the people, but especially in the sixteenth century—a "splendid period because of the close union between the new Tudor kings and their people; because England armed herself to face dangers from foreign foes."

The bonds between king and people made it possible to build an empire. Kipling incorporated the myth of the white man's burden into nineteenth-century history. "The natives everywhere," he wrote, "welcome the mercy and justice of our rule." In India British rule "has been infinitely to the good of all the three hundred millions of the different races." His history is racist; it follows Thomas Carlyle's lead. Kipling tossed aside Carlyle's anti-industrialist and anti-commercialism writings, and revived the Carlyle who established the ideological basis for empire. In "The Nigger Question" (1849) Carlyle observed of the colonies:

> For countless ages . . . till the European white man first saw them some three short centuries ago those Islands had produced more jungles, savagery, poison-reptiles and swamp-malaria: till the white European first saw them . . . their noble elements of cinnamon, sugar, coffee, pepper black and grey, lying all asleep, awaiting the white enchanted who should say to them, Awake!

For Carlyle the Negro was

> A swift, supple fellow; a merry-hearted, grinning, dancing, singing affectionate kind of creature, with a great deal of melody and amenability in his composition.

Carlyle proclaimed that it was "the everlasting duty of all men, black or white . . . to do competent work, to labour honestly." But he argued that the Black man would not work. He depicted the West Indian Blacks "with their beautiful muzzles up to the ears in pumpkins . . . while the sugar-crops rot round them uncut, because labour cannot be hired." Carlyle's solution was the enslavement of Black men. Carlyle wanted free white labor and slave Black labor. In *A History of England* Kipling observed that

> The prosperity of the West Indies, once our richest possession, has very largely declined since slavery was abolished in 1833. The population is mainly black . . . lazy, vicious, and incapable of any serious improvement, or of work except under compulsion. In such a climate a few bananas will sustain the life of a Negro quite sufficiently; why should he work to get more than this? He is quite happy and quite useless, and spends any extra wages which he may earn upon finery.

Generations of English schoolchildren derived their sense of the Negro from Kipling's history.

In *Puck of Pook's Hill* Kipling depicted the rise of the empire. In "Weland's Sword" imperial might is forged. In "The Knights of the Joyous Venture" Kipling's warriors voyage to Africa in quest of gold. On the shores of the Dark Continent the white knights are worshiped as gods and given gold as a token of their courage and moral fortitude. Kipling explains that the Englishmen do not have to exploit or steal. They are freely offered money by the conquered in return for bearing the white man's burden. In the last story, "The Treasure and the Law," wealth is the mechanism which ensures justice and social order. People do not struggle for rights. History is created through political deals in private chambers. It moves slowly and deliberately up a staircase. Puck offers the lesson of the tales:

> Weland gave the Sword! The Sword gave the Treasure, and the Treasure the Law. It's as natural as an oak growing.

One step leads to another. Kipling saw no conflict or strife in history. He observed no economic changes. He simply did not think in terms of economic systems, of exploitation, of transitions from one form of society to the next. In his history there is no time, there is no change. The present recedes infinitely into the past—the figures become smaller and smaller. The British Empire grows out of the imperial seed planted in primitive times. And he concludes his history with a program for the future, with the view that the future will be like the present and like the past, only it will be writ larger. History is a cone, men march up from the base to the apex, along an inclined plane. For the future Kipling demands a "Federation of the whole British Empire": more expansion, more aggrandizement, more bureaucracy, more hierarchy. "There can be no doubt that the only safe thing for all of us who love our country," he concludes, is "to learn soldiering at once, and be prepared to fight at any moment." He wants his reader to put down his history, pick up the gun and fight for England.

Kipling's history is neat and tidy because he is afraid of the reality of change. He did fear that the empire would be attacked and destroyed, as Rome was sacked, and for this reason he ends his history with a plea for a federation of the British Empire and for an armed population. To Kipling and his crew, the barbarians were the bad guys. But the anti-imperialist rebels called for vandals to sack the mother country. Friedrich Engels noted that "every vital productive germ with which the Germans inoculated the Roman world, was due to barbarism . . . only barbarians are capable of rejuvenating a world laboring under the death throes of unnerved civilization." Engels looked down toward Rome from the German forests; but from the walls of Rome Kipling looked fearfully at the barbarians ready to descend. Engels welcomed the fall of empire; Kipling barricaded the imperial fortress.

Kipling felt the swirling water in the cone. In the vortex he felt that only empire could preserve civilization. When G. K. Chesterton and D. H. Lawrence wrote their histories, they too searched for an escape from crisis and fragmentation, but neither of them rallied around the empire. They created imperia, moments in history when order, balance and wholeness prevailed. Their imperia are utopias, alternatives to the crises of their time. In creating these they stopped time, they denied the dialectic of history, but they offered history as a critique of the corruption and decadence of imperial England.

G. K. Chesterton, in *A Short History of England* (1917), defined the Middle Ages as an imperium which allowed for human growth. Chesterton's ideal was medieval Europe—the high tide of Christianity and the Church, which had re-imposed order after the descent of the Huns and the destruction of the ancient world. He claimed that "the mediaeval man's vision of Christendom was something much larger than our empires and races and vested interests." His utopian imperium incorporated the church and the trade-union movement—"the English expression," Chesterton called it, "of the European effort to resist the tendency of Capitalism." Chesterton favored the development of guilds. He wanted to see the gradual restoration of "the personal property of the poor, and the personal freedom of the family." He believed that modern Europe was in the midst of a crisis matched only by that which had struck Europe after the descent of the barbarians on Rome. He wanted the creation of a new Holy Roman Empire, a Christian society.

In *Movements in European History* Lawrence looked hopefully toward the future. He believed that Europe was "moving toward a oneness, the circle has almost been completed again . . . the national spirit brings us to this, which is ultimately the international or universal spirit." Lawrence believed that there would be "a great united Europe of productive working people," rallying around "one great chosen figure, some hero." His view of history was mechanical. The empire of the future would take the place of the commercial empires, which had taken the place of the medieval empire, which in turn had supplanted the Roman Empire.

> So the cycle of European history completes itself, phase by phase, from imperial Rome, through the mediaeval

> empire and papacy to the kings of the Renaissance period, on to the great commercial nations, the government by the industrial and commercial middle classes, and so to that last rule, that last oneness of the labouring people. So Europe moves from oneness to oneness, from the imperial unity to the unity of the labouring classes, from the beginning to the end.

Here Lawrence stops time. He halts history. But in his novels he offers a complex sense of time—of past, present and future. In the late works, especially in *The Plumed Serpent* (1926), he speaks for a world "organically united." He wants the "First Men of every people" to form "a Natural Aristocracy." He feels that the "earth might rejoice, when the First Lords of the West met the First Lords of South and East, in the Valley of the Soul . . . the earth has Valleys of the Soul, that are not cities of commerce and industry." Lawrence's empire becomes a kinship in spirit. Both Chesterton and Lawrence, in seeking an alternative to the commercialism of the British Empire, created imperia which were hierarchical, elitist. Chesterton defended trade unions but insisted on a high priest, a pope, to lead his empire. Lawrence wanted a united Europe of productive working people, but demanded "an absolute *Dictator* and an equivalent *Dictatrix*." Kipling re-created the past to solidify and ensure the continued existence of the British Empire. History for Kipling became an escape from the realities of the present. He could rewrite the past, he believed, so that England, unlike Rome, would never fall. His histories offer fictions of order which attempt to suppress the conflicts of reality.

6

Kim: *The Middle Way*

In *Kim* the contrasts operate forcefully; there is a sense of conflict and struggle which is lacking elsewhere in Kipling's work. As George Moore noted, Kim is Kipling himself. Kim is the distillation of Kipling's dreams. He is an adolescent who explores the world, delights in life and, at the same time, is a slave to the government. *Kim* is Kipling's best work because it comes from the core of Kipling's being. The range and complexity of experience is wider and deeper than in any other place in Kipling's work.

Kim has been widely read and appreciated, especially by Americans—Mark Twain, T. S. Eliot, Henry James, and Frank Norris—but it has never achieved the status of a modern classic. It is an unusual work in English fiction. There are fine parts in the book, but the novel as a whole is disappointing. *Kim* is severely marred. The exuberance and sense of fraternity which spurts to the novel's surface is continually contained by the stern, upright hand of authority. The tension in *Kim* is between freedom and joy in India and discipline for the empire. The contradiction is imbedded in the form of the novel itself. When the characters are in Her Majesty's Service, the novel follows a rigid pattern. When the characters jump from the wheel of empire and explore India, the structure becomes expansive and flexible.

Kipling was habitually troubled by the question of form. India presented especially severe problems for his imagination. He sought details; his eye rested on the local, not the universal. Kipling was unable to synthesize, unable to create complex patterns. He had difficulty writing novels, and produced mostly short stories because the novel demanded sustained organization. The boundaries of the short story were much clearer. Kipling worked best with a sense of restriction. His first stories were published in newspapers. The space or "canvas," as he called it, offered him was determined by the columns available in that edition. Kipling was trained to cut, to edit, to work in a small area. His habit of seeing isolated things, the parts rather than the wholes, derived from his Indian experience. India was enigmatic. Kipling called her the Sphinx of the Plains. In his newspaper reports in the 1880s he spoke often of his difficulty in comprehending the Indian scene. In Jodhpur in 1887 he wondered whether it was the "backwater of the river of Anglo-Indian life" or the "main current, the broad stream that supplies the motive power." In 1888, when he returned to Calcutta after traveling across India, he called himself "a wandering savage adrift." He discovered that "the eye has lost its sense of proportion, the focus has contracted . . . and the mind has shrunk with the eye . . . The eye," he concluded, "loses itself in a maze." He noted that the European visitor's first reaction to India is "extreme bewilderment"; the white man's mind "fails to take in the situation."

Although he found forms hard to handle, he was sensitive to color. "Colour holds the eye more than form," he wrote. He was especially aware of light and dark because of his poor eyesight, because he was preoccupied with seeing and observing. Kipling's reaction was common to Europeans in the East. They were baffled by Eastern nature and Eastern people, as Indian writers have noted. Nirad C. Chaudhuri, the Indian novelist, writes that Indians reject "the Western sense of measure" (especially Hindus, for whom "neither time nor space had any limits"). So, the English were usually unable to comprehend the Indian sense of time and space.

This view of India is reflected in Kipling's casual comments in *Kim*. He refers to the "happy Asiatic disorder," to "great, grey, formless India"; he tells us that Indians are not bothered by random noise, as Europeans are, that all twenty-four hours of the day are alike to Indians. He is convinced that the people have no sense of measurement. But novels require form: beginnings, middles and endings. His reasoning is that if India is formless and the West all form, then the artistic structure imposed on the material will have little to do with the East. Kipling saw India with the Englishman's sense of time and space. For the Indian writer, the land has its recognizable patterns. The forms he chose elicited the social structure.

Kipling was also concerned about his English reader's preconception of and perspective on India. He wanted to leave the reader with a lasting impression of the land. Alfred Lyall, an imperial official and literary critic, suggested that the English reader "must be able to realize the points and the probabilities of a plot and its personages; he wants a tale that falls more or less within his own experience." The reader had seen English drawing rooms, churches, schools and factories, but he had never seen Indian temples or mosques, Indian cities, mountains or plains. His curiosity would be aroused by the outlandish, unfamiliar Indian scenes, but he would also be dubious of them. He would wonder whether the author dealt in fantasies or realities. Very often a barrier was raised between the artist and his material, on the one hand, and his audience, on the other. This is a problem faced by all writers who present new worlds—it could be Black Africa, or the junkie's mind and environment. He must convince the reader of the emotional and social truth of his realm. Kipling often tried to convince his readers of the authenticity of his fictional world by heaping detail upon detail, but that in itself was not enough to dispel the reader's skepticism. Lyall recognized that stories which provided "close description of native Indian manners or people" would "find scant favour in England," that documentary works would be of primary interest and value to people already familiar with India. Lyall played down the importance of the sociological novel that presents a new area of life. His radical insight was that the traditional English novel had no roots in Indian culture. He knew that a new vision of life would be most powerfully dramatized by using unconventional techniques, rather than familiar, conventional forms. Kipling never articulated a formal theory, but his views were close to Lyall's. He labored under nearly identical assumptions.

Kipling had denied himself several approaches. He would not write a novel about Hindus and Muslims because he felt they were not average Indians. He wanted to be able to write about the English and the Indians together, and so in *Mother Maturin* he turned to the Eurasians to include both worlds. One of Kipling's friends who read *Mother Maturin* wrote that the novel offered:

> The story of an old Irishwoman who kept an opium den in Lahore but sent her daughter to be educated in England. She married a Civilian and came to live in Lahore—hence a story how Government secrets came to be known in the Bazaar and *vice versa.*

There is little similarity between *Mother Maturin* and *Kim,* but both novels juxtapose the secret conspiracies of the government with the open Indian marketplaces. The Eurasians are a social group; Kim is a mythical hero, an orphan born during an earthquake and fated for greatness. But he too explores both the Indian world and the British world. Kim shuttles back and forth from the English to the Indians. He is a puppet in Kipling's hands; Kipling changes his costumes, his voice, gives him new roles to play. Kim's parents were Irish, but he is raised by Indians. He is a white boy adopted by Brown men and women. In the course of the novel Kipling gives him a variety of parents. The men:

Mahbub Ali, the Pathan; Huree Babu, the Bengali; Creighton, the English military man; and the lama, a Buddhist monk. And the women: the sahiba, an old woman; Huneefa, a lady with mystical powers; and the Lady of Shamlegh, a Himalayan. But there is not as much variety as appears at first. Most of the characters are stick figures who stand in the background and have only a few lines to say. There are, therefore, few valid alternatives open to Kim.

The novel describes Kim's initiation into manhood, his explorations in the world of white men and Brown men. It is a novel about education—the theme Kipling traces in *The Jungle Books, The Just So Stories,* and *Stalky & Co.,* the volume of stories about a boys' public school. Kim is an Irish boy, a familiar type to British readers. He is also an Easterner, a foreign type. Kipling gradually introduces his readers into the Indian world. Throughout the book Kipling keeps his English audience in mind. He is explicit and overbearing with them, rarely allowing them to explore the world he has created. He takes the reader in hand every step of the way.

Kim is Kipling's mask. He gives the illusion that we penetrate into strange, foreign places. Kim is Kipling's defense. He really does not know the inside of the Indian world, but he gives an illusion of intimacy. Kim is the work of an Englishman, not an Indian; it exhibits the characteristic limitations of English novels about India. When Kipling tries to give depth of information and depth of awareness he strikes a false note. When he records what he as a sensitive observer has seen the writing is sharp and moving. When the lama speaks privately with the sahiba in her cart, Kipling draws the curtain closed. Kim does not see or hear what transpires between them. Kipling does not know how his characters would act or what they would say in that situation, and he wisely does not try to fake it. Instead, he describes the sights before Kim's gaze:

> It was a strange picture that Kim watched between drooped eyelids. The lama, very straight and erect, the deep folds of his yellow clothing slashed with black in the light of parao fires precisely as a knotted tree-trunk is slashed with the shadows of the long sun, addressed a tinsel and lacquered *ruth* which burned like a many-coloured jewel in the same uncertain light. The patterns on the gold-worked curtains ran up and down, melting and reforming as the folds shook and quivered to the night wind; and when the talk grew more earnest the jewelled forefinger snapped out little sparks of light between the embroideries. Behind the cart was a wall of uncertain darkness speckled with little flames and alive with half-caught forms and faces and shadows.

Kipling is on much firmer ground when he describes situations available to the eye of the Western traveler in India. One of the best scenes in the novel defines Indian reactions to the railway. It is one of the few places where individuals of different castes sit together in close confines. In the third-class railroad carriage Kipling entertains a Sikh artisan, a Hindu moneylender, his haughty wife, an Amritzar courtesan and a Dogra soldier. The railway disrupts the Indian caste system. "There is not one rule of right living which the *te-rains* do not cause us to break," one of the travelers says. "We sit . . . side by side with all castes and peoples." Kipling recognized in India two opposing ideas about the railway: one articulated later by Gandhi, the other by Nehru. Gandhi noted that railways "accentuate the evil nature in man," but Nehru said that "the coming of the railway to India brought the industrial age on its positive side." The lama is wary of the railroad; like Gandhi, he would rather walk. But Kim, the materialist, the advocate of progress, is at home in a third-class railway carriage. Sometimes Kipling wants to walk side by side with the lama. But he is at heart the poet of the machine. He celebrates the dynamo and the railway.

In the scene in the railway carriage Kipling suggests the heterogeneity of India. He saw no dominant single culture in the land. Kim moves in the midst of India's diverse peoples and cultures. The novel has two main, connected plots: the lama's religious pilgrimage (his Search on the Road for a miraculous river of healing) and Kim's travels across India. Kim is the lama's companion and an agent for the British secret service. Kim is the master of the disguise. He dresses and talks now like a Hindu, now a Muslim, now a Eurasian. Kipling's saw himself as a man of many parts, a ventriloquist. He liked and was influenced by Browning's poetry—especially the dramatic monologues—for he admired Browning's ability to speak with equal eloquence and power as an Italian duke, a Renaissance painter, a bishop or a savage. Like Kim, who uses his disguises for the British secret service, Kipling is the imperial ventriloquist. He can speak for the empire with the dialect of a white soldier, an Indian servant, an old woman. The ability to play different parts is a political asset. The disguise enables the warrior to infiltrate the enemy camp. Kim is taught to mimic men of each sect, to repeat the Koran, to speak the language of the Buddhist priest. He blends into the environment, takes on its protective coloration and sees and hears secret conspiracies. He is a government spy. Large parts of *Kim* read like popular boys' adventure stories about imperial politics. The Irish boy, disguised as the lama's begging boy, uncovers and stymies the foreign conspirators. The imperial fabric is protected by an orphan and a handful of secret-service men. To work for the empire is a game, the Great Game, a series of romantic adventures. The agents are lawless, but lawlessness in defense of imperial law is legal. In the Great Game, kinship between Brown men and white men is tolerated. Between the English and the Indian spies who pursue England's enemies there is a rough fellowship.

Kim gives the appearance of freedom, but the characters are governed by Kipling's ideas about race, culture and politics. Kim changes costumes but he is fixed in his ways. When we first see Kim he is "burned black as any native." In the manuscript version Kipling noted that he looked like a child who had one white and one Brown parent. He changed the description because he felt that of all people half-castes were the most despicable. Miscegenation is the primary crime in Kipling's penal code. It is to Kim's credit that he *looks* Black. But he is pure white at his heart. Kim is "a poor white of the very poorest." In the manuscript Kipling advised his readers that to be poor white trash in India carried more of a stigma than in any other nation on earth. He is the defender of the poor white man against the Black man. He sympathizes with the poor white but not with the Black man in slave society. He seeks the unity of rich and poor whites against all Blacks. Kim's training in the service of the empire teaches him to imitate others and at the same time never to forget that he is white. Kipling originally entitled the novel *Kim O' the Rishti,* Kim of the Irish. He changed the title, but Kim's acts are defined in terms of his Irish heritage. When Kim first meets the lama, Kipling notes, "the Lama was his trove and he purposed to take possession. Kim's mother had been Irish too." When Kim accepts money offered to him, Kipling explains, "He was Irish enough by birth to reckon silver the least part of any game. What he desired was the visible effect of action." Since Kim is supposed to be part-Indian his character is also defined in terms of the East: "Kim could lie like an Oriental," Kipling insists. The climax of the novel, which takes place in the Himalayas, relies heavily on Kipling's sense of race. Unknown to the lama, Kim tracks down two foreign agents who have come to India to instigate a rebellion against the English. When they encounter the foreign agents and one of them strikes the lama, the blow awakens "every unknown Irish devil in the boy's blood." Only after his Irish anger is aroused can he act to defend the lama and then tend his wounds. At school Kim is taught that one "must never forget that one is a Sahib, and that some day, when examinations are passed, one will command natives." His severest test places him in a situation contrived to make him forget he is white. The smells, the sounds, the objects which surround him—"Tibetan devil-dance masks, hanging above the fiend-embroidered draperies of those ghastly functions—horned masks, and masks of idiotic terror"—nearly overwhelm him. His teacher takes a jar, smashes it and tries to force Kim to believe that the pieces of the jar have reassembled, that the broken jar has magically been made whole. But Kim refuses to accept that view. He is saved. At the crucial moment "Kim had been thinking in Hindi, but a tremor came on him, and with an effort like that of a swimmer before sharks who hurls himself half out of the water, his mind leaped up from a darkness that was swallowing it and took refuge in—the multiplication table in English." Kipling believed that the white man's mind was superior to the Indian's mind, that the syntax of the English language and the multiplication table were products of a rational and higher race.

Kim is introspective. He wonders about his identity. Kipling notes that to wonder about one's identity is an Eastern rather than a Western phenomena. "A very few white people," he wrote, "but many Asiatics can throw themselves into amazement . . . by repeating their own names over and over again to themselves, letting the mind go free upon speculation as to what is called personal identity." Kipling speaks as if the concept of doubt about the self is entirely foreign. The English know their place; they never question it. Kipling wants us to think of the Westerner as confident, active, extravert, aggressive, the Easterner as meditative, introvert and passive. He uses the racist stereotypes.

Kim moves along a conveyor belt. He is guided through a series of initiation rituals. Kim's life is broken into cycles. He falls asleep each night and awakes a different person in the morning. He is reborn into a new caste, a new religion; Kipling uses the concept of reincarnation to elaborate on the pattern. Kim's initiations—complete with magical amulets, chants and ceremonial dress—are enacted by a long series of motherly women. Many of the women are prostitutes; Kim's relationship to them has a strong current of sexuality. In one scene a blind prostitute paints his body, disguises him to look like the lama's follower. She also uses her magic to protect him:

> . . . the room filled with smoke—heavy, aromatic, and stupefying. Through growing drowse he heard the names of devils—of Zulbazan, Son of Eblis, who lives in bazaars and *paraos,* making all the sudden lewd wickedness of way-side halts; of Dulhan, invisible about mosques, the dweller among the slippers of the Faithful . . . the boy lost his senses.

Kim is drugged and loses consciousness. Huneefa calls upon "devil after devil in the ancient order of the ritual, binding them to avoid the boy's every action." When he awakes, it is "after a sleep of a thousand years." Kipling likes this Black Mass. He was fascinated with primitive rituals, interested in anthropology, but the description he offers here is mumbo-jumbo, Masonic Lodge nonsense.

The final ritual and rebirth is enacted by the sahiba. She rejuvenates him after the long march across the Himalayas by "laying him east and west, that the mysterious earth currents which thrill the clay of our bodies might help and not hinder." When Kim's strength returns, she "laid him down full length along in the shadow of the wooden-pinned cart. And Mother Earth was as faithful as the Sahiba. She breathed through him to restore the poise he had lost . . . His head lay powerless upon her breast, and his opened hands surrendered to her strength." His proximity to the wheels of the cart tells us that we have come full circle. The orphan alone in the world is reborn through Mother Earth.

These sentimental initiation rituals are obvious and clumsy. Rather than growing out of the characters' lives, these rituals are imposed upon them. Kipling describes no Indian rituals, no Hindu marriages or Muslim weddings, burials or births; he presents only archetypal rituals divorced from Indian life. Kipling's rituals carry Kim into the secret service, into manhood, without allowing him to grow on his own.

Kim is an allegory. The Indian novelist Mulk Raj Anand said of *Kim:*

> It may be accepted as a book for children, a fairy tale, but the *dramatis personae,* the Lama, the Babu, the Pathan horse dealer . . . are the stock characters of any United Services Club conversation of that period, without much reality of their own.

All of the characters, except Kim and the lama, are stock figures. They have emblems and epithets, but almost nothing else. Colonel Creighton is the Whip of Calamity, Mahbub Ali is the Hand of Friendship, the Anglican minister and the Catholic priest are the Twins, the sahiba is the Dispenser of Delights. Kim is called the Friend of the World and the Friend of the Stars; the lama, Old Red Hat. The novel begins at the museum—the Wonder House—where the museum director, the Keeper of the Images, is in charge. The characters move through the House of the Bull (war) and under the Gates of Learning (school) until they reach the Gates of Deliverance (the end).

There is another very different view of the world imbedded in *Kim*. It is a world of freedom and friendship. The initiation rituals and allegorical patterns are swept aside, and the characters move on their own initiative. They cease to be puppets. Kipling called *Kim* a picaresque novel. The picaresque form allowed Kipling scope and permitted his characters the breathing space denied by the stifling allegory and initiation rituals. But Kipling was disappointed about his use of the picaresque. "As to its form," he wrote in his autobiography, "there was but one possible to the author, who said that what was good enough for Cervantes was good enough for him." *Kim* is like *Don Quixote* only in that it describes the adventures of two contrasted characters. The invocation of Cervantes was an evasion of the problem, as Kipling's mother recognized. "Don't you stand in your wool-boots hiding behind Cervantes with *me*!" she scolded. "You *know* you couldn't make a plot to save your soul." He accepted his mother's criticism. In his own view *Kim* had "opulence of detail" and paucity of form. It was "nakedly picaresque and plotless—a thing imposed from without."

When Kipling lets himself go, when he forgets about the empire, the secret service, the novel quivers with life. At these moments Kim stops mimicking the Indians in the service of the empire and thrusts himself into Indian life. When he has finished school and returns to the lama, we see him "forgetting his white blood; forgetting even the Great Game as he stooped Mohammedan-fashion, to touch his master's feet in the dust of the Jain temple." Kim is no longer the boy we first met.

> He sat, in defiance of municipal orders, astride the gun Zam-Zammah on her brick platform opposite the old Ajaib-Gher—the Wonder House, as the natives call the Lahore Museum. Who hold the Zam-Zammah, that "fire-breathing dragon," hold the Punjab; for the great green-bronze piece is always first of the conqueror's loot.
>
> There was some justification for Kim,—he had kicked Lala Dinanath's boy off the trunnions,—since the English held the Punjab and Kim was English.

It is right for English children to lord it over Indian children, Kipling assumes, because England owns India. From the start he makes sure that we know there are conquerors and conquered, that there is loot and imperial might. Indians are presented as unsophisticated folk who think of guns as fire-breathing dragons and museums as wonder houses.

But when these imperial values are dropped, the Indian city is no longer an evil place, no longer an underworld of the grotesque and the horrible. It is, instead, a place of ancient dignity:

> The clamour of Benares, oldest of all earth's cities awake before the Gods, day and night, beat round the walls as the seas roar round a breakwater.

The finest parts of the novel describe Kim and the lama on the open road. The joy that wells up in the novel derives from Kipling's experience as a loafer traveling freely across India. Eliot claimed that

> . . . there are two strata in Kipling's appreciation of India, the stratum of the child and that of the young man. It was the latter who observed the British in India and wrote the rather cocky and acid tales of Delhi and Simla, but it was the former who loved the country and its people. In his Indian tales it is on the whole the Indian characters who have the greater reality, because they are treated with the understanding of love. One is not loving between seventeen and twenty-four. But it is . . . the four great Indian characters in *Kim* who are real . . . As for the Britons, those with whom he is most sympathetic are those who have suffered or fallen . . . He might almost be called the first citizen of India.

Eliot is mistaken. It was Kipling's experience as a journalist during the 1880s which made *Kim* a joyful book. Kipling remembered his childhood only as a series of grotesque and bizarre events. His experience as a journalist brought him into contact with India and allowed him to travel. Kipling observed that his own "sedentary and civilised nature" experienced a new emotion when he traveled across India's plains and mountains. "Some day," he predicted, "a novelist will exploit the unknown land." He also suggested that "a small volume might be written of the ways and tales of Indian loafers of the more brilliant order." Those ideas from the 1880s were finally embodied in *Kim*. "There is no life so good as the life of a loafer who travels by rail and road," he explained, "for all things and all people are kind to him." The epigraph to *Life's Handicap,* which Kipling identified as a native proverb, captures that feeling:

> I met a hundred men on the road to Delhi and they were all my brothers.

Observing sunset on the open road, he said:

> This moment of change can only be felt in the open and in touch with the earth, and once discovered, seems to place the finder in deep accord and fellowship with all things on earth. Perhaps this is why the genuine loafer . . . shows such a genial tolerance towards the weaknesses of mankind, black, white, or brown.

Kipling idealized the loafer, as he idealized the bohemian, because his own life was narrowly confined. His notion of freedom was of complete abandon, of wandering without a direction or aim. Freedom is for him the absence of restraint. Kim's and the lama's freedom does not involve any struggle or participation with others. They delight in each other and in nature. "There is no country in all the world as beautiful as the Himalayas," Kipling wrote. The rhythms in the novel change when Kipling describes his two characters in Northern India:

> "Who goes to the Hills goes to his Mother." They had crossed the Siwaliks and the half-tropical Doon, left Mussoorie behind them, and headed north along the narrow hill-roads. Day after day they struck deeper into the huddled mountains, and day after day Kim watched the lama return to a man's strength. Among the terraces of the

> Doon he had leaned on the boy's shoulder, ready to profit by wayside halts. Under the great ramp to Mussoorie he drew himself together as an old hunter . . . and walked as only a hillman can. Kim, plains-bred and plains-fed, sweated and panted astonished.

The first sentence is false; it sets a wrong tone. But the passage suggests the vast spaces in India, the characters in contrast with nature. Behind the description, too, is a false sense of the impurity of the plains and the purity of the Hills, the push and pull of humanity in the plains and a still world without men in the Hills. Kim walks along the Grand Trunk Road and Kipling describes what he observes and how he feels:

> The Grand Trunk . . . was built on an embankment to guard against winter floods from the foothills, so that one walked . . . a little above the country, along a stately corridor, seeing all India spread out to left and right. It was beautiful to behold the many-yoked grain and cotton wagons crawling over the country roads: one could hear their axles, complaining a mile away, coming nearer, till with shouts and yells and bad words they climbed up the steep incline and plunged on to that hard main road, carter reviling carter. It was equally beautiful to watch the people, little clumps of red and blue and pink and white and saffron, turning aside to go to their own villages, dispersing and growing small by twos and threes across the level plain.

Here Kipling offers the land as he sees it. The people are picturesque and colorful, not sharply defined or deeply understood. There is a tone of prudery in the reference to the "bad words" spoken by the peasants. But the characters bask in Kipling's enthusiasm. The novel captures the sense of "the bustle and stir of the open road." Kim is at the center of activity. "In all India," Kipling writes, "there was no human being so joyful as Kim." In school he yearns for

> . . . the caress of soft mud squishing up between the toes, as his mouth watered for mutton stewed with butter and cabbages, for rice speckled with strong-scented cardamoms, for the saffron-tinted rice, garlic and onions, and the forbidden greasy sweetmeats of the bazaars.

His desires are suppressed in school, released on the road. "This broad, smiling river of life," Kim thinks while walking the Grand Trunk Road, "was a vast improvement on the cramped and crowded Lahore streets. There were new people . . . at every stride." The novel celebrates diversity, the multiplicity of life. Here Kim is unconscious of the empire and curious about all people. Kipling often merely catalogs the people Kim sees and gives no pattern to the continuous stream of events, but the catalog suggests the heterogeneity of India. We see Sanis with lizards and dogs, an ex-prisoner, a Sikh devotee, whole villages, women and babies, Hindus, Muslims, female railway laborers, a marriage procession, a juggler with his monkeys, a moneylender, Indian soldiers and a seller of Ganges water. The novel passes over the surface of reality. In the manuscript version of *Kim* Kipling described one of Kim's meals as "not a common feeding but a royal gorge, an imperial stuffing." It is this sense of richness, of imperial delight and exuberance, rather than the political imperium, which gives the novel its power.

Kim is at the center of everything. "India was awake, and Kim was in the middle of it," Kipling writes. The image of the wheel and the concept of the Middle Way pervade the entire novel. The lama is a Buddhist and the Middle Way is his fundamental religious concept. "To those who follow the Way," he tells Kim, "there is neither black nor white, Hind nor Bhotyal. We be all souls seeking escape. No matter what the wisdom of the Sahibs. When we come to my River thou wilt be freed from all illusion." Like many Westerners, Kipling thought that for Buddhists, salvation was the result of self-reliance and strenuous activity. The lama is an individualist; he is an Oriental Emersonian. Kipling appropriates the Buddhist concept of the Middle Way. He places Kim at the middle of India, between white and Brown, England and India. Kim is the hub of the wheel. He is himself a small wheel in a larger wheel; the novel is a series of wheels within wheels. As the lama says to him, "Thou hast loosed an Act upon the world, and as a stone thrown into a pool so spread the consequences thou canst not tell how far." The wheel turns and re-turns endlessly. The circles expand outward. Experience is a never-ending process, with human action involving an infinite number of possibilities. The novel abounds in wheels. "All India was at work in the fields, to the creaking of well-wheels," Kipling writes. We hear the endless noise of wagon wheels, water wheels, the wheels of machinery. There is also the idea of the wheel, the wheel of fortune. The lama draws picture-parables of the Great Wheel. He traces "in clearest, severest outline the Great Wheel with its six spokes, whose center is the conjoined Hog, Snake, and Dove (Ignorance, Anger, and Lust), and whose compartments are all the Heavens and Hells, and all the chances of human life." When he is struck by the foreign agents the lama tells us that "Ignorance and Lust met Ignorance and Lust upon the road, and they begat Anger."

Kim and the lama are contrasting characters. While the lama draws his picture-parables and meditates about the Great Wheel, Kim watches water wheels and cartwheels. While the lama is concerned with metaphysics, Kim's "mind was distracted; for by the roadside trundled the very Wheel itself, eating, drinking, trading, marrying, and quarreling—all warmly and alive." The lama's world is the life of the mind, Kim's is the world of action. Kim is at home in the hot, turbulent plains, close to the surface of things; the lama is at home in the cool, placid hills, in the metaphysical heights.

Kim offers contrasts between the East and the West. The

lama is the meditative Easterner, Kim the active Westerner. The distinction Kipling makes between the two characters goes deep into his habits of mind. Kim is "the eyes and ears of the Lama." The lama is Kim's mind. In his newspaper reports about Indian landscapes Kipling continually spoke of the eye and its realm and the mind and its realm as distinct territories. Kipling's sensibility was dissociated. His own mind worked in terms of seeing and watching on one hand, and theorizing and analyzing on the other. He built a wall between perception and thought. Because of his dissociation, it was difficult for him to merge details into pattern, the concrete with the abstract, difficult to create symbols, difficult to forge unified works of art. Kim and the lama are the products of an artist who could not yoke the sensual with the philosophical, who could not reconcile thought and emotion. Kim describes colors and shapes, the lama talks of Heaven and Hell, Ignorance, Anger and Lust. We see India divided in two. The power of seeing is not synthesized with the faculty of abstraction and organization. They are balanced one against the other, but they do not merge to form a new whole. Kipling's own being is divided into territories of East and West, Brown and white, the territory of the mind and the territory of the senses. But on the open road, where everything is transformed, the lama and Kim become more complex. The lama acquires a body and develops physical strength. He ceases to be an old meditative priest. He is no longer the stereotype of the introspective Oriental, as opposed to the stereotype of the active Westerner.

Kipling's treatment of the lama changed in the course of the novel. Originally the lama was a frightened child, terrified of modern machines. But he gradually acquires dignity and respect. He becomes a serene holy man. Kipling's new attitude toward the lama is signified by a change in the scene at the beginning of the novel. In the manuscript version of the novel Kim opens the museum door and the lama drops to his knees in humble adoration, but in the final text "Kim clicked round the self-registering turnstile; the old man followed and halted amazed." The two men share their knowledge of the East and then exchange gifts. The lama gives the museum curator a pen. In the original draft of the novel the curator patronizingly hands the lama a third-class railway ticket. In the final text he gives the lama a pair of spectacles. Much of the paternalism is sponged away.

The lama is respected as an artist. He knows the "secret of the conventional brush-pen Buddhist pictures which are, as it were, half written and half drawn." Kipling admires the lama's picture-parables, but he finds them inferior to Greek art. Kipling thought that Indian art was second-rate: Greek painting and sculpture were the measure of all art. He accepted the prevailing British ideas about Indian art. John Ruskin claimed that Indian artists sought "pleasure first and truth afterwards (or not at all)," while European art sought "truth first and pleasure afterwards." Indian art was beautiful in color and line, but had "no natural form" and was "systemless," according to Ruskin. He believed that most Indian art represented the "barbarous grotesque." John Lockwood Kipling, who taught art in India, was a poor teacher because he was an imperialist. He felt that the plastic arts in India were inferior to the plastic arts in Europe. At a time when Indian artists were beginning to experiment and find new forms, he claimed that the "spirit of its artistic prime has been dead for centuries." Kipling liked the Taj Mahal, but he perverted its quality and noted that "it was the realization of the gleaming halls of dawn that Tennyson sighs of." He also noted that there was "no repose" in Indian architecture, that "the entire effect is one of repulsion." He felt, as Ruskin did, that the art was idolatrous and "frankly obscene." Indian art was "unholy." In *The Naulahka* Indian buildings are decorated with "monstrous and obscene pictures." The stone pillars which dot the land are "carved with monstrous and obscene gods." In a bat-infested temple Kipling's hero observes "how entirely the life, habits, and traditions of this strange people alienated them from all that seemed good and right." Indian art, religion and morality in Kipling's eyes are all equally vile and immoral. It is hardly surprising that E. B. Havell, the leading English student of Indian art at the turn of this century, noted correctly that "Indian art is still very little understood by Europeans," and that the Indian critic Syed Ross Masood was sorely puzzled in 1920 about "why Englishmen make no serious attempt to study our various literary and artistic movements." Masood felt that 1880 marked the rise of a "new era in the literary annals of our literature," and that 1895 marked the beginning of a renaissance in Indian painting.

Kipling's limited view of Indian art distorted his portrait of the lama. It also meant that he rejected the forms and the patterns used by traditional Indian artists. In *Kim* when we first meet the lama he stands in the entrance hall, where there are figures of the "Greco-Buddhist sculptures done, savants know how long since, by forgotten workmen whose hands were feeling, and not unskillfully, for the mysteriously transmitted Grecian touch." Kipling does not want to accept any help from Indian artists because he thinks their work is second-rate.

The story of Kim and the lama on the Grand Trunk Road has similarities with Mark Twain's description of Huck Finn and Jim on the Mississippi River. Kim and the lama never go by raft on the Ganges or the Huegli, but the Grand Trunk Road is described as a river: "Such a river of life, as nowhere else exists in the world," Kim says. The brotherhood between Huck and Jim on the raft is matched by the love between Kipling's travelers on the open road. Kim and the lama do not flee from civilization as directly as their American counterparts, but their journey takes them from the cities of the plains to the villages of the Himalayas. Both

Twain and Kipling wrote about the childhood of white men, about the friendship between a white child and a Black man. Both created nostalgic pictures of boyhood in a racist society. Back on shore, and off the open road, Huck and Kim are corrupted by a society which makes the Black man subservient to the white man. Both Kipling and Twain enjoy disguise, games, the picaresque as a literary form. But Twain wrote about his own land, Kipling wrote about a foreign land. Twain was rooted in the culture he described; Kipling was alien to Indian culture. With bitter satire Twain attacked the life on the shore, but Kipling offered no social criticism. Kipling had only enthusiasm for the machine, while Twain had ambiguous feelings about it. In "Among the Railway Folk" Kipling wrote:

> Huckleberry Finn says of a timber raft, "It amounted to something being captain of that raft." Thrice enviable is the man who, drawing Rupees 220 a month is allowed to make Rupees 150 overtime out of locomotives numbered 325, 432, or 8.

Twain envisioned the destructive power of the machine, especially the Mississippi steamboat, but Kipling delighted in the steamboat and the locomotive.

Kipling and Twain took great pleasure in each other's work. "The deep and subtle and fascinating charm of India," Twain wrote, "pervades no other book as it pervades *Kim* . . . Kipling is just about my level." Kipling wrote to Frank Doubleday: "I love to think of the great and godlike Clemens. He is the biggest man you have on your side of the water." Kipling had high praise for *Huckleberry Finn.* On his trip to the United States in 1889, when he was traveling by steamer on a California river, he observed, "All I can remember is a delightful feeling that Mark Twain's Huckleberry Finn and Mississippi Pilot were quite true, and that I could almost recognize the very reaches down which Huck and Jim had drifted."

Kipling was excited by Twain's language, by the "Mississippi Pilot's talk." He too used colloquial speech and dialects. Kipling's language is unusual in several respects. For one thing, he handled many words and phrases which were in common usage in the eighteenth century but, by the late nineteenth century, were out of circulation in England. Anglo-Indian written and spoken language was old-fashioned. Kipling sensed the archaic quality of Anglo-Indian speech. In 1889 he noted that

> India still lacks a dictionary of marine vernaculars—the sea language that the thousands of coasting sailors . . . use. It is a quaint tongue to listen to . . . I should be disposed to conclude that seventy five per cent of it is blasphemy, and the remainder fossilized sea terminology long since obsolete in both the French and Portuguese navies.

Not only the sailors, but soldiers, administrators and society ladies spoke a language which sounded outdated to the newly arrived traveler from England. The Anglo-Indians also had unique colloquial speech patterns. When Kipling began to write they were becoming increasingly conscious of it. *Hobson-Jobson,* the first dictionary of Anglo-Indian usage, appeared in 1886—at almost the same time as Kipling's first stories. In his newspaper articles for the Anglo-Indians, Kipling used dialects and slang. But when the pieces were collected and published in England, the Anglo-Indian and Indian expressions were deleted, and standard English was substituted. The language in *Kim* is stylized. One has the feeling that Kipling went through his writing with a pair of tweezers, applying dialect and colloquial speech at regular intervals in the text. He thought that the Indians and the Anglo-Indians were a quaint folk. The characters address each other as "thee" and "thou." They speak in proverbs. "For the sick cow a crow, for the sick man a Brahmin," Kim says. "The husbands of the talkative have a great reward hereafter," the lama observes. Kipling sought a poetic level of speech. He wanted his characters to be chanting their words, to offer them in a musical, singsong fashion.

> "Where goest thou?" he called after Kim.
> "Nowither—it was a small march, and all this"—Kim waved his hands abroad—"is new to me."
> "She is beyond question a wise and a discerning woman. But it is hard to meditate when—"
> "All women are thus." Kim spoke as might have Solomon.

The dialogue is flat and pretentious.

In *Huck Finn* the language is the language of the real world. It is not archaic. It beats out rhythms of joy, creativity and the possibilities for human freedom. In *Kim* Kipling defends the vernacular and condemns "clumsy English," but his actual writing does not match his theoretical preference. At school Kim hears stories

> . . . told in the even, passionless voice of the native-born, mixed with quaint reflections borrowed unconsciously from native-foster mothers, and turns of speech that showed they had been that instant translated from the vernacular. Kim watched, listened, and approved. This was not insipid, single-word talk of drummer-boys. It dealt with a life he knew and in part understood.

Kim often reads like a poorly translated novel.

Kim is also significantly different from *Huck Finn* because, unlike Huck, Kim is not forced into a crisis. Huck's values as a poor white Southerner are brought into question by his relationship with Jim. Freedom in *Huck Finn* means the anarchy on the raft, a world without government, an idyllic society. It also means freedom from slavery, from slave masters, from a plantation system. Freedom in *Kim* has nothing to do with colonial liberation, or even specifically freedom of Indians from the English. It means wandering—freedom from material things. There is much less sense of freedom in *Kim* than in *Huck Finn* because while Kim walks freely he is also the imperial agent. For Kim there is no direct confrontation, no conflict. He is not a rebel in the way that Huck is. He enjoys getting out of crowded city streets, but he does not perceive the vicious nature of his society. At the end of the novel Huck says:

> I reckon I got to light out for the territory ahead of the rest, because Aunt Sally she's going to adopt me and sivilize me, and I can't stand it. I been there before.

Kim does not light out for the territories. He does not return to the Himalayas. He is revived by the sahiba and Mother Earth. He is "sivilized."

The end of *Kim* presented severe problems for Kipling. He used the image of endless ripples in a pool to express his idea of human action, but he also wanted a terminating point, a shore which would halt the ever-widening circles. It is likely that he had the endings of *Huck Finn* and *Tom Sawyer* in mind while he was finishing his own book. When in 1889 Kipling interviewed Twain in America he asked if "Tom Sawyer married Judge Thatcher's daughter and whether we were ever going to hear of Tom Sawyer as a man." Twain replied, "I haven't decided. I have a notion of writing a sequel to *Tom Sawyer* in two ways. In one I would make him rise to great honour and go to Congress, and in the other I should hang him." Kipling wanted his hero to succeed; he wanted him to achieve social status. Kim acts like an Anglo-Indian Tom Sawyer when he works for the empire.

The two main metaphors in the novel—the wheel and the road—suggest an ongoing and never-ending process. But the lama's search ends. He finds the miraculous river of healing and he reaches the infinite. "As a drop draws to water, so my soul drew to the Great Soul which is beyond all things," he says in the best Emersonian tradition. His soul passes "beyond the illusion of Time and Space." Kim's journey is completed, he is initiated, but he is reborn through the sahiba and Mother Earth. He is ready to start again. After his revival he feels that "his soul was out of gear with its surroundings—a cog-wheel unconnected with any machinery, just like the idle cog-wheel of a cheap Beheea sugar-crusher laid by in a corner." Kim knows that he "must get into the world again." He cries, he hears

> . . . the wheels of his being lock up anew on the world without. Things that rode meaningless on the eyeball an instant before slid into proper proportion. Roads were meant to be walked upon, houses to be lived in, cattle to be driven, fields to be tilled, and men and women to be talked to. They were all real and true—solidly planted upon the feet—perfectly comprehensible—clay of his clay, neither more nor less.

The novel celebrates physical reality, movement, work, conversation, the texture of life.

Kim excludes two kinds of energy. One comes from the richness and diversity of all creation and human fellowship. The other is imperial heat. They are very different phenomena, though Kipling makes no conscious distinction between the two. He thinks that Kim can walk freely among men of all castes and creeds as their brother, and at the same time act as a government agent. He speaks of the "Irish and the Oriental in Kim's soul." But there is no conflict between these two parts of his mind. The climactic scene of the novel is cunningly arranged so that Kim defends the East and the empire in the same stroke. The lama is attacked by Russian and French agents who are out to subvert the British Empire. Since it is Kim's task as a spy to defeat them, he does so, and in the process he also defends the lama. Kipling arranges the plot so that there is no conflict between Kim's commitment to imperialism and his love for the lama. Kim is always in the Middle Way. He repeatedly questions his identity. "What am I?" he asks, "Mussalman, Hindu, Jain or Buddhist? That is a hard knot." He is "Kim—Kim—Kim—alone—one person—in the middle of it all." At the end of the novel he is still at the hub. "I am Kim. I am Kim. And what is Kim?" he asks in the final moments. It never comes to his attention that he must choose between East and West, Indians and the empire. He does not see that a white man who is an imperialist cannot simultaneously be a friend to the colonized people.

Kipling was unaware of the conflict he created in *Kim*. In the only place where there is conflict in his work it is unintentional. Kipling did not see that Kim's love for the lama and his exuberant love of Indian life threaten his work for the British government. Kipling thought he could be a racist and love Buddhists at the same time. At the end of the novel the lama and Mahbub Ali—representing the open road and the empire—stand on either side of Kim. It is the lama who has the final word. The last description in the novel is of the lama: hands crossed and smiling, he is a man "who has won salvation for himself and his beloved." This ending offers more of a sense of fellowship than the original ending, in which the lama looks like a man "who has gone through the valley of the Shadow and knows what is beyond."

Kim's future has been decided. Mahbub Ali says to the lama, ". . . now I understand that the boy, sure of Paradise, can yet enter Government service, my mind is easier." In the first draft of the novel Kipling did not intend Kim to enter government service and become an obedient servant of the empire. He envisioned his hero growing restless with a settled, domestic life, and again taking to the open road to ramble about the whole earth. For a moment it seems as if Kipling has resolved Kim's dilemma. He would let him wander freely on the open road. But he changed his mind. He insisted that Kim work for the government. The novel ends with Kim beside the lama and the British Empire off-stage. To serve the empire Kim will wander. That is not freedom at all, but bondage.

Kipling capitulated to the imperialist demands. He refused to let Kim wander freely. Like Mowgli, Kim must take his place in the imperial hierarchy. Kipling did not open up and flow with the only genuine conflict in the novel. Kim is ready to break loose, but Kipling won't release him. He does not allow the two Kims to clash, nor does he allow India and England to come into conflict. He betrayed his heart and mind for the British Empire.

7

Conrad's Contradictions

I. "WITHOUT CONTRADICTIONS NOTHING WOULD EXIST."

In Conrad's world contradiction is all-pervasive and never-ending. Not sterile contradictions, which are the toy of the cloistered academic, but the flesh-and-blood contradictions between living men and women, between ideas walking about in the minds of men, the contradictions in the pulsing tissue of social organization. In the knowledge of this truth he labors: in reality, contradiction; in contradiction, reality. There is "nothing uncontradicted," he wrote; in all men there is an "alliance" of "irreconcilable antagonisms." Struggle exists everywhere: on a ship on the open sea, in the tangled jungles of Africa, in the dark, ancient cities of Europe. Conrad's society generates violence between rich and poor, Europe and Africa, Black and white, royalists and revolutionaries, exploited and exploiters, colonizers and colonized. The battles are fought to bloody finishes. Nostromo is killed by a shotgun blast as he forages in the dark for the silver he has stolen; Mr. Verloc, the secret agent, is stabbed to death by his wife with a kitchen knife; Heyst, the hero of *Victory,* commits suicide by setting fire to his bungalow and burning himself to death in the flames. Peace comes on rare, deceptive moments. Beneath the calm surface of the sea lies a storm ready to break loose. Under the peaceful society a revolution is about to erupt. Everything on Conrad's planet earth is defined in terms of its opposite. A relentless warfare is carried out between opposing forces. One set of contradictions leads to another. Reconciliations are brief. The synthesis is always shattered. Conrad was the master of the dialectic.

When he sat down at his desk, took his pen in his hand and laid out the clean white sheets of paper, his assumption was that the writer wrote about struggle. Conflict was the stuff of fiction. "The only legitimate basis of creative work," Conrad wrote, "lies in the courageous recognition of all the irreconcilable antagonisms." Only then did the "barren struggle of contradictions assume the dignity of moral strife going on ceaselessly." There is a spectacle that Conrad watches—an endless cycle of dialectical change, a law of nature. He is spellbound by, sometimes in awe of, violence. Occasionally he thrives on violence for its own sake. But when he was on target he revealed contradictions in their moral settings and historical conditions.

Conrad was torn, caught in conflict and struggle. When he wrote he saw himself engaging in armed struggle. He fought to create, to bring the truth to light, to uncover the hidden. On one side, as he saw it, was himself—man the artist. On the other side was his opponent—nature. Conrad tells us that the act of writing *Nostromo* was

> . . . a creative effort in which mind and will and conscience are engaged to the full, hour after hour, day after day, away from the world . . . a material parallel can only be found in the everlasting sombre stress of the westward winter passage round Cape Horn. For that too is the wrestling of men with the might of their Creator, in a great isolation from the world.

Writing was labor. By this Conrad did not mean that the work of art was the product of struggle with God. There was no God; the universe was not an ethical construct. But the novel was the outcome of warfare with nature for survival. The artist wrestled with himself and with the material world around him.

There are two men, not one. Mr. Joseph Conrad sits down before a mirror, looks straight ahead and sees Mr. Korzeniowski, his other self. They are two warring selves. The two continually engage in dialogue. The curtain rises. The drama unfolds. First there is Mr. Korzeniowski, the Pole, born in 1857 in territory controlled by the Russians. His parents are landowners; his father is a poet, playwright and translator who fights in the Polish national liberation struggle. This first self, this Mr. Korzeniowski, feels he is part of a colonized people struggling for independence and self-determination. He is David against Goliath. He hates the imperial powers—Russia and Germany—the militaristic giants invading Poland from the East and the West. And so Korzeniowski, the Pole, identifies with all colonized peoples, the Congolese, the Mexicans, the Malays.

His parents die. The orphan becomes a rover. He leaves Poland, leaps out of his past into a strange and foreign world. Geneva, Paris, Marseilles, Gibraltar, the Azores, the Cape of Good Hope, Singapore. Poland recedes further and further into the distance as the railway car speeds across Europe, as the steamboat passes over the seven seas. A sailor, he wanders about the earth. He is a modern Odysseus embarked on his own odyssey, battling with the gods of the sea and the devils of foreign lands, in love with his own Nausicaä. His ancestor is the primeval sailor. He is a hero in an unheroic age. He fancies himself an adventurer, the last of the romantics, a Latin lover, a gunrunner, fighting for lost causes. He is an anomaly in the world of imperialism, in the hour of super-capitalism; commerce and industry are hateful to him. "Such was my abominable luck," he jests bitterly, "in being born by the mere hair's breadth of twenty-five centuries too late into a world where kings have been growing scarce with scandalous rapidity, while the few who remain have adopted the uninteresting manners and customs of simple millionaires." He is closer to the peasant in the fields than to the financier in the counting house, an admirer of the horseman, not the mechanic. There is an aristocratic bias in his outlook. He is an intellectual, a European humanist, with a sense of continental traditions and culture. He is morose, cynical, despairing. He is taciturn, belligerent, aloof, isolated. He hates complacency, fat German burghers, sentimental English cockneys.

And then there is Mr. Conrad. Korzeniowski changes his name, becomes Mr. Conrad, joins the British merchant marine, receives his Master Mariner's Certificate and is made a British subject. He is an Englishman. A celebrated author, he writes for the popular magazines, is the friend of H. G. Wells, John Galsworthy, Henry James. His temple is the British Empire, the rock of stability in a sea of change. Admiral Nelson is his god. He is a domestic animal. He is married to a quiet English girl and has two sons. He has a few small investments abroad and complains about his meager bank account. He is practical, conservative, patriotic and optimistic.

This contradictoriness accounts for the unevenness of Conrad's work: the trash—*The Rescue, The Arrow of Gold;* the mediocre work—*The Secret Agent* and *The Nigger of the Narcissus;* and the works of power—*Heart of Darkness* and *Nostromo*. It explains the pervasive irony, the instinctive habit of saying two things at the same time, of affirming and denying, of resting on the surface and plunging into the depths, of proclaiming victory and announcing defeat. The contradictoriness is productive. The dialogue, the struggle between Mr. Conrad and Mr. Korzeniowski, yields novels which explore the extremes of experience. Conrad's heroes, like himself, do battle with themselves. They are betrayers and betrayed, victims and victimizers, totally isolated and completely involved. They make history and are destroyed by it. These conflicts tear them apart. They must choose, decide, take sides. They are forced to throw in their lot with one force, one group, one party or the other. There are no neutrals.

Conrad wrote about conflicts which polarized society and at the same time split the individual man into two men. "The bitterest contradictions and the deadliest conflicts of the world," he wrote, "are carried on in every individual breast capable of feeling and passion." He felt the worldly contradictions in his own mind and body. "The human heart," Conrad observed, "is vast enough to contain all the world." In this sense he is like Honoré Balzac, who in 1844 wrote, "as for me, I shall have carried a whole society in my head." Balzac incorporated all of Restoration France within his solid frame, digging into one corner of his brain for a book on finance, another for a book about publishing, a third on provincial manners. Conrad, too, could draw out of himself whole continents, historical eras and societies.

Conrad was an autobiographical writer. He wrote out of and about himself, but he did not create a private world. The contradictions he discovered in his own inner landscape are illuminations of the contradictions in the outer landscape. He believed that when the writer sat down to write he withdrew into a "lonely region of stress and strife," but in that lonely, turbulent region the wide world expanded before him. Conrad linked the most intensely social and political experience of his life with his own intensely inward and private experience. In *Heart of Darkness* Marlow, speaking for Conrad, notes that his Congo voyage was "the farthest point of navigation and the culminating point of my experience. It seemed somehow to throw a kind of light on everything about me—and into my thoughts." When Conrad wrote he saw himself stepping into a territory of the mind which resembled the Congo territory of King Leopold. In the inner landscape, he claimed, "there are no policemen, no law, no pressure of circumstances or dread of opinion to keep" the writer "within bounds." This interior world is like the Congo of "utter solitude, without a policeman . . . where no warning voice of a kind neighbour can be heard whispering of public opinion." In creating his self he simultaneously creates society, and in creating society he simultaneously creates his self.

Conrad lodged himself at the heart of historical conflicts. He was, as Thomas Mann described him, the "Polish Englishman," a Western Easterner. Conrad burrowed to the center of rival European nationalisms. He embodied contradictory national cultures in his own being. He claimed that his was "the only case of a boy of my nationality and antecedents taking a . . . standing jump out of his racial surroundings and associations." One of a kind, but his singularity reveals the condition of European man. In his dossier were these recommendations: knowledge of the Slavs, the Anglo-Saxons, expert on autocracy and democracy, Russian orthodoxy and English nonconformity. Conrad also boasted that he was the "last seaman of a sailing vessel." If he could only live long enough, he claimed, he would "become a bizarre relic of a dead barbarism, a sort of monstrous antiquity, the only seaman . . . who had never gone into steam." In his own lifetime he had seen the machine transform the sea. The age of sail passed, the age of steam was inaugurated; his biography cut across the history of the industrial revolution. He remembered nostalgically the old sea, the

> . . . sea before the time when the French mind set the Egyptian muscle in motion and produced a dismal but profitable ditch. Then a great pall of smoke sent out by countless steamships was spread over the restless mirror of the Infinite. The hand of the engineer tore down the veil of the terrible beauty in order that greedy and faithless landlubbers might pocket dividends. The mystery was destroyed. The heart changed. The once loving and devoted

> servants went out armed with fire and iron and conquering the fear of their own hearts became a calculating crowd of cold and exacting masters.

Finally, Conrad situated himself on the border between industrial, commercial society and tribal, agricultural society. He is on the frontier where the African chief and the European trader clash, where both missionary and the shaman hold their own rituals, where the warrior with his spear dies before the soldier with his rattling gun. The frontier is in his own mind, as well as in the world of flesh-and-blood men and women.

In his last and unfinished essay, "Legends" (1924), he noted that there was "material for a fine legend" in the golden era of sailing, which lasted from 1850 to 1910. "The pathos of that era," he wrote, "lies in the fact that when the sailing ships and the art of sailing them reached their perfection, they were already doomed." The legend he wanted to tell would be the "celebration of the era of fair ships sailed with consummate seamanship—an era that seems as distant now as the age of miracles." As he saw it, the roots of legends were entwined "fancifully about the facts of history." The facts "need not be literally true," but they "ought to be credible and must be in a sort of fundamental accord with the nature of the life they record."

Legends and myths inevitably distort and simplify. They interpret, electrify, call to arms. Conrad's novels create new legends, destroy old myths, sustain others. In his sea tales and in his novels of the South Seas, *The Nigger of the Narcissus* and *The End of the Tether,* the legend is static. The house of contradiction collapses and in its place is an edifice of compartments, of neatly setoff rooms. *The Nigger of the Narcissus,* for example, presents a sharp dichotomy between life on the old clipper ships and life on new steamships—the old reliable salts and the modern proletarian sailors. Old Singleton is a sage, a hard worker, respectful, uncomplaining. James Wait, the young West Indian Black, is lazy and degenerate, and Donkin, the radical orator from London's East End, brings dissension when unity is essential. It is an all-too-facile attack on radicals and Blacks and a plea for the old times when sailors knew their places, respected their captains.

Conrad never wrote well about the past. He became nostalgic, sentimental. In his two avowedly historical late novels, *The Rover* and the unfinished *Suspense,* both dealing with the Napoleonic era, his drama is plotted every inch of the way and for every second. There is no breathing space. In *The Rover,* old Peyrol, the sailor, and the only man who has had absolutely nothing to do with the French Revolution, returns to France, outwits the English, destroys Screvola, the terrorist (the embodiment of the revolution), and frees the two young lovers, both victims and orphans of the revolution. He dies so that they can live. Out of old France comes a new society. It is too elaborate, too refined. Dead, dead, dead. There, as in *The Nigger of the Narcissus,* the patterns of conflict, which are dialectical, are missing, and in their place are the patterns of change, which are mechanical.

Conrad was wary of making neat and tidy diagrams, paradigms, which stifled contradiction. He was disappointed with *The End of the Tether* because it lacked a complex pattern, because the form was static. Captain Whalley, the central figure, is defeated by the social conditions he sets in motion. The captain is the "pioneer of new routes and new trades." He belongs to the old sea, the old East, and outlasts "the conditions that had gone into the making of his name." Conrad depicts the historical changes in the East. Once a fishing village with "a few mat huts erected on piles between a muddy tidal creek," the settlement becomes a city with courts of justice, a colonial treasury, and a cathedral. Captain Whalley makes a fortune as a trader, but he is abruptly impoverished by the crash of a banking corporation, "whose downfall had shaken the East like an earthquake." He returns to work, but in the new commercial society where individual initiative is restricted, he is "an amazing survival from the prehistoric times of the world." He reminisces about the "efforts of small men, the growth of a small place." But Whalley himself believes that there has been progress, that life is more orderly, lawful, more peaceful than it once was. He is certain that "a disposition for good" exists in all men and at all times, but he discovers that while material conditions have improved, men still perpetuate evil deeds. The moral pattern in *The End of the Tether* is nakedly transparent. There is a skeleton but no flesh.

When Edward Garnett, Conrad's friend, reviewed *The End of the Tether* in 1902 he called it "a study of an old sea captain, who, at the age of forty years' trade exploration of the South Seas, finding himself dispossessed by the perfected routine of the British Empire overseas he has helped to build, falls on evil times, and faces ruin calmly, fighting to the last." Conrad was intrigued by his analysis and in a letter to Garnett said, "You are the Seer of the Figures in the Carpet. The Figure in the Carpet of the E of this T [*Heart of Darkness*] you have seen so perfectly and described in a line and a half with so much precision that even to me it has been a sort of revelation. As to the E of T [*The End of the Tether*], you have seen the Figure—but the miserable threadbare warp and woof of the thing had fascinated them [the critics] already."

Conrad took the phrase "the Figure in the Carpet" from Henry James's short story of that title, published in 1896. In "The Figure in the Carpet," James's main character, a novelist, says:

> There's an idea in my work without which I wouldn't have given a straw for the whole job . . . It stretches, this little trick of mine, from book to book, and everything else, comparatively plays over the surface of it. The order,

> the form, the texture of my books will perhaps some day constitute for the initiated a complete representation of it.

James saw a pattern which extended across and unified the whole of his work. In "The Lesson of Balzac" he further explored the metaphor and the concept:

> The figured tapestry, all over-scored with objects in fine perspective . . . symbolizes to me . . . the last word of the achieved fable. Such a tapestry, with its wealth of expression of subject, with its myriad ordered stitches, its harmonies of tone and felicities of taste, is a work above all of closeness.

Conrad appropriated James's image. He located a figure in the carpet in James's work: "Nobody has rendered better," Conrad wrote of James, "the tenacity of temper, or known how to drape the robe of spiritual honour about the drooping form of a victor in a barren strife." This Jamesian ambiguity—"inner triumph in the face of outer defeat"—Conrad found greatly appealing. His own heroes—Lord Jim, Nostromo, Kurtz—are triumphant in the face of loss. The figure in James's carpet embodies conflict. But Jamesian conflict is unlike Conradian conflict. Conrad observed that there was "too much perfection of *method*" in James's work. The elaborate configurations, forms and patterns were far more important than the dramatic conflicts—the contradictions which formed the matter of the work of art. The patterns Conrad shaped, unlike James's, pivot about historical contradictions. *The End of the Tether* disappointed Conrad because its pattern was bluntly visible in the threadbare tapestry, because there was too much framework and not enough of the web of social forces.

"The struggles Mr. Henry James chronicles," Conrad wrote, "are, though only personal contests, desperate in their silence, none the less heroic (in the modern sense) for the absence of shouted watchwords, clash of arms and sound of trumpets." These conflicts constitute for Conrad the vitality of James's work, an indication of the seemingly endless stream of creativity in James. But the struggles Conrad chronicles, unlike James's, are not only personal contests. They are both public and private, individual and historical. Jamesian heroism is the heroism of the drawing room, the heroism of Isabel Archer in returning to Rome to live with evil Osmond. In Conrad there are shouted watchwords, the sound of trumpets, the clash of arms. His heroes change the course of history.

"As the picture is reality," James wrote in "The Art of Fiction" (1884), "the novel is history." Taken literally and applied to James's work, that definition makes no sense. *The Portrait of a Lady* and *The Ambassadors* are clearly and obviously not history. What James means is that readers have got to take the novel seriously. He aims to give the novel sacred status by calling it history. The novelist writes about that which is true. His work is a play of substance, not shadows, of flesh-and-blood characters, not wooden marionettes. "The subject matter of fiction," he said, "is stored up . . . in documents and records . . . it must speak with assurance, with the tone of the historian." You must believe what the novelist shows you, not toss it aside as the diversion of an entertainer.

"The Art of Fiction" was a crucial essay for Conrad, but he applied James's definition to his own situation. In his piece on James he wrote:

> In one of his critical studies published some fifteen years ago, Mr. Henry James claims for the novelist the standing of the historian as the only adequate one, as for himself and before his audience. I think that the claim cannot be contested . . . the position is unassailable.

And Conrad goes on to say that "Fiction is history, human history, or it is nothing. But it is also more than that; it stands on firmer ground, being based on the reality of forms and the observation of social phenomena, whereas history is based on documents, and the reading of print and handwriting—on second hand impressions. Thus fiction is nearer truth . . . A historian may be an artist too, and a novelist is a historian, the preserver, the keeper, the expounder, of human experience." Again, James speaks of documents and records to impress upon his reader that behind fiction is a solidity, an actuality, something which has in truth happened. He does not mean that fiction is literally based on historical documents. For Conrad that was true. He was a historical researcher, burrowing through memoirs, monographs, autobiographies of statesmen, generals, famous ladies, soldiers of fortune, explorers. What is important for him is not the documentary quality, but the essential—the fundamental and enduring. He extracts the core of meaning from the tangled web of history. He offers "the spirit of an epoch." He picks out the key fact or situation from the historical storehouse and transforms it into the material for his novel.

In the "Author's Note" (1917) to *Nostromo* he explains the meaning of his assertion that "fiction is history," that "a novelist is a historian." First, in 1875 or 1876, Conrad hears a tale about a man who during a revolution steals a lighter full of silver. A quarter of a century later he reads a book casually picked up in a secondhand bookshop. It is the story of an American seaman, who describes that robbery. The thief, as Conrad describes him, is "an unmitigated rascal, a small cheat." Conrad is uninterested in that situation and has "no particular interest in crime *qua* crime." He writes, "It was only when it dawned upon me that the purloiner of the treasure need not necessarily be a confirmed rogue, that he could be even a man of character, an actor and possibly a victim in the changing scenes of a revolution . . . that I had the first vision of a twilight country which was to become the province of Sulaco." The historical situation brings to life the episode of the theft, transforms a curious incident into a crucial struggle in a historical conflict. Next, Conrad tells us that his "principal authority for the history of Costaguana is . . . my venerated friend, the late Don José Avellanos . . . in his impartial and eloquent *History of Fifty Years of Misrule*. That work was never published . . . and I am in fact the only person in the world possessed of its contents." This is Conrad's way of saying that he is first the historian of Costaguana, and second its novelist, that there is a historical base below the superstructure of the fiction. The novel is based on the essentials of nineteenth-century South American history. Behind the color and sound, the loves and hates, the dilemmas and solutions of the characters there is a historical framework. And the actual historical allusions in the novel—to Napoleon III and Charlotte Corday—he noted, "are never dragged in for the sake of parading my unique erudition, but that each of them is closely related to actuality—either throwing a light on the nature of current events or affecting directly the fortunes of the people." Finally, Conrad wrote that "as to their own histories I have tried to set them down, Aristocracy and People, men and women, Latin and Anglo-Saxon, bandit and politician, with as cool a hand as was possible in the heat and clash of my own conflicting emotions. And after all this is also the story of their conflicts." What produces conflict in Conrad's novels is the antagonism between classes, races, sexes, cultures, man and nature, man and the machine, the economic base and the cultural superstructure.

James was, as Conrad defined him, "the historian of fine consciences." He zeroed in on the thought processes, the moral dilemmas of aristocrats, of refined ladies and gentlemen. James's characters think, think, think. Their infinitely complex deliberations are as monumental in James's cosmology as historic events—as the seizing of the Bastille or the opening guns of the American Civil War. He has the psychologist's interest in a patient's life history. Conrad too is the historian of consciousness, but his characters do not have the "fine consciousness" that James's have. Of Willems, the central figure in *An Outcast of the Islands,* Conrad writes:

> He was not . . . able to discern clearly the causes of his misery; but there are none so ignorant as not to know suffering, none so simple as not to feel and suffer from the shock of warring impulses. The ignorant must feel and suffer from their complexity as well as the wisest.

On these grounds Conrad parted company from James. James's heroes and heroines are intellectuals, conversationalists; they are cultured, well-mannered. Conrad creates characters like Singleton or Jim—simple sailors who are as torn by conflicts, by "warring impulses," as are the most cerebral and fine of James's women. Conrad knows that the sailor can feel conflicts as keenly as the American businessman or the European aristocrat of whom James was so fond. James restricts conflicts to an elite. For Conrad conflicts in consciousness are not experienced by only one social class.

James's characters are ahistorical figures who pass before but who are beyond the influence of the historical scene, whereas Conrad's characters weave in and out of that historical fabric. Conrad's history is contemporary history. He looks at the events of his time with the eye of the historian. But he does not kill the present. He does not drive a nail through it so that it cannot move. His history breathes. He assumes that the present—along with its confusion and chaos—springs dialectically from the past, is propelled into the future, has its meaning in struggles.

Conrad concludes his essay on James with a few remarks on the endings of James's novels. "His books end as an episode in life ends," he wrote. "You remain with the sense of the life still going on." Conrad profited from James's discovery. His novels, too, end with "the sense of the life still going on." But they do not end on a note of ambiguity, as James's do. Conrad's novels end with new historical struggles rising out of the old. His novels are about cycles: the new cycle on a higher level than the old, spinning faster than the old, going into motion. The conflicts of the novel are restated at the conclusion in a new key. The struggle between man and nature, man and the machine, man and his fellowmen is not finished; it will be played out on a new stage between different actors. One illusion is destroyed, one corruption revealed, but in their place sprout new lies and new corruptions to be cut down. In the end is the beginning.

II. THE MONSTROUS MASTER MARINER

There is only one element for Conrad. Water. Earth, air and fire are of no consequence. The sea is his home. He is touched all over by it, immersed in it—the universal bath—carried by its currents, torn by its storms, sucked down into its depths by maelstroms and buoyed up on its calm surface. He is the son of the sea. For the oceans he has a passion. They are his opponents. The sea is his teacher. On its mirrored surface he looked deep into his own self. Henry James called him the Monstrous Master Mariner. In plain English, a sailor. Without the sea Conrad is a nowhere man. But the sea also erodes his power; its endless rocking lulls him to sleep, its thundering waves batter down his rocky walls.

It is the sea—the world of ships and sailors, mainsails and jibs, anchors and rudders, dry docks and barnacles—which waterlogs him with a sense for things, for material objects. His hands touch and grasp ropes, anchors. He gets a feel for surfaces, angles and corners. He works, holds tools, changes the sizes and shapes of objects. The world of water makes him a materialist. If he gets lost in reverie at sea then he is a drowned sailor. If he falls asleep in the crow's-nest then he tumbles to a dark watery grave. He must be awake. The ship and the things aboard it come to have special meaning. They are transcendent. The ship's voyage is a symbol of existence, a passage through time from one place to another; the spokes of the ship's helm stand out as "a symbol of mankind's claim to the direction of his own fate." In the darkness of night out at sea, the light in the lighthouse, indicating the path outward or homeward bound, is his symbol for the imagination—a light guiding man, revealing the hidden.

In an essay on "The Secret Sharer" Professor Guerard tells us that for Conrad and for all writers since the "beginnings of literature and symbolism" the sea is "an image for the unconscious life." For Conrad, however, the sea is wet and salty; it is not an image for the unconscious life. It carries ships, fish swim in it, if you drink it, and no other water, you die. In *The Mirror of the Sea,* a holy book of the waters, and of the men and ships who passed over their surface, he tells us (in the chapter "Emblems of Hope") that "it is not so much that the anchor is a symbol of hope as that it is the heaviest object that he [the sailor] has to handle on board his ship at sea." An anchor is not a link to the unconscious life. No, it is a forged piece of iron that holds the ship fast.

But it is on the sea too that his idealism floats. There, intangible ships float on tangible oceans. Sailors hear unhearable music—the orchestra of the seven seas. They see phantoms. The sea is mysterious, inexplicable, unpredictable. It is on Conrad's sea, like Coleridge's, that there are haunted ships, curses, strange creatures which fly and crawl and swim. It is on ships that Conrad especially feels the "spell of moonlight." He looks "upon the mystic nature of material things."

On the sea Conrad learned his alphabet and vocabulary, letters and numbers. The merchant ships of the late nineteenth century were his Oxford and Cambridge. He acquired the tools of two trades at sea—sailing and writing. He met the word, followed its power, was charmed and fascinated by it. From the language of sailing men he learned to be a craftsman with words. In *The Mirror of the Sea* he tells us about the first mate. His task, it seems, is to watch "the growth of the cable." This is a sailor's phrase, Conrad tells us, and it has "all the force, precision, and imagery of technical language that, created by simple men with keen eyes for the real aspect of the things they see in their trade, achieves the just expression seizing upon the essential, which is the ambition of the artist in words." And at night he spent hour after hour on deck or in the hold listening to masterful storytellers, old salts, with white beards flavored by the sea, who could remember Napoleon shipped off to exile on Elba and the Battle of Trafalgar. His own chief storyteller is Marlow, the sailor. In *Nostromo* another sailor, Captain Mitchell —known to his shore friends as Fussy Joe—is a chief narrator, exuberant and rambling in his tales. Marlow is compelled to talk, like Coleridge's Ancient Mariner. The sea lays an awful burden on men. Conrad listens to the legends of the sea with his jaw hanging open. The moral character of the old sailors is shady, their disposition is reckless, but their language is vivid. From these men Conrad drew his conclusion that the man rich in imagination is a poor citizen, an antisocial type. The tales are oral history, experience passed on by word-of-mouth from one generation of sailors to the next. It is a culture in which the spoken word, not the written word, is primary. We are active listeners rather than passive readers.

On the sea the sailor is isolated. He is in a world barren of women. There are no cities, no streets, no grog shops, no whorehouses, no forests, no crowds of men. As far as the eye can see there is only water and sky—and occasionally another ship. At sea Conrad is like a hermit in his cave, like a medieval saint in his cell. The ship is a jail which bars him from the world. And to be at sea—in solitary, as it were—is to be high. The voyage is a trip. The mind loses contact with itself. The mind seems to hover over the waters. And this solitude, with the ship at the center of the world, has the effect of magnifying all experience. The ship becomes the world. The sailor is imbued with a sense of his own importance. It is an ego trip, but it is also a brotherhood trip, a collective experience. The crew works, eats, sleeps, together. The sea, the true democrat, fosters a spirit of democracy among the sailors. Each man is dependent on his mate. All sailors are brothers. Italian sailors extend greetings to Arab sailors. In port the flags of all the nations of the world flutter beside one another in the wind. Liberty, Equality, Fraternity, are the sailor's watchwords.

Men are thrown together against nature, against threats from storm and calm. But, as Conrad notes, "all those brothers in craft and feeling . . . have been also more than once fiercely engaged in cutting each other's throats." The ship is a microcosm of the world, a little society in which conflict and dissension are rampant. There are mutinies at sea, just as there are rebellions in cities. On board the ship there is a hierarchical society, a captain who looks down from Olympian heights, or who remains secluded in his cabin. Like a king, he is surrounded by an entourage—his first, second and third mates. The cards of democracy are passed out only among the lower decks. His ships fly the flags of liberty and democracy, but they have jails; sailors are lashed. The captain has his special table, the crew have their hammocks in the hold.

Conrad is no Ishmael sleeping beside his chosen Queequeg. His white sailors do not embrace Black sailors. "A certain enormous buck nigger encountered in Haiti," he says, "fixed my conception of blind, furious, unreasoning rage, as manifested in the human animal, to the end of my days. Of the nigger I used to dream for years afterwards." The sea takes him to all places. It opens the world to Conrad. He circumnavigates the globe, meets Arabs and Mexicans, Englishmen, Japanese, Black Haitians. He starts as a Pole, a Central European who had never before seen a Black man. And so when he does, it comes as a shock. "Nigger" is the word that comes to his tongue. He is afraid of Black sailors; they seem to darken the air with rage, hate. They are mysterious to him, as if they have contact with supernatural powers. He wants to avoid the Black sailor, to stay out of his reach. They are Jonahs placing evil spells on ships.

The sea is a clock; on its face Conrad reads the story of time. In *The Mirror of the Sea* he writes:

> If you would know the age of the earth, look upon the sea in a storm. The greyness of the whole immense surface, the wind furrows upon the faces of the waves, the great masses of foam, tossed about and waving, like matted white locks, give to the sea in a gale an appearance of hoary age, lustreless, dull, without gleams, as though it had been created before light itself.

The ship is a time machine that takes him back into the past, to a world without cities. He sails off into the primitive past, to the age when the first man aboard a log pushed out into the sea. He looks at the sea through the eyes of the cave man, of the Viking rovers, of the Norsemen rowing through rough seas. It is the world of Odin and Thor. The sea tides carry him out and back into all mythologies: into the cultures of all peoples who worshiped the oceans, poured libations to still angry waters, sacrificed young calves before embarking on quests for golden oranges, golden fleeces, or Helens abducted by foreign tribes. He worships Neptune and the Kings of the East and West Winds. On them he is entirely reliant. "The West Wind is the greatest king," he says in *The Mirror of the Sea.*

> He is a barbarian, of a northern type. Violent without craftiness, and furious without malice, one may imagine him seated masterfully with a double-edged sword on his knees upon the painted and gilt clouds of the sunset, bowing his shock head of golden locks, a flaming beard over his breast, imposing, colossal, mighty-limbed, with a thun-

> dering voice, distended cheeks, and fierce blue eyes, urging the speed of his gales.

With these mighty gods standing beside him in the ocean, the mightiest of the elements, man becomes godlike too. He is baptized a hero in the salt waters of the Atlantic and Pacific. When he is lifted out he is a giant. The sailor's tale is an epic; the sailors are knights on quests, on crusades, at war, in a Homeric battle with nature. Conrad is Odysseus, a wanderer on his own odyssey, meeting strange tribes, fighting giants, loving foreign princesses.

The only direction his sea-bound time machine will not take him is forward. Conrad will not go by sea into the future. He looks back to ancestors, to his fathers, but not to his descendants or children. That way, up the gangplank into the modern luxury liners, he refuses to go. And he gets a kind of perverse pleasure in knowing that the *Titanic* sinks. The sinking of the ship is nature's victory over a decadent, overrefined civilization.

The sea makes the roving youth a man. On the sea Conrad has a "vision of evil," an end to his romantic view of nature. He is initiated into the sea's "cynical indifference" to human suffering and to human courage. The sea does not care. You can drown and it does not care; you can survive a storm which wrecks your ship and the ocean shows no sign of emotion on its surface. From Poland the sea looks gentle and friendly to man, but in the Indian Ocean or the Yellow Sea its fury and power are terrifying, its windless nights are unnerving. Conrad first saw the sea at Venice, the city of canals: a city sinking into the sea, a city of death and decay, its ancient buildings, its palaces of art threatened by the rage of the waters.

On the sea Conrad caught his first glimpse of England: the sailing ship *James Westoll,* its red ensign flying in the wind. The sea brings him to his exile island home. He is a sailor in the merchant marine under the reign of Queen

Victoria, under the British Empire. He is a sailor in the imperial fleet. He idealized England because England ruled the waves, because he thought that the English, more than any other people, were sea creatures, an island people dependent on the surrounding waters. The Union Jack spoke to him of tradition and security, optimism, trade, conservatism and progress. Through the sea he acquired his patriotism, his love of Lord Nelson. The conclusion of *The Mirror of the Sea* is a holy psalm for Nelson, the sea and England:

> All passes, all changes: the animosity of peoples, the handling of fleets, the forms of ships; and even the sea itself seems to wear a different and diminished aspect from the sea of Lord Nelson's day. In this ceaseless rush of shadows and shades . . . we must turn to the national spirit, which, superior in its force and continuity to good and evil fortune, can alone give us the feeling of an enduring existence of an invincible power against the fates.
>
> Like a subtle and mysterious elixir poured into the perishable clay of successive generations, it grows in truth, splendour, and potency with the march of ages. In its incorruptible flow all round the globe of the earth it preserves from the decay and forgetfulness of death the greatness of our great men, and amongst them the passionate and gentle greatness of Nelson.

The sea which takes him around the world brings him to England, his last port of call. The sea, the truly internationalist element, binds together men and land, and becomes Conrad's English lake, carrying English ships, men and goods around the world.

Conrad's sea is the universal element: the waters of contradiction. The rhythms and patterns of the sea regulate his life on shore: landfall and departure, east winds and west winds, full tides, ebb tides, calms and storms. Conrad's is a Manichean universe in which the two halves are land and water rather than light and dark. When he writes he thinks of the sea, of the ship leaving the harbor. Putting down the first word on the page is like shoving off into the ocean. After the safety and security of the port, man is alone on the sea; the writer at his desk is away from his fellow-man. As he writes he is alone in his craft, paddling along, flowing with the current, tacking, steering, floating, reaching his destination, refueling before the outward voyage again. Ports of call are only temporary resting places. The sailor's challenge is in the midst of the storm at high sea; the writer's is in the midst of gales and whirlwinds in the lives of his characters.

The years at sea taught Conrad the barrenness of the aesthete's creed. In *Romantic Image* Professor Kermode notes that the symbolist believed that "to be cut off from life and action" was "necessary as a preparation for the vision." And while Conrad believed that the lonely sailor, like the isolated hermit, experienced "sudden revelation of the profane world," he felt that the "artist is a man of action, whether he creates a personality, invents an expedient, or finds the issue of a complicated situation." Conrad is an action painter. He works against "cross gusts of wind swaying the action" of mankind.

The sea stretches and enlarges everything Conrad thinks about, reads and feels. The sea flows through his mind, washes around his heart, agitates his intellect and his passion. "Books are an integral part of one's life," he notes. And especially his "Shakespearean associations are . . . with the year of hard gales, the year in which I came nearest to death at sea, first by water and then by fire." He had helped his father translate Shakespeare into Polish, and Lear, Hamlet, Falstaff, Antony and Cleopatra became living figures on the ship's stage. He carried his one-volume, five-shilling edition of Shakespeare around the world, reading it in his cabin at night, and in port "at odd moments of the day, to the noisy accompaniment of caulkers' mallets driving oakum into the deck-seams of a ship in dry dock."

Shakespeare penetrated his skin along with the salt water of the ocean. And both flowed out simultaneously in his work: in *Nostromo* in the scenes on the Golfo Placido, which recall the storms, the isolation, the madness, the chaos of *Lear*; and in *Victory*, for Axel Heyst's magical island recalls Prospero's island in *The Tempest*. Conrad's tempests, the storms in the minds of his heroes, are Shakespearean.

But Conrad's best books are not principally about the sea. Although *Heart of Darkness* takes us down the Atlantic and up the Congo River, it is the cities of Europe, the jungles of Africa, life on the land, not on the sea, which shock and enrage. But everything Conrad wrote of the land is seen from the harbor, from the sea, from under the sailor's cap. It is that sense of the interpenetration of polar opposites —land and sea, change and permanence—which Conrad, the sailor on land, the seaman out of his natural element, docks in the harbor of the English novel. The sea is the timeless, the land is the empire of time; the sea is ahistorical, the land the territory of history. On the sea man faces nature, on the land man fights in society.

Only land and sea together brought complexity and wholeness to Conrad's fiction. The sailor's view of the land revealed its kernel of truth.

8

Season in Hell

Heart of Darkness (1899) is a voyage into hell, the hell of colonialism. On the trip we meet devils of violence, devils of greed, devils of desire, devils of folly, devils of rapacity. It is a somber study, a fugue on Blackness and whiteness. A tale of horror, of the grotesque and macabre. Screams and shudders, strange beasts, the unknown. *Heart of Darkness* terrifies the reader. It instills a form of madness in him. It haunts the reader, tears asunder that truce he has made with mediocrity, with the appearance of things. *Heart of Darkness* grasps for everything. Nothing must be excluded. Conrad wants to encircle all history, all time, all places, all kinds of men. Half the time he screams. He is in a frenzy, or he is drugged. Banging his hands, kicking his feet. His images flow in wild confusion. It is a quick, spontaneous outburst, and Conrad rushes to get it all down on paper. It is almost too much for him. He tries to embrace it all, the whole universe, and it slips away from him. His discoveries knock him off the face of the earth. Sometimes he does not know how to tell it as it is. One word after the other, in a line, one sentence following another, paragraph after paragraph—this does not seem adequate to the task. How can words make you feel the lash of the whip on a man's body, how can they make you smell the stench of rotting flesh, how can they make you feel the man-made scars cut deep into the green jungle.

Marlow, the voyager into the Congo, Conrad's establishment self, has his mind wrecked. In telling his tale, Conrad aims to transform the consciousness of his listeners. Freak them out. Marlow is a mysterious figure. He sits alone, aloof, almost lifeless: an idol, an allegorical figure—"trustworthiness personified." He is mystical, motionless—"in the pose of a meditating Buddha"—a magician who casts spells, exorcises ghosts. He believes that words are like bullets; they are the "swift black mercenaries" Sartre fires *rat-ta-ta-ta*. They carry destructive power in time through space. His words bring meaning, but that meaning "was not inside like a kernel but outside, enveloping the tale which brought it out only as a glow brings out a haze, in the likeness of one of these misty halos that sometimes are made visible by the spectral illumination of moonshine." The setting for Marlow's tale is primitive. Three men are huddled together against the darkness, brought together by the sea: an accountant, a lawyer, a director of companies—three fat cats of the bourgeoisie, living comfortable lives, protected by the police, repressed sexually and emotionally. Marlow wants to take them out of quiet, placid England, beyond the rows of decent shops and complacent shopkeepers and into the heart of Africa. Marlow rages at this bourgeois trinity; he snorts, pounds his fists. In *Lord Jim*, too, he attacks them again. He fears his story will be "dwarfed . . . in the hearing." He mistrusts not his words, but his listeners' minds. "I could be eloquent," he says, "were I not afraid that you fellows have starved your imaginations to feed your bodies." They lead "safe—and profitable—and dull" lives.

Marlow himself is a middle-class Englishman. He is chummy. "By Jupiter," he exclaims in the best pompous English manner. He sits around a fire with his mates talking like a schoolboy about Sir John Franklin and Sir Francis Drake. And he describes a map of the world, "marked with all the colours of a rainbow" to indicate which colonies in Africa belong to whom. "There was a vast amount of red," he says, "good to see at any time, because one knows that some real work is done in there, a deuce of a lot of blue, a little green, smears of orange, and, on the East Coast, a purple patch, to show where the jolly pioneers of progress drink the jolly lager-beer." He believes that the British colonialists bring the justice of English courts, the progress of British values, while German progress is measured by the exportation of lager beer. Marlow talks about sacred flames, the flag, the indomitable British spirit. It's Korzeniowski the Pole aping the British, insinuating himself into British culture, trying to disguise that foreign look, that Eastern European accent. But he is also an explorer, a middleman with contacts at the end of the road. He is out to bombard the British. His tale is like one of Mao's big character posters—it initiates a cultural revolution.

Heart of Darkness is about Marlow's education. European man, the white man, finds out about the Third World, the Black man. In *Heart of Darkness* Conrad unravels and uncovers. He takes the twisted and gnarled sailor's knot and untangles it. He rips aside the white winding sheet and reveals the decaying corpse. His is a destructive voyage, with the express purpose of annihilating the European's belief in civilization, in the colonial enterprise. Conrad saw how language—the words used by orators, newspapermen and admen—masked society. The novelist unmasks. Behind "high-sounding names," such as *Welt-politik,* was the violent reality of the factory system and the banking house. Noble words made men betray themselves, persuaded them to participate in atrocities. "The words one knows so well," one of his heroes says, "have a nightmarish meaning . . . liberty, democracy, patriotism, government—all of them have a flavour of folly and murder." While the president speaks of democracy, tyranny is in practice; when newspaper editors speak of patriotism, they are trying to mask genocide. This is Conrad's sense of the corruption of language by the state. Words mean the very opposite of what they once meant. In *The Inheritors* (1901), written with Ford Madox Ford,

Conrad shows how a European financier named De Mersch buys up an English newspaper for the sole purpose of extolling his international enterprises. The narrator of the tale, a journalist, writes "a paean to a great colonizer." He dignifies exploitation. But he is also a muckraker, and he does a story which shows the "real horrors stripped naked . . . the famines, the vices, the diseases and the crimes."

Conrad occasionally wrote for the press, but he thought of journalism as "a sort of intellectual death." There was no place for "effective truth" in the pages of the daily newspaper. "Everyone knows that the bourgeois press is one of the most powerful weapons of the bourgeoisie," Lenin wrote. "It is impossible to leave it in the hands of the enemy at a time when it is no less dangerous than bombs and machine guns." Conrad felt that the press's "feverish exploitation" of news robbed men of "the power to reflect and the faculty of genuine feeling." His own prose, he declared, offered the "unsentimental truth stripped of the romantic garment the Press had draped around its harsh form." In *Chance* (1914) he demonstrates the social power of language, the difference between the journalist's work and the novelist's craft. "You know the power of words," Marlow tells us. "We pass through periods dominated by this or that word—it may be development, or it may be competition or education, or purity or efficiency, or even sanctity. It is the word of the time." For Conrad language was a record of the changes in social and intellectual history. Thrift is the word Marlow unmasks in *Chance*. While the "press was screeching . . . that the financier . . . was helping the great moral evolution of our character towards the newly discovered virtue of thrift . . . by promising to pay ten per cent interest on all deposits," Marlow strips away "the rags of business verbiage and financial jargon" and exposes the naked commercial dealings. The financier De Barral is caught in his corrupt schemes. He goes on trial. Both Marlow, the novelist, and his counterpart, the newspaper man, sit and watch the proceedings. While the journalist sticks to the "actualities which are the daily bread of the public mind," Marlow is treated to "a glimpse," a "burlesque revelation." He possesses that faculty James described in "The Art of Fiction" —the "power to guess the unseen from the seen, to trace the implication of things, to judge the whole piece by the pattern." Marlow finds that the "merest starting point becomes a coign of vantage, and then by a series of logically deducted verisimilitudes one arrives at truth." Unlike the newspaperman, the novelist reflects, and he is rewarded with "a moment of detachment from mere visual impressions."

Conrad assumes that the truth is hidden, that the essentials are below the surface, that the language used by reporters, presidents and business executives depicts reality as the opposite of what it actually is. The novelist dives below the surface and brings up the fundamental truth. And Conrad feels that there are moments when, in a flash, one's vision is qualitatively changed. In a second the hidden truth is revealed.

Heart of Darkness is an epiphany. It takes us behind the words "civilization" and "empire." Behind the door of civilization is European barbarism; behind the door of empire is exploitation, death, disease, exile. *Heart of Darkness* is a vision of evil. The heart of darkness is the core of truth beneath the surface. It is the moment in which all is revealed. There is all the "rot let loose in print" by the press—about the imperial enterprise. He sweeps it away. There is the pretense of the philanthropic enterprise. He pricks holes in that bag. There is the face of the jungle; he goes into the interior. There is the accountant with his oiled-down hair, starched white shirt and cuff links. His cool exterior hides his heart of avarice and greed. He would rather kill a Congolese than make an incorrect entry in his account book. "When one has got to make correct entries," he says, "one comes to hate those savages—hate them to death." There are the African masks—those masks which inspired Picasso's "Les Desmoiselles D'Avignon"—which hide the features of the Black man. Conrad unmasks.

Heart of Darkness turns everything inside out, upside down. Light is dark, up is down, good is evil, death is life. The agents of civilization are barbarians. The Enlightenment thinkers are torturers. The Christians are devils. Everything turns into its opposite, denies, then destroys itself. Marlow makes two important discoveries on his trip. The first is that European civilization rests on the exploitation of Black people by white people, that European society rests on the annihilation of the wretched of the earth, on the theft of the riches of the planet.

Heart of Darkness signals the end. It is about the decay of European civilization. The whole world is in gloom, in mourning. The sun is setting. It is dark everywhere—in the Congo, in London. Hell is the eternal season. In the manuscript version of the novel the "heart of darkness" specifically referred to the planet earth—the center of blackness in the universe. Conrad performed surgery on that image, but darkness is still embedded in the tale. Paint it black, Conrad exclaims. It is the end of a historical era. In the colonial territory one sees the heart of imperialism; the truth of the metropole is revealed in the Third World.

Conrad was working for a European trading company in the Congo in 1890. His Congo diary and his letters back home record his feelings. "Everything is repellent to me here," he wrote in September 1890, "men and things, but especially men." He described the colonial trader as a "common ivory-dealer with sordid instincts." At first he grumbled and muttered under his breath about the stupidity of packing ivory in crates, but gradually he came to attack the colonial setup as a whole, and shake his fist at that "big (or fat?) banker who rules the roost at home." One letter he received from his Uncle Bobrowski reveals how Conrad himself was feeling. "I see from your last letter," Bobrowski wrote, "that you feel a deep resentment towards the Belgians for exploiting you so mercilessly." Conrad ended up thinking of himself as one of the Congo's "white slaves," in common bondage with Black slaves—bound to the imperial machine. The agent of colonialism, the victimizer, becomes conscious of his own victimization, his own oppression, and becomes a rebel. Conrad is the white nigger.

The Congo voyage transformed him. To discover that behind your affluence lies another man's poverty, that behind your ease lies another man's exploitation, that behind your life lies another man's death, that your fate is inextricably connected with the fate of millions of Black men and women whose existence you had denied—all this is mind-blowing. It drives Marlow mad. His madness is illuminating. It is the insanity that clears the decks of falsehood and produces reformations, renaissances and revolutions. Traveling down the coast of Africa to the Congo, Marlow sees a French gunboat firing shells into the jungle. There is no one visible on the coast or in the interior. But the sailors continue to fire because they have been told that the enemy, the criminals, the outlaws, are hiding in the dark bush. That description of the French gunboat is like the film clips of Amerikan warships off the coast of Indochina, firing shells into the jungle. It is a reign of terror. There is a colonial war going on; genocide of Black people by white people. To Marlow it is absurd.

He describes the destruction of the earth by white men. Marlow indicts Europe. Before the tribunal of man he files a brief that lists the atrocities. There is the Eldorado Exploring Expedition, which in fact has no interest in exploring. "To tear treasure out of the bowels of the land was their desire." Then there is the International Society for the Suppression of Savage Customs. A humane society, you may think. The report prepared for the society suggests as the solution to the problem: "Exterminate all the brutes." You eliminate savage customs by eliminating savages. There are the impressionistic descriptions of shapes and forms which once were men, but which are now only loose gatherings of flesh and broken bones. There is the chain gang and the law. The law, "like bursting shells," is as essential for the exploitation of the Africans as loaded carbines in the hands of white guards. *Heart of Darkness* describes the building of the railway through the Congo in 1890: The jungle is dynamited to clear a space for the tracks—each one laid at the cost of a human life. The railway: the machine of the nineteenth century, the engine of progress and civilization, pulling the cargo of death, the caboose of destruction.

In *Heart of Darkness* Marlow shoves Europe and Africa together, puts the spheres of white beside the spheres of Black. They are connected. He is Atlas, holding the planet, and changing the shape of the globe and man's sense of the world. It is the geography of the mind which Marlow expands. He takes the charted mind of European man, which looks like one of those fifteenth-century maps, and fills in new territories, plots uncharted areas. *Heart of Darkness* is a voyage into the mind. It is about thinking—why you think as you do, how you think—about human consciousness and mind explosions. "The mind of man is capable of anything—because everything is in it, all the past as well as all the future." Marlow's mind is cleared of tangled roots, just as the jungle is cleared of thick undergrowth. In this world fat men become thin, elegantly dressed men walk naked. Their bodies are stripped of the "cloak of time," their minds sheared of excess growth. Marlow takes us back to the beginning, to an unearthly earth, to prehistoric times. Before he leaves Europe for the Congo he visits a doctor—"an alienist," Marlow calls him—who studies the mind. He measures the crania of all white men going to Africa. "This is my share in the advantages my country shall reap from the possession of such a magnificent dependency," the doctor says. But the real "changes take place inside." Marlow sees the white man without bourgeois institutions, totally alone, thrown back on himself—in a vacuum. He sees the white man as the complete product of his society: a person who is taught when and how to think, whose mind is stamped with the images of the dollar sign and the pound sterling, the eagle and the lion, the scales of justice and the gun. In Africa there are no protective walls of the mind. The flying buttresses tumble, the edifice crumbles. The high priests languish. Society is repressive, Marlow discovers. It keeps each man in his own cell. In Africa there is a jailbreak. The prisoner saws away the bars of his cell and escapes. His emotions escape. His thoughts go free. And in his freedom he becomes a criminal, a devil.

Marlow sees for the first time that Africans are men, that their minds are like the minds of Europeans. All along he has been taught that the brain of the white man is superior, that it is physiologically different from the brain of the Black man. But Marlow finds his brothers in Africa. What blows his mind is that whites and Blacks are kin. He rejects the claims of the Victorian novelists Charles Kingsley and William Thackeray that Blacks are not men, that they are a subhuman species. He watches Black men:

> They howled and leaped, and spun, and made horrid faces; but what thrilled you was just the thought of their humanity—like yours—the thought of your remote kinship with this wild and passionate uproar. Ugly. Yes, it was ugly enough; but if you were man enough you would admit to yourself that there was in you just the faintest trace of a response to the terrible frankness of that noise.

After the corruption of Europe, the decadence of the West, the artificiality of Paris, the beauty of the society lady, the quietude of the cabinet meeting, the decorum of the middle-class sitting room—the wildness, the grotesqueness and the chaos are liberating. To the beauty of the stock market, the quietude of law and order, Marlow says *no*. The discovery he makes about African men and women, about the mind of man, is shattering. It means that exploitation of Africans by Europeans is a crime. It deflates the whole morality of imperialism. He, that Black man, whipped as he works, must feel and think as I think and feel, Marlow realizes. That is the weight of the burden he feels.

No Africans, no Third World men or women, are major characters in *Heart of Darkness*. They are a moving force in history, they are a power, but they are not seen as specific individuals. In *Heart of Darkness* they are in the background—Black arms and legs glimpsed through the dense jungle. There is a Black primitive rebel who turns to arson and burns down a company warehouse as an attack on the colonial enterprise. There is the jumped-up Black servant whose white master provokes him to mock other whites. There is the Black guard with rifle in hand, making sure that his Black brothers do not escape from the chain gang. There is also the Black woman who steps out of the jungle: the Earth Mother, sensual, fertile, fecund. She is a creature out of cheap romantic fiction. She is the embodiment of Conrad's dream fantasies.

At the center of this hell is Kurtz. In Kurtz all the contradictions, the most extreme conflicts, are concentrated. "All Europe," Marlow says, "contributed to the making of Kurtz." He is the quintessence of Western man; he is a "universal genius." He is Mr. Enlightenment—an "emissary of pity, and science, and progress." He is Mr. Monopoly Capitalism. He wants profit and power. He is a dictator in his little kingdom in the Congo, an arch criminal, a murderer, a cannibal. He becomes a god on earth. His is the sin of egotism. His self expands to fill the universe. There is only I, I, I. Kurtz is terribly alone. Kurtz is the force of energy itself. He consumes himself till there is nothing left. In this fable about wealth and life Kurtz becomes capital personified. He becomes cold, lifeless, white, "an animated image of death carved out of old ivory." He becomes a fetish. He becomes the thing he worships. He has kicked the earth to pieces, and in vengeance the wilderness gets back at him. It invades him. Kurtz is Conrad's portrait of Rimbaud (whose works he had been reading in the late 1890s), the French poet who went to Africa, became a gunrunner, a slave trader, a plantation overseer. Like Rimbaud, Kurtz has his season in hell. He is an artist, an orator, a painter, a poet.

Conrad looks into his heart and finds there a spirit of perversity. He is fascinated by evil. What he remembers most about Kurtz are the skulls of slain Black men on posts outside his camp. Victims of progress, Africans killed during rituals in Kurtz's honor. And the heads are ornamental, they are decorated. Kurtz is the force of evil which men worship and lust after. Cruel, malicious, destructive. Sympathy for the devil—that is what Conrad demands. He invites us to a Black Mass. Kurtz is loved, worshiped. The simple, innocent Russian boy in the Congo—an anomaly in the dark jungle—adores Kurtz. So do the Africans. They adore he who exploits and degrades them. In this is Conrad's own malicious spirit, his cruel joke. He is laughing up his sleeve, making a bitter jest at the expense of mankind. Slaves love their masters. The two men—Kurtz, the devil, and the angelic Russian—are as one. It is that inextricable link between good and evil which drives Conrad mad. The Russian is led by an "absolutely pure, uncalculating, unpractical spirit of adventure." Kurtz is possessed by ivory, the crown and the gun. The ring we hear is the emptiness of bourgeois man, the hollow echo of colonialism. Nothing. A whole culture—nothing but a sham. So why not, he thinks, blow the whole thing up. Desperation. Acts of desperation and creation.

Kurtz is Conrad's hero because he judges, because he speaks out. He chooses and acts. He rebels. He is no liberal. He does not tolerate. He is not like the hypocritical pilgrims on Marlow's ship. Kurtz is an extremist. He wants no compromises—only hostilities, battles. At the end death is the only possibility for him. He cannot go home and sit in a quiet room sipping tea, writing his memoirs—"My Colonial Experience." He must die so that we can begin to make an outcry. To Marlow Kurtz confesses his own sins, his crimes against humanity. Just before he dies he sees it all pass before him, and he bequeaths his legacy to Marlow—the horror of colonialism, the terror of progress, the horrors men make.

Conrad makes himself hysterical. He is melodramatic. He wants the sky to darken, the rain to descend on his naked skin, thunder to crack in the heavens. The villain crouches behind a dark wall. It is all too horrible. Weepings, sobbings. Conrad compounds mysteries. It is inscrutable, unspeakable. Something so horrible that he cannot say. "The inconceivable ceremonies of some devilish initiation." The mystification of evil. Something so terrible, he *will* not say.

Where is the evil? What is the horror? All along he shows it to us—the mad scientist, the French warship lobbing bombs into the jungle, the slave labor, the decimation of the jungle, the mass deaths, the perverse passions and lusts, the lie of democracy and Christianity. But then there is all that blackness, all that mystery about black. Conrad is scared. Kurtz is white, pure white. He goes bad, becomes evil. He is corrupted by the Blacks. His is the heart of darkness. The Africans are black. Blacks are evil, he implies.

In *Heart of Darkness* there is a paradox. Conrad says two things about corruption and evil. He seems to say that imperialism is responsible. But then he turns away at the last minute and says it is the Black man. In that moment he fails us. He does not look with steadfast eyes. It is as if there is too much that is evil about colonialism, too much horror about the white man and his history for Conrad to place all the blame only on colonialism. He must find the Black man guilty too, guilty because that is his innate nature. For Conrad, the Black man, his newfound brother, is something unknown, mysterious, not to be trusted: blackness is badness. He sees blackness in white men, blackness in all men—the horrible, the ugly, the wild, the grotesque. And he celebrates it; he makes blackness sacred. His novel is a paean on blackness, on the core of darkness.

Then comes the end. Kurtz has two mistresses. One is white, virginal, cold. The other is a Black queen—passionate, sensual, warm. Both women yearn for him. Conrad presents the stereotype of the Black and white sisters—neither of whom know about the other, both of whom are appendages—with the man at the center of the circle. After Kurtz dies Marlow must return to Europe and visit his white fiancée. He lies to her. We know the truth, but she never will. Kurtz's fiancée is the blind citizen of the mother country. She knows nothing of the truth about colonialism. Her existence rests on the Third World, but to her that world is invisible. Conrad has no intention of soothing our nerves, of calming us. Marlow feels that the roof is going to crash down on his head because he has lied. The black-and-white keys on the piano seem to be his enemies—dominoes at war, ready to lurch at him. It is an extravagant and lavish ending, with everything pushed to the point of absurdity. Everything that has happened is repeated at a faster speed. We are in a madhouse, in a prison, living a lie, and there is a man telling us to break out. He is screaming at the top of his lungs. Then silence.

9

Lord Jim: *White Skins*

Lord Jim is a lord without power. The scepter, the crown, the throne—even these signs of power are denied him. A lord only in name. He is soft, vacillating, not steadfast. Bending easily. The feeble last survivor of a once-powerful race. Jim lacks Kurtz's aggressiveness, his violent passions, his vision of might. Kurtz becomes a god; he rules a kingdom, amasses wealth. Jim has a love affair with a Brown woman, acts kindly and gives up. He is intimidated by real strength. He will not fight for what is right.

Jim wants to be a hero. His image of the hero comes straight out of boys' adventure stories. He reads about lonely white men on desert islands battling the elements and winning. He sees himself rescuing beautiful maidens who are about to be raped. On board ship he imagines himself quelling mutinies, throwing the rebels in the hold and receiving rewards from the captain. Finally, he envisions himself ruling over Black men. From behind a wooden stockade, flintlock rifle in hand, he shoots down charging Black men with spears raised above their heads. But Jim does not fulfill any of these dreams. He is an anti-hero. He rescues no one, saves no one, defends no one. Jim is admirable because he does not fight savages to the death, because he does not stop mutinies. He is appealing because he does not become a racist or an imperialist. But he is equally disappointing because he does not combat racism and imperialism. He does not fight for colonial liberation.

In the East Jim finds work on the *Patna,* an old broken-down ship. The crew is white—a gang of derelicts. Europeans who want easy jobs, the privilege of being white, of having Brown servants and Black laborers. They are lazy—parasites on the poor islanders of the East. White trash. The ship strikes bottom; she cannot move. The white crew members jump overboard, leaving in the hold their live cargo—hundreds of Arab pilgrims. Jim is faced with a choice. He decides to leave the *Patna* with the other Europeans. He betrays the code of the sea; he betrays his fellowman. Courage is lacking in Jim's heart. But the ship does not sink. Jim again sees the Brown faces. They haunt him, for they are a living reminder of his failure to live up to the code he set for himself. On the *Patna* Jim is offered the opportunity of becoming a hero—of staying with the ship. He can throw in his lot with the poor Brown pilgrims; like all mankind, they are travelers on the move from one port to another. The moment passes him by. He does not snatch heroism out of the air.

Marlow keeps insisting that Jim is a solid citizen. He says he is all English: blond hair, blue eyes, six feet tall. He is the boy next door, from a *petit bourgeois* family. He seems bound for success. It is written on his forehead. However, the leap from the *Patna* is the first strike against Jim. After it he seeks to redeem himself in the eyes of the world.

In Patusan, a country in the interior, Jim gets a second chance. Patusan is a never-never land: paradise. There are no telegraph wires, no mailboats, no "haggard utilitarian lies" of civilization. It is earth untrammeled. Imperialism has not fouled its waters, stripped its forests, or bound its people in servitude. Here Jim falls in love with a beautiful Malay woman named Jewel; he makes friends with the royal family. Jim is the knight. Jewel is his lady. They meet in haunted Gothic ruins in the jungle. It is like W. H. Hudson's *Green Mansions.* The moon glitters on the river, spectral shapes abound:

> The world was still, the night breathed on them, one of those nights that seem created for the sheltering of tenderness, and these are moments when our souls, as if freed from their dark envelope, glow with an exquisite sensibility that makes certain silences more lucid than speeches.

Cheap romance.

In Patusan Jim becomes a kind of Peace Corps volunteer. To do good unto others is his aim. Here Jim becomes a lord. He is worshiped. But he does little except pick up litter, and make the lives of a few individuals a bit more comfortable. Jim doesn't exploit the people. He brings no industry, establishes no British government. Earlier, he is given the chance to become an overseer on a guano island, but he turns it down. Chester, an Australian who is a whaler, trader, pearler, wrecker, outlaw, discovers an island of bird shit. His idea is to dump coolies on the island, have them dig the guano, ship it to Australia and sell it to farmers for fertilizer. He wants Jim to wear two six-guns and lord it over the men, make sure they work fourteen hours a day and do not try to escape. He is to be the boss of the chain gang. Jim is not morally or politically opposed to this type of work, but he is temperamentally unsuited for it. It is too difficult. He could never pull the trigger on the fugitives from the slave labor camp because he would be lost in thought about the state of his own soul.

Jim also can never become like his seventeenth-century ancestors who came to Patusan in quest of pepper. Conrad tells us that

> For a bag of pepper they would cut each other's throat without hesitation, and would forswear their souls, of which they were so careful otherwise: the bizarre obstinancy of that desire made them defy death in a thousand shapes; the unknown seas, the loathsome and strange diseases; wounds, captivity, hunger, pestilence, and despair. It made them great! By heavens! it made them heroic; and it made them

> pathetic, too, in their craving for trade with the inflexible death levying its toll on young and old . . . They left their bones to lie bleaching on distant shores, so that wealth might flow to the living at home. To us, their less tried successors, they appear magnified, not as agents of trade but as instruments of a recorded destiny, pushing out into the unknown in obedience to an inward voice, to an impulse beating in the blood, to a dream of the future. They were wonderful; and it must be owned they were ready for the wonderful.

Jim lacks their determination, their sense of destiny, their bravery against all odds—in the face of death. Jim is a pioneer without the pioneering spirit. He is a hollow shell of the once-powerful and terrifying white men who lorded it over the islanders of the South Seas.

Jim is meant to be a latter-day Natty Bumppo. Conrad set out to write the South Sea version of James Fenimore Cooper's *Leatherstocking Saga*. "F. Cooper is a rare artist," Conrad wrote Arthur Symons. "He has been one of my masters. He is my constant companion." And in 1902 he recommended to David Garnett that he read first *The Last of the Mohicans,* second *The Deerslayer,* and third *The Prairie,* for Conrad had read them in that order. Lingard, who is the hero in three of Conrad's novels, and who is Jim's brother, is Conrad's frontier hero. *The Rescue,* the last novel he published about Lingard and the South Seas, is about his hero's earliest days. At the end of the novel Lingard has "the shape of a giant outlined amongst the constellations." He is a mythical figure. He saves a group of wealthy white globe-trotters, but in the process kills his closest friends, the last in the line of a royal Malay family. The first novel Conrad published, *Almayer's Folly* (1895), presents the final days of Lingard. While Almayer, the last white man on the islands, dies alone—his wife already buried, his daughter on the run with a Brown man—Lingard mysteriously disappears, "as though he had been a common coolie." In *An Outcast of the Islands* he is at the height of his power. But even though he is the leading British trader in the area, he is on the first step of his downhill slide, since he is challenged by both the Arabs and the Dutch. The Lingard cycle encompasses his initiation, manhood and fall. In *Lord Jim* Conrad runs through the full cycle.

Maxim Gorky, the Russian novelist, saw Natty Bumppo as an outlaw:

> . . . as an explorer of the forests and prairies of the "New World" he blazes new trails in them for people who later condemn him as a criminal because he has infringed their mercenary and, to his sense of freedom, unintelligible laws. All his life he has unconsciously served the great cause of the geographical expansion of material culture in a country of uncivilized people and—found himself incapable of living in the conditions of this culture for which he had struck the first paths.

Conrad saw Natty Bumppo as more of an innocent, unsophisticated type—a skilled backwoodsman. He did not view him as a rebel or a battler. Conrad's epic of the frontier and the pioneer lacks dynamic energy.

Jim's is a short, happy life in Patusan. Another white man appears on the scene. Gentleman Brown is his name, but he is no English gentleman. No dandy is he. He is a cutthroat; he murders and rapes. He executes acts of evil for their own sake. Brown lands in Patusan to burn and destroy. Wherever he goes he leaves people homeless, earth scorched and barren, a trail of cold bodies in the warm jungle. Brown is trapped by the army of Patusan. He cannot escape. But Jim meets with him and provides him with a safe-conduct pass through the battlefield to the sea. Brown plays on Jim's whiteness. He makes the color of their skin the common ground between them. During his conversation with Brown, Jim remembers the *Patna.* At this point he tries to act the hero to erase his lack of heroism on ship. Brown is allowed to leave peacefully, on condition that if any harm should come to the Malays they may take Jim's life. But Brown is not honest; no contract is binding on him. He betrays Jim and takes a toll in human life by murdering the king's son. It is a repeat of the *Patna* incident in that no matter what Jim does, the Malays are left stranded; they are shot down. The kindly Peace Corps volunteer is part of the imperial machinery whether he likes it or not, whether he intends it or not. Jim is on the side of the white criminals living on the backs of poor Brown men, on the side of the cruel European assassins, the agents of genocide.

Lord Jim cannot exist in the twentieth century because he is not equipped to handle war, revolution, alienation, isolation. And Conrád's own machinery in *Lord Jim* is outmoded. It belongs to the nineteenth century. *Lord Jim* is like an opera, like something from Verdi's libretti. Fatal passions, love and death, picturesque settings, Oriental and Western races romantically contrasted. There is a liberal creed which also dates the book, which is meaningless in the age of imperialism. In his autobiography Conrad noted that

> An impartial view of humanity in all its degrees of splendour and misery together with a special regard for the rights of the unprivileged of this earth, not on any mystic ground but on the ground of simple fellowship and honourable reciprocity of services, was the dominant characteristic of the mental and moral atmosphere of the houses which sheltered my hazardous childhood.

This is a patronizing, paternalistic, feudalistic perspective which is criminal when bombs are dropped on peasants, when children are napalmed, when colonial peoples work long hours, starve and die young.

In the middle section of the novel Jim visits with Stein, a participant in the German revolution of 1848, a naturalist and a merchant—the whole man of the nineteenth-century bourgeoisie. Stein is a philosopher. He knows his men and his beasts. Stein asks us to see Jim in the light of the insects he collects—butterflies and beetles. Jim wants to be a butterfly, a beautiful, soaring creature; he wants to be a free man, a hero, with no ties to the perishable earth. But Jim never takes off. He is a beetle caught in the mire, stuck on a guano island. Stein's advice to him and to us—the philosophy which brought him to power—is:

> A man that is born falls into a dream like a man who falls into the sea. If he tries to climb into the air as inexperienced people endeavour to do, he drowns . . . The way is to the destructive element submit yourself, and with the exertions of your hands and feet in the water make the deep, deep sea keep you up . . . To follow the dream, and again to follow the dream.

Jim does not live in accord with Stein's philosophy. He never tangles with the destructive element. He does not struggle; he retreats rather than pushes ahead. He sinks rather than swims. Jim represents the failure of liberal capitalism. He does not succeed. He gains no power, accumulates no capital, no territory. All he can do is die, sacrifice his life. An unheroic hero. Who would want to follow his example? His death is meaningless. Conrad tries hard to give Jim dignity, stature. But try as hard as he can, there is no way. Jim is no hero to the colonized Brown people. Nor is he a hero to the imperial people. He can neither fight for the liberation of Brown mankind from the European oppressors, nor exploit the colonial people to aggrandize the mother country. Better to live as Kurtz did, in the extremes, than to have rambled along Jim's path. Kurtz discovers and understands the death force of imperialism. He has let go all the way. He has danced in the jungle with the very blackest Black man. Kurtz changes. Jim goes to his death with his mind clogged with romantic illusions, with his emotions and passions still in deep freeze. That being a Peace Corps volunteer means being connected with imperialism, Jim never sees. He tries to do good, live right, act nobly, and as he does, men starve, women and children die. In all its ugliness, the romanticism of imperialism is transparent in *Lord Jim*.

10

The Darkness of the Gulf

I. MATERIAL INTERESTS

Nostromo contains the whole world. It begins slowly, steadily, calmly. On the wide cinema screen the place is surveyed: the dark gulf, the orange trees, the ships in port, the mountains, the treacherous rocks in the sea, the winds bearing tempests, the silver clouds. Seemingly out of nothing, Conrad builds a substantial world with the weight of things heavy and deliberate. First the stage is set—a stage unbounded by brick walls or wooden floors; not the stage of Ibsen's domestic dramas, but the stage of his epic *Peer Gynt*. It is cast in the open air—the sky above, the earth below. Conrad's eye is the eye of the motion-picture camera, compressing time, moving back and forth in space over mountain and plain, from continent to continent, hemisphere to hemisphere. The moving images flow together organically. Conrad the master builder creates the South American country of Costaguana and its capital, Sulaco, on the coast, isolated by mountains—a peaceful, backward territory with a seaport. Beyond the harbor is the gulf, the silent, windless horizon where sea and sky meet. Then the plains, the woods of the interior. "There was not a single brick, stone, or grain of sand of its soil," Conrad writes, that "I had not placed in position with my own hands . . . all the history, geography, politics, finance . . . men, women, headlands, houses, mountains, town, *campo*." He creates a universe, carves day out of night, the land from the sea, the metropole from the hinterlands. A giant moving slowly, amassing, assimilating, shaping. And then the homes for the men and women: Indians in their tents in the interior, the shacks for the mestizos, the shanties for the European workers—railway men and dockers—the ancient elegant *casas* of the Spanish aristocrats, the homes of the English businessmen. The masses dancing and fighting in the plazas and the courtyards.

All these forces and men affected by one thing: Costaguana's silver mine. "Silver," Conrad wrote, "is the pivot of the moral and material events, affecting the lives of everybody in the tale." The silver of the mine covers everything, it is everywhere: silver-gray horses, silver spectacles, silver bullets, silver buttons, bars of silver, silver crosses, silver-colored clouds in the evening sky. Men fight and die for the silver. Touch something and it turns to silver. Conrad the geologist and geographer creates the earth and fills it with riches. It is cold, naked, raw wealth that Conrad handles—not factories or houses of commerce. He is at the mine where the stuff is brutally ripped out of the earth, the raw stuff taken and transformed into objects of beauty and grace. Behind the silver ring on a woman's hand is the death of an Indian, a starving mestizo family. In Conrad's scheme Europe is at the apex of the pyramid, and Africa, Asia and Latin America are at the base. The raw minerals are at the bottom, the silver rings at the top. After Conrad the geographer comes Conrad the historian, who shows us men and the silver at war:

> Worked in the early days mostly by means of lashes on the backs of slaves, its yield had been paid for in its own weight of human bones. Whole tribes of Indians had perished in the exploitation; and then the mine was abandoned, since with this primitive method it had ceased to make a profitable return, no matter how many corpses

> were thrown into its maw. Then it became forgotten. It was rediscovered after the War of Independence. An English company obtained the right to work it, and found so rich a vein that neither the exactions of successive governments, nor the periodical raids of recruiting officers upon the population of paid miners they had created, could discourage their perseverance. But in the end, during the long turmoil of pronunciamentos that followed the death of the famous Guzman Bento, the native miners, incited to revolt by the emissaries sent out from the capital, had risen upon their English chiefs and murdered them to a man.

Costaguana is the treasure house of the world. The land of silver, robbed by every international power. The mark of the Spanish conquistadors is left on the face of the land: "the heavy stone work of bridges and churches left by the conquerors proclaimed the disregard of human labour, the tribute labour of vanished nations." The churches, their cast-iron bells ringing violently, are monuments to the annihilation of heathen Indians by Christian conquerors. The marble statues of kings on horseback a mark of the tyranny of European rule over the primitive Indians. Costaguana is bound into the yoke of poverty; its silver is rocketed to Europe. The mine uproots the Indians and the mestizos; it destroys their tribal life, wipes away the individuality of small towns and creates a national economy. Out of the peasantry a proletariat is created. Where there were serfs and masters, there are now union organizers and strikes. The miners, created by colonialism, become the agents for its destruction. "Nobody had ever heard of labour troubles" before the English reopening of the San Tomé mine, a citizen of Costaguana notes. In turn, the system creates its aristocracy of workers, the kings of labor who serve the masters of capital. Once they wore sandals, ponchos and bright sashes. Now, in their affluence, they sport tweed suits imported from London. When the toilers strike, they force them back to work at gunpoint.

Mr. Gould, the mine owner, is an English engineer, the last in a long series of Goulds who have worked South America. The Goulds are the foot soldiers of that bourgeoisie who, in Marx's words, "played a most revolutionary part," the capitalists who destroyed feudalism. "The bourgeoisie," Marx wrote in *The Communist Manifesto,* "has left remaining no other nexus between man and man than naked self-interest, than callous 'cash payment.' It has drowned the most heavenly ecstasies of religious fervour, of chivalrous enthusiasm, of philistine sentimentalism in the icy water of egotistical calculation . . . In one word, for exploitation, veiled by religious and political illusions, it has substituted naked, shameless, direct, brutal exploitation."

Charles Gould, member of the international bourgeoisie in Costaguana, does his part, as Marx described it, to make the "country dependent on the towns . . . barbarian and semi-barbarian countries dependent on the civilized ones, nations of peasants on nations of bourgeois, the East on the West." He labors for the "subjection of Nature's forces to man, machinery, application of chemistry to industry and agriculture, steam-navigation, railways, electric telegraphs, clearing of whole continents for cultivation, canalization of rivers, whole populations conjured out of the ground." Costaguana is Marx's universe. Conrad's characters spout Marx, so it is likely Conrad himself had sat up late at night poring over *The Communist Manifesto, Das Kapital* or *The German Ideology.* Michaelis, the anarchist, tells us in *The Secret Agent* that

> History is made by men, but they do not make it in their heads. The ideas that are born in their consciousness play an insignificant part in the march of events. History is

> dominated and determined by the tool and the production —by the force of economic conditions.

The revolutionary Goulds in turn become counterrevolutionary; the silver mine oppresses men. And Gould himself dries up. We see him on horseback, or walking in the wild interior, or in his home in the capital—always with his silver spurs jingling. The sound of money, the spurs digging into the flanks of his mare, or into his wife. Gradually Gould the man disappears. All we hear is the sound of the spurs, the sound of silver.

In the mine he creates a Frankenstein, but he never realizes what a monster he has brought to life. His wife, Emilia, does. She knows that the San Tomé mountain, the source of the silver, hangs

> . . . over the whole land, feared, hated, wealthy, more soulless than any tyrant, more pitiless and autocratic than the worst government; ready to crush innumerable lives in the expansion of its greatness.

Gould has faith in the mine; but let the material interests take hold, he says, and justice, peace, law and order will follow. After economic power, democracy, culture—the virtues of civilization—he assumes the people will come trailing obediently behind. He is a pawn. Behind him are two men: the British Sir John and the American Holroyd. The Englishman is a gentleman, the representative of the railway interests. He must convince the conservative, landed Spanish families that the railway will benefit them. The American, crass but puritanical, is a cowboy-billionaire. He speaks like L. B. J., with his Texas drawl, and thinks like Cecil Rhodes, who proclaimed, "I would annex the planets if I could." Holroyd is an insatiable emperor ruling a worldwide empire. "Time itself," he says, "has got to wait on the greatest country in the whole of God's Universe. We shall be giving the word for everything; industry, trade, law, journalism, art, politics and religion, from Cape Horn . . . [to] the North Pole. And then we shall have the leisure to take in hand the outlying islands and continents of the earth. We shall run the world's business whether the world likes it or not. The world can't help it—and neither can we, I guess." The Pacific Ocean is his lake; South America is his playground. He plants the seeds of puritanism as he exports capital. The Protestant ethic becomes universal. God is his partner, and gets "his share of profits in the endowment of churches."

Who will control the material interests? Who will own the silver mine? Those are the questions *Nostromo* asks. On one hand there are the Goulds, Holroyd, Sir John, the Latin American aristocrats, the aristocracy of labor. Then there are the jumped-up, self-appointed *petit bourgeois* generals, the masses in the streets, the popular politicians who speak in the plaza at high noon. *Nostromo* describes an unsuccessful revolt, a coup d'état, which fails to unseat the Goulds and the Holroyds. In Costaguana there is an endless cycle of dictators, president-dictators and military dictators; dictators in silk hats, dictators in bowlers, dictators wearing no hat at all. The silver is there, permanently. One dictator succeeds another, each as anxious as the other to secure control of the San Tomé mine. Political barbarism, too, is permanent. In the past, Conrad says, the savages "went about yelling, half-naked, with bows and arows." Today the barbarians "wear the black coats of politicians." Under the fifteen-year dictatorship of Guzman Bento there is a reign of terror, political repression, a twentieth-century Inquisition. Under President Don Vincente Ribiera the political prisoners of past regimes are released, but there remains the tyranny of organized society.

The crimes of Guzman Bento's terror machine are written on the body of Dr. Monygham, once an "officer and a gentleman," a surgeon in Her Majesty's Army. Bento shoots his way into political power. He gives the order for the murder of Charles Gould's uncle, the former President of Sulaco. Mr. Gould is "put up against the wall of a church" *boom, boom, boom,* and shot dead. But before the bodies of the dead have been carted away in tumbrils and buried, Dictator Bento sees the ghosts of his slain enemies haunting him. He divines a conspiracy. He sees plotters everywhere, working in the night to unseat him. His chief inquisitor—the man whose job it is to ferret out the conspirators—is Father Beron, a priest whose "inquisitorial instincts suffered but little from the want of classical apparatus of the Inquisition." He uses a piece of string and a ramrod, a few muskets, a length of rope and a mallet of heavy hardwood. He lacks only modern technology to be as cruel, as sadistic, as monstrous as any torturer in a Greek prison camp or a Brazilian jail.

Dr. Monygham is his chief victim. "Confess, confess," the priest pleads. Confide in me. What was the plot? Who are the enemies of the state? Where were they going to strike? Dr. Monygham has nothing to say, for there is no plot, no conspiracy. The conspiracy is a lie. The forms of torture become increasingly severe, the torture sessions more frequent. The pain stimulates "the fertility of his imagination." He confesses to the good priest. He invents a story out of whole cloth. The conspiracy exists. Once he has uttered the lie, the screw is withdrawn. Monygham is taken down from the rack and left to rot in a solitary cell in prison; in jail, within a jail. But Bento dies and Monygham is released. For the rest of his life he walks with a limp and his body trembles. He is a walking victim of fascism; his limp is the outward sign of his inner weakness, his torture and his confession.

That is all history: a part of Monygham's and Sulaco's past. For the present they must deal with the two Montero brothers and the rebellion they lead. General Montero, the oldest of the brothers, is like one of D. H. Lawrence's Mexican generals in *The Plumed Serpent*—half man, half primitive god. He appears as "some military idol of Aztec conception" who dons "European bedecking." He is the god of war. His brother Pedrito is more complex. He has a vivid imagination, he has read historical novels and he sees himself as the Napoleon III of Costaguana, surrounded by a brillant court. "He would associate the command of every pleasure with the conduct of political affairs and enjoy power supremely in every way"—that is his dream. Pedrito believes that tyranny is compatible with democratic elections. "The highest expression of democracy was Caesarism," he believes, "the imperial rule based upon direct popular vote . . . Imperial democracy was the power of the future." So the masses elect their dictators in Sulaco. Pedrito wants a progressive-sounding, yet conservative-based, state which ensures peace, secures prosperity and pays him in fame and glory. He is the totalitarian wrapped in the robes of democracy.

About the causes of the Monterist revolution in particular —and all revolutions in general, about the role of the masses in history—and the part of the radical left in shaping it, Conrad is snide, cynical, venomous. For Conrad, the masses of the modern age are the rabble, the mob, armed with pikes, marching with torches in the streets, looters and burners who have no idea why they loot or burn. As he sees it, it merely reflects a childlike, primitive instinct of destruction. At the same time that Conrad sees all about him exploitation and oppression, tyranny and decadence, he perversely tells us that the fundamental causes of the Monterist revolution were the same as those of all revolutions— it was "rooted in the political immaturity of the people, in the indolence of the upper classes and the mental darkness of the lower." He dismisses the Montero brothers with the racist allegation that in their veins there was "the presence of some negro blood." It is that primitive fluid inside that prompts them to rebel. And he mocks the radical Senator Gamacho, makes him a stereotype of the demagogic rabble-rousing soapbox orator. In *The Secret Agent* he ties the rhetoric of the radical politicians to moral nihilism. Mr. Verloc, the police agent who dabbles in anarchist circles, we are told, is "too lazy even for a mere demagogue, for a workman orator, for a leader of labor." Señor Gamacho's address to the crowd is as "thin as the buzzing of a mosquito" and "like the uncouth howlings of an inferior sort of devil cast into a white-hot furnace." There is the radical orator on the platform, gesticulating and ranting, and before him the crowd, understanding not a word, nor an idea, but transplanted into a realm of violence by the current of emotional energy. Gamacho incites to riot. Revolutionary times, Conrad lamented, are "intoxicated with oratory." But Conrad does not denounce all orators or rhetoricians. He defends Marlow's long-winded narrative in *Lord Jim* on the grounds that M.P.s in the British House of Commons often talk as much as six hours at a stretch. And he admired the British parliamentary orators of the nineteenth century, Gladstone and John Bright. It is the orators of the streets that Conrad suspects.

In *Nostromo* and also in *The Secret Agent* there is a gallery lined with portraits of radicals and revolutionaries. The last man to see Nostromo before he dies is a Costaguanan communist. "Have you any dispositions to make, comrade?" he asks Nostromo. "Do not forget that we want money for our work. The rich must be fought with their own weapons." Conrad describes him as a "pale photographer, small, frail, bloodthirsty, the hater of capitalists." Like everyone else in the land, he is preoccupied with the silver; communists are no exception to the rule of mastery by the material interests. It is hate which impels Conrad's revolutionaries; not one of them feels, as Che felt, that "the true revolutionary is guided by great feelings of love." The Marxists of Sulaco, like Madame Defarge and the Jacquerie of *A Tale of Two Cities,* wait impatiently for the day when blood will flow through the streets like wine. Conrad makes Nostromo's last visitor a photographer because he thought that photography —unlike the motion picture—was a mechanical process, an industry, not an organic art form. The man who snapped black-and-white photographs was concerned with the surface, not the underlying reality. That is how Conrad saw the communist. Almost all his revolutionaries are hairy hunchbacks. They are grotesque types. Those pictures hanging in the gallery depict bomb-throwers, orators, propagandists. They have jagged noses, twisted ears. Conrad drags out all the clichés. "The most ardent of revolutionaries," he confides to us in *The Secret Agent,* were only seeking the "peace of soothed vanity, of satisfied appetites, or perhaps of appeased consciences." In all revolutionaries he saw rampant egotism. "The way of even the most justifiable of revolutions is prepared by personal impulses disguised into creeds."

At the Place de la Concorde or the Bastille, at the Finland Station or the Winter Palace, Conrad would have been as fierce an opponent as Robespierre, Babeuf, Lenin or Trotsky ever had. For Conrad, the French Revolution led to the "degradation of the ideas of freedom and justice." He saw Napoleon spring out of the leveled Bastille. Conrad is a fanatic about Napoleon; he dates history before and after Napoleon. Napoleon is the product of the revolution: a dictator, the father of empire, the victimizer of Poland, a warrior, an exile, a parvenu. He never forgot that during the invasion of Russia his uncle was starving and was forced to eat dog. Conrad saw the ideals of the French Revolution—liberty, equality, fraternity—become desecrated in the streets. He could have learned a great deal from another sailor—Herman Melville—for Melville understood that the French Revolution made good on some of its promises; that, though the revolution brought with it the terror and Napoleon, and entrenched the capitalist, it freed Frenchmen from feudal tyranny. Melville was more of an internationalist than Conrad. When he thought of the revolution, he saw

Anacharsis Cloots leading genial and brotherly sailors, from an assortment of tribes and complexions, before "the bar of the first French Assembly as Representative of the Human Race." In *Billy Budd* Melville noted that the French Revolution rectified "the old world's hereditary wrongs," but then became "a wrongdoer, one more oppressive than the kings." Conrad nodded his head in agreement, but Melville did not stop at that point. He went on to say that the eventual outcome was "a political advance along nearly the whole line for Europeans." Conrad saw no humane cosmopolitanism in the French Revolution; he observed no advance.

The Conrad paradox is that he detests both empire and revolution. He sees the two inextricably connected. The French Empire is forged in the crucible of the French Revolution, and the Russian Revolution is hatched out of the egg of the Czar's empire. "The nineteenth century," he wrote in "Autocracy and War," "began with wars which were the issue of a corrupted revolution . . . the twentieth begins with a war which is like the explosive ferment of a moral grave, whence may yet emerge a new political organism to take the place of a gigantic and dreaded phantom." In 1905, after the Russo-Japanese War and the first Russian revolution, he predicted that there would "be some violent break-up of the lamentable tradition, a shattering of the social, of the administrative—certainly of the territorial unity" of Russia. In 1917, he wrote with casual irony: "Can't say I'm delighted at the Russian Revolution." In his political life, in his essays and letters, he failed to recognize that radical revolution was the poisoned arrow in the flesh of empire.

But in *Nostromo* he accepts that truth. The ending of the novel is revolutionary. It is a prophetic ending, a prediction about things to come. The men and women who will create the future are sketched roughly for us. Conrad speculates on the year 2001. What next? he wants to know. Who will be the descendants, literal and figurative, of today's workers, women, peasants and intellectuals? The oracle says: Revolution will again erupt in Sulaco. On both sides of the barricades the forces are massing. In revising *Nostromo* from the magazine version to the final text, Conrad made this point more explicit. He added the passage in which Father Corbelàn, the radical Cardinal Archbishop of Sulaco, tells Mrs. Gould, "Let them [the imperialists] beware, then, lest the people, prevented from their aspirations, should rise and claim their share of the wealth and their share of the power." For a brief period the mine had offered material benefits to the miners of Costaguana. And they had marched and fought for Charles Gould and Holroyd to defend the interests of the ruling class. During the Monterist rebellion "the relations of those imported workmen with the people of the country had been uniformly bad from the first." The European workers are kept divided from, and are encouraged to be hostile to, the workers of Costaguana, who cry "death to foreigners" whether they are foreign bosses or foreign workers. Now there begins to be an affinity of interest between the Italian socialists working in the harbor and on the railway and the Indians at the mine. Now, as Dr. Monygham says, the San Tomé mine weighs "as heavily upon the people as the barbarism, cruelty, and misrule of a few years back." The coming revolution in Sulaco will be an anti-imperialist revolution, a revolt against foreign control. Peasants, workers, intellectuals and the national bourgeoisie will come together to fight for independence.

Costaguana's revolutionary forces are growing. Children are turning against their parents. Antonia, the daughter of Costaguana's leading social democrat, rejects her father's liberalism and turns to revolution. The anarchist and socialist Italian workers are not as preoccupied as were their fathers with amassing wealth, with acquiring and spending.

What Conrad says of the present and what he predicts about the future come from his reading of the past. Almost all of the characters in the book are seen in relation to historical figures—Charlotte Corday, Napoleon Bonaparte, Napoleon III, Garibaldi, Bolívar. And Conrad's sense of the future is locked in place by his key to the past; he sees cycles. But there is no indication that there will be a new Bolívar, a new liberator of twentieth-century South America. Conrad had read and written about guerrilla warfare in "Gaspar Ruiz." Yet there is no sense that there will be Tupamaros robbing banks or kidnapping ambassadors in the cities of Costaguana; and while Hernandez, the bandit of the plains, is similar to Pancho Villa, it does not seem that there will be guerrillas fighting in the mountains near Sulaco.

If Conrad could have looked ahead a bit further than his own times, he would have seen that Decoud's descendant is Regis Debray. Like Conrad's character Decoud, Debray is a Frenchman, an intellectual, a writer, a philosopher and a participant in the revolution. While Decoud literally takes his life because he is totally isolated, disengaged and alienated, Debray metaphorically commits suicide. Decoud is destroyed by his past. Debray destroys his past and is reborn a revolutionary with the guerrillas in the mountains. Decoud, once he has left Sulaco, cannot return to become an actor in the revolution. It has no meaning for him. But for Debray, there is meaning in ending his life as an upper-middle-class intellectual. The alienated intellectual becomes an *engagé,* an *enragé,* a guerrilla.

There is no Debray, and neither is there a Che. Dr. Monygham, the victim of Bento's prison camps, understands oppression, exploitation, tyranny. He rejects the material interests of capitalism, for he believes they are founded on expediency; they are inhuman. He knows the San Tomé mine holds back development of the power of the peasants, Indians and workers. Monygham is cynical, ironic; he is "disillusioned as to mankind in general, because . . . he was well aware . . . of the crushing, paralyzing sense of human littleness, which is what really defeats a man." Because of that cynicism, that pessimism, that disengagement from revolutionary movements, he cannot see victory in the cavern of death. He settles for littleness, and refuses to believe in heroism. Che the doctor healing the sick becomes the revolutionary fighting for oppressed mankind. Monygham remains a doctor dispensing pills, giving kindly advice. He cannot hear what Che says to us:

> Wherever death may surprise us, it will be welcome, if this our battle cry finds some receptive ear, if another hand reaches out to take up our weapons, and other men come forward to intone our funeral dirge with the staccato of machine guns and new cries of battle and of victory.

There are no machine guns yet in Costaguana, but there are rebel forces. There is a conspiracy, a people conspiring for their freedom, for liberty and for land. Nostromo's parting words to Mrs. Gould are a battle cry for revolution. And so while there are no Ches, no Debrays, in the mountains of Costaguana, there is the sense that history is on the side of the oppressed and exploited. Revolution is in the offing.

II. INCORRUPTIBLE

In Costaguana two wheels, throwing off sparks, generating fires and explosions, are ever grinding against each other. One is the circle of humanity; the other is an empire of things and forces. There are men; and there are also mines and banks, Houses of Parliament, railways, dictatorships. Nostromo is the leading warrior in this battle. He is Our Man, the "unchanging Man of History," and, at the same time, the twentieth-century workingman. He is an orphan, a sailor, an Italian, the king of the workers, a natural aristocrat. He lives for public recognition: he is an exhibitionist. At the fiesta he rides his white stallion through the crowd and kisses pretty Morenita before a thousand watching eyes. With a silver knife he cuts the silver buttons from his jacket and gives them to her. It is like a scene in a grade-C movie. A thousand throats in unison Ah.

Nostromo is adopted in Costaguana by the Violas—by old Giorgio and his wife, Teresa. Giorgio was a follower of Garibaldi; he was one of his Red Shirts, a revolutionary nationalist, a republican, a sworn enemy of kings and priests. All his life he despised wealth and the wealthy. The Violas' only son died in infancy. If he had lived he would have been Nostromo's age. So, the adopted Nostromo is special to Mrs. Viola—almost her own son. When she is on her deathbed she asks for him, since he is her protector, but he refuses her request. He has been asked to put the silver from the mine onto a lighter to prevent it from being captured by the rebels. He accepts the challenge. It brings him onto the stage of history, into the limelight, and keeps him out of the hushed, darkened chamber of a dying old lady. Nostromo never returns the silver to the mine owners. He keeps it himself, but tells the Goulds and Dr. Monygham that it is lost somewhere below the surface of the Golfo Placido, on the ocean floor. He buries the silver on an island in the gulf, where later a lighthouse is built, and where Giorgio Viola becomes the lighthouse keeper. At night Nostromo—now a thief—creeps through the jungly ravine on the island to take silver bars, a few at a time. He must hide them, grow rich slowly, protect that secret part of his life. One night he is shot and killed by old Giorgio, who takes him for what he is—a common thief. The old nineteenth-century worker, who depises gold and silver, kills his twentieth-century son, who is mastered by his passion for wealth.

Before he is shot, Nostromo becomes a "wealthy comrade." Paradoxically, he is both a comrade and a wealthy man. He goes to the meetings of the socialists and the anarchists, but does not participate in their movement. He is a patron, a figurehead. He is also a businessman. He is the worker who betrays his own working-class heart. He is a member of the select, infamous club Lenin investigated—the labor aristocracy. Nostromo is manipulated by the foreigners, by the big politicians and big businessmen. More than any other single individual, he prevents the success of the demagogic populist forces. He brings back General Barrios, who defeats the rebel forces. But Nostromo is discarded by his ruling-class employers. He is victimized by the Goulds and Dr. Monygham. Nostromo is divided. He is caught and ground down by the competing wheels of oppressor and oppressed.

In *Nostromo* Conrad asks, Will the material interests defeat man, or will man control the forces he has created? Nostromo conducts a lifelong and life-destroying battle against the silver. By refusing Teresa Viola's deathbed plea, he submits to the power of the silver. He becomes its slave. Nostromo is superstitious. He believes the Azuera legend—a tale recounted by the poor folk of Sulaco which expresses their political and moral experience. Two gringo prospectors, so the legend runs, went looking for buried treasure on the Azuera peninsula. And they found it, but never returned because they were faced with an unacceptable choice. "The two gringos," the story goes, "spectral and alive, are believed to be dwelling to this day amongst the rocks, under the fatal spell of their success. Their souls cannot tear themselves away from their bodies mounting guard over the discovered treasure. They are now rich and hungry and thirsty . . . tenacious gringo ghosts suffering in their starved and parched flesh of defiant heretics, where a Christian would have renounced and been released."

Nostromo is born a Catholic in the land of the Pope, but he is not religious; he does not attend Mass. The story of Azuera, which he hears at the very start of the novel and which shapes our whole sense of the mine, of the economics of modern imperialism, expresses Nostromo's basic assumption that wealth is evil. He sees himself becoming like the gringos. He, too, has death in life. He is killed by his passion for the silver. He had chosen the deadly silver over the living Mrs. Viola, the deadly silver over the living Decoud, and now in the end the silver takes his life.

On his deathbed he speaks with Emilia Gould, the unmercenary good fairy of the novel. Conrad thoroughly revised this scene. In the magazine version (published in serial form during 1903 and 1904 in *T.P.'s Weekly*) this is the outcome:

> "Nostromo!" Mrs. Gould whispered, bending very low. "I, too, have been guilty of deception about that very silver."
>
> "Marvellous!" breathed out the Capataz with an imperceptible irony.
>
> "Señora, nobody knows where it is. It is lost!"
>
> His transgression had eaten up his life, seemed to have decomposed, corrupted his personality. A grimace of effort and pain settled on his face.
>
> "Shall I tell you where it is to be found? Is it your wish? I will try to."
>
> Mrs. Gould averted her head in obscure sympathy, in dread, in pity:
>
> "No, Capataz," she said. "Let it be lost for ever."

Conrad revised the scene. In the final text we see and hear this:

> "Nostromo!" Mrs. Gould whispered, bending very low. "I, too, have hated the idea of that silver from the bottom of my heart."
>
> "Marvellous!—that one of you should hate the wealth that you knew so well how to take from the hands of the poor. The world rests upon the poor, as old Giorgio says. You have been always good to the poor. But there is something accursed in wealth. Señora, shall I tell you where the treasure is? To you alone . . . . Shining! Incorruptible!"

> A pained, involuntary reluctance lingered in his tone, in his eyes, plain to the woman with the genius of sympathetic intuition . . .
>
> "No, Capataz," she said. "No one misses it now. Let it be lost for ever."

Nostromo the worker talks with Mrs. Gould the financier's wife. Between the two of them class conflict is transcended. It is a moment of stillness, tranquility and calm. But it is also the crescendo of the novel. It is the moment when the force of the silver, of material interests, is held in check. Human love, the sympathy between Mrs. Gould and Nostromo on the basis of their common struggle against the corrupting silver, is supreme. Nostromo, our man, triumphs against wealth. In the second version the irony and the cynicism is more controlled, more contained. Nostromo is more class-conscious. He talks with Mrs. Gould, but for the first time he points to the rich as his enemy. He identifies with the poor. Every day old Giorgio has been telling him how rich people oppress poor people. Only now, after Giorgio has shot him, does he recognize and accept that view. "There is something accursed in wealth," he says. Despite all pretentions to efficiency, culture and science, capital corrupts in the age of imperialism, as riches did in slave and in feudal times.

Conrad was an economic determinist. He had read his Marx but had misunderstood him. He did not grasp the Marx who defined a dialectical relationship between base and superstructure, between economics and culture. He believed that money corrupted, that material interests shaped men's lives. He saw a struggle between ideals and material realities, with ideals becoming corrupted. It is not just the silver which stifles life. It is railways and steam engines, man-made machines. The telegraph poles which bear "a single, almost invisible wire far into the great campo" are "like a slender, vibrating feeler of that progress waiting outside for a moment of peace to enter and twine itself about the weary heart of the land." But in the scene between Mrs. Gould and Nostromo, Conrad undercuts that feeling that the human heart is strangled by infernal machines and cold wealth.

At the tail end of the novel the struggle between man and his world is reaffirmed on a higher level. Revolutions for the control of the mine, the railways, wealth, property and political power are to come. Nothing is settled in Costaguana's future except the certainty of a revolution, of conflict and war. And while Nostromo has cut loose the burden of the silver that weighed him down, the struggle between man and nature will go on in a different form tomorrow and the day after that. The last paragraph of the novel was also carefully revised. In *T. P.'s Weekly* the ending read:

> From the deep head of the gulf, full of black vapor, and walled by immense mountains from Punta Mala round to the west of Aznexa, where the obscure gringos, dead in life and living in death, guard the legendary treasure, out upon the ocean with a bright line marking the illusory edge of the world, where a great white cloud hung brighter than a mass of silver in the moonlight, in that city of a longing heart sending its never-ceasing vibration into a sky empty of stars, the genius of the magnificent Capataz de Cargadores dominated the place.

But in the final version of the novel, with short staccato sentences replacing the one long sentence, we read:

> Dr. Monygham, pulling round in the police-galley, heard the name pass over his head. It was another of Nostromo's triumphs, the greatest, the most enviable, the most sinister of all. In that true cry of undying passion that seemed to ring aloud from Punta Mala to Azuera and away to the bright line of the horizon, overhung by a big silver white cloud shining like a mass of solid silver, the genius of the magnificent Capataz de Cargadores dominated the dark gulf containing his conquests of treasure and love.

A super-charged symbolism is at work here. Linda Viola calls out Nostromo's name: Gian Battista. She proclaims her undying love for him. Hung out on a line in the night sky, G I A N B A T T I S T A; and opposite it on another line—a silver cloud—S I L V E R. Nostromo/ the silver. On and on and on, his death an ending, but no ending; still struggle, conflict, more and always.

Conrad felt that some key word was necessary for every novel—"a word that could stand at the back of all the words covering the pages, a word which, if not truth itself, may perchance hold truth enough to help the moral discovery which should be the object of every tale." The key word in *Nostromo* is "incorruptible." In revising his manuscript Conrad added the word at critical points, consistently connecting it with both Nostromo and the silver. The contradictions of the novel are contained in this word. In the scene in which Nostromo meets with Mrs. Gould, Conrad added "incorruptible." In the magazine version he says that Nostromo's transgression had "corrupted his personality." In the final version of the novel Nostromo says, "Señora, shall I tell you where the treasure is? To you alone . . . Shining! Incorruptible!" Nostromo thinks of the silver but we think of Nostromo and the silver, each one separate and yet inextricably bound together. Nostromo is corrupted. But the contradiction of the scene, which is also the contradiction of the novel, is that Nostromo is *in*corruptible. He dies innocent, dies reborn, and in that sense he is resurrected. He is whole and new again, as he was in the beginning. He gets things straight, rejects wealth, joins with the oppressed, the poor.

Conrad pursued the *mot juste* to capture the essence. From Flaubert and Maupassant he learned the importance of craftsmanship. It is control he wants—mastery of the word. In his essay on Maupassant he presents his view on the *mot juste*. Conrad distinguishes between the "master of the *mot juste*," represented by Maupassant, and the "dealer in words," the shoddy workman. The master of the *mot juste* is no juggler, no aesthete. Conrad studied Maupassant's manuscripts; he compared the early with the final drafts of Maupassant's short stories and said that the first drafts were weak not because of the form of expression or the technique itself, but because the conception of the work was faulty. "His vision," Conrad wrote, "by a more scrupulous, prolonged, and devoted attention to the aspects of the visible world discovered at last the right words as if miraculously impressed for him upon the face of things and events." The craftsman studied his society; he changed words not for alliterative effects, nor to dazzle the reader, as if the words were glass beads dangled before a wide-eyed kitten, but to elicit the truth. Since language in the age of imperialism—the language of the press, of advertising, of politicians—presented the very opposite of what existed in reality, he saw it as his task to recover reality, to rescue it and preserve it through truth in language.

The dominant place in *Nostromo* is the Golfo Placido. It is the center. When we return—and we always return—we return to the gulf. In his essay "Books," published the year after *Nostromo,* Conrad said that the incidents and characters, scenes and images of a novel should be encompassed "in one harmonious conception." A novelist subsisted on a regular diet of contradictions, but he unified his novel through harmony of form. *Nostromo* is the most carefully organized of Conrad's novels. Basic to the form of the novel is the image of the dark gulf. *Nostromo* marks a departure from his earlier works, which were written with a belief in the spontaneity of the imagination. Recalling the writing of *Almayer's Folly* seventeen years after it was published, Conrad said that "the conception of a planned book was entirely outside my mental range when I sat down to write." In 1895, the year *Almayer's Folly* was published, he told Edward Garnett, "all my work is produced unconsciously . . . and I cannot meddle to any purpose with what is within myself

. . . It isn't in me to improve what has gotten itself written." But he discarded that theory. To interpret the world of imperialism, to capture its complexity and its pattern, the artist had to organize his material. He had to create a universe. "In truth," he wrote in 1905, "every novelist must begin by creating for himself a world, great or little, in which he can honestly believe. This world cannot be made other than in his own image . . . yet it must resemble something already familiar to the experience, the thoughts and the sensations of his readers." He rejected his earliest ideas: that consciously planned books were bad, that a work of art sprang spontaneously into being and that one should not revise. A novel, like a film, was a "logical succession of images," images of discord and strife which eventually fuse into a world.

Conrad's section of *Romance* is a blueprint for *Nostromo*. It is a trial run. It shows Conrad at the planning stages, getting his ideas, characters and themes in running order. The major part of Conrad's portion of the book (the other parts were written by Ford Madox Ford) is set in an underground cavern. The darkness of the cavern anticipates the darkness of the Golfo Placido. The cavern in *Romance* has the "amazing vast emptiness of a temple," just as the Golfo Placido is an "enormous semi-circular and unroofed temple." The cave is "an abode of darkness, enormous"; it inculcates "a feeling of being in the open air on a night more black than any known night had been before," anticipating that "fatal night" on the gulf which "no intelligence could penetrate," and which, in Captain Mitchell's words, "will never be seen again." The cave's darkness is of "infinite space . . . big enough to contain in its black gloom of a burial vault all the dust and passions and hates of a nation." There is a legend associated with the cave—a "legend of men who had gone in and had never come back any more," which becomes the Azuera legend of *Nostromo*.

In *Romance* Conrad's universe becomes empty of God.

The narrator watching "the magnificent ritual of sunset" feels that it is "like some gorgeous and empty ceremonial of immersion belonging to a vast, barren faith." *Romance* marks a length of Conrad's long march into darkness, pessimism, alienation. The descriptions of the cave suggest infinite space and the open air, but the physical dimensions of the cave itself, with its walls, floor and ceiling, imply a confined area. By moving his drama from the cave to the open air of the gulf in *Nostromo,* Conrad unfetters his men and women, breaks their chains. They are free. They are liberated to commit any and all deeds of good and evil, to become heroes or victims, bandits or generals, to remain incorruptible or to be corrupted. *Romance* is the seed of a discovery, which in *Nostromo* develops into a healthy organism. Since the universe is godless, man is at its center. Man is free to make his own world. History becomes the novelist's driving passion; history is the record of man on the earth. By writing the novel *Romance* Conrad gave expression to his underlying desire to write romantic fiction. It came to the surface, was recognized and exorcised. After *Romance* he could forget about the romance as a form and romanticism as a concept, and concentrate on the historical, on history.

The world of *Nostromo* is dark, but it is not the darkness of *Heart of Darkness.* It has no connection with dark racial pigmentation. In *Nostromo* the great darkness of the night sky covers Sulaco after the sun goes down. At the start of the novel Conrad tells us that "The eye of God himself . . . could not find out what work a man's hand is doing in there; and you would be free to call the devil to your aid with impunity if even his malice were not defeated by such a blind darkness." In this case, the darkness is the force of the universe which is alien and hostile to man. It embodies Conrad's sense that the "ethical view of the universe involves us at last in so many cruel and absurd contradictions, where the last vestiges of faith, hope, charity, and even of reason itself seem ready to perish, that I have come to suspect that the aim of creation cannot be ethical at all. I would fondly believe that its object is purely spectacular: a spectacle for awe, love, adoration, or hate, if you like, but in this view—and in this view alone—never for despair!" The darkness of the gulf is neither evil nor good. It is morally and ethically neutral. It is the universe Decoud and Nostromo inhabit in the dark night they spend on the gulf.

In contrast with the first part of the novel, which begins in the silver mine and which is heavy, below the surface, the middle section of the novel gives us a feeling of lightness, of disembodiment. We float on the surface of the gulf, unable to see, with the sense that we have left the material world. There is a feeling of alienation. A sense of dislocation, of loss. It is not the real world. Everything is unsubstantial. Minds are separated from bodies. There seems to be an existence apart from material conditions. Man is alienated from himself, divided against himself, estranged from nature and from his fellow-man. He lives in fear, in a strange universe. *Nostromo* is about social forces and conflicts, but it is also about isolation and loneliness. The originality of form derives from this: Conrad's ability to write of human alienation and dislocation, of man alone in the universe, at the same time that he writes of men at work, men tied to each other in the fate of their society.

During the revolution on shore, men and women are taken out of themselves. The eruption reveals people who in normal times live undisturbed lives. In the explosion disparate forces and people are thrown together. Extremes touch. Hernandez the bandit becomes a general, fighting on the side of Charles Gould, the bandit who is sanctioned by the law. And Decoud, the upper-class French writer and intellectual, is thrown together with Nostromo, the working-class Italian. Conrad focuses on Nostromo and Decoud in the darkness of the gulf because he believes that "exceptional individualities . . . are true to the general formula expressing the moral state of humanity." There is a classic balance to the irreconcilable antagonisms in the novel. In Nostromo there is audacity of action, in Decoud, audacity of intellect. Two outcasts. In the darkness of the gulf Nostromo and Decoud float over the still water in a lighter packed with the silver:

> The two men, unable to see each other, kept silent till the lighter, slipping before the fitful breeze, passed out between almost invisible headlands into the still deeper darkness of the gulf . . . The change from the agitation, the passions and the dangers, from the sights and sounds of the shore, was so complete that it would have resembled death had it not been for the survival of his thoughts. In this foretaste of eternal peace they floated vivid and light, like unearthly clear dreams of earthly things.

The world is silent and hushed. It is here that something "deeper, something unsuspected by everyone, had come to the surface." It is here that Conrad articulates the symbolism of the book: "the silver of the mine had been the emblem of a common cause, the symbol of the supreme importance of material interests."

Decoud, the Frenchman, the journalist, the cynic, is alone in the midst of the revolution. There is his death in the solitude of the gulf—the great, hollow, empty space of nature. And there is the triumph of the counterrevolution, of the forces of law and order. His death and the triumph of his class—we hear of these two separate events simultaneously. Nostromo leaves Decoud alone on the island with the silver, promising to return. Decoud is a creature of Saint-Germain-des-Prés, of boulevards and cafés, of the Left Bank. Alone on a desert island he is a cripple. He is totally unprepared to face solitude, the sands of the shore, a world with no other men. He goes mad. The universe seems to him a series of senseless, incomprehensible images. Everything is chaotic. Decoud makes the existential decision and chooses death. He takes four bars of the stolen silver, puts them in his pockets and drowns himself in the gulf. Silver, the material interests, overpower man once more. Decoud, the intellectual, is trapped by his own mind. A defeated Robinson Crusoe of the twentieth century, unable to create society on his little island. No more Robinson Crusoes, no more island paradises, no more little colonies, Conrad says. Decoud dies of bad faith. He eventually doubts his own self. He sees no pattern or meaning in life. He cannot grapple with himself. Waiting, waiting; he tires of waiting and then takes his life. He sees life stretched out before him and a narrow umbilical cord which connects him to it. The cord is silent, unbearably silent. He is receiving no messages. When he commits suicide he breaks the cord, ends the silence. Nothing is worthwhile: that is Decoud's conclusion. Conrad is close to Decoud. He feels this barrenness, this emptiness, the longing for silence, the temptation to suicide, but he pulls himself back, strives to make sense of the senseless images, dives into the political arena. He creates a world in which he can exist, the world of *Nostromo*; he decides, No, I will not commit suicide, I will live.

III. GREAT TRADITION

Thirty-two years elapsed between the publication of *Middlemarch* (1871–1872) and the publication of *Nostromo* (1903–1904). They illuminate worlds fully antagonistic. Joseph Conrad and George Eliot both have, as F. R. Leavis argued in *The Great Tradition,* technical originality and moral concerns, but the structure of Conrad's novels and the moral discoveries and historical patterns in *Nostromo* and *Heart of Darkness* are foreign and distasteful to George Eliot. Both she and Conrad considered themselves historians: both rejected mechanical and accepted organic metaphors for the imagination, both wanted art to illuminate rather than simply reflect or mirror life. But the society they explore, their analyses of it and the staging of their dramas is qualitatively different.

Between Eliot's world and the world of Conrad and D. H. Lawrence lies revolution, world war, colonialism. Her language rests on a static sense of society, while theirs grows out of a sense of society in crisis. For them language shares in the general process of upheaval and fragmentation. It both camouflages and exposes. For George Eliot language is a tool used by rational men to understand and describe society. Her world is similar to Jane Austen's but unlike Conrad's or Lawrence's in that it suppresses rhetoric, melodrama, the lyric and the symbolic. George Eliot is confident; she assesses things and people in the cold light of reason. Lawrence's statement at the conclusion of *Women in Love,* his optimism when faced with the thought of the end of man, is beyond her ken:

> The mystery could dispense with man, should he too fail creatively to change and develop. The eternal creative mystery could dispose of man, and replace him with a finer created being. Just as the horse has taken the place of the mastodon. It was very consoling to Birkin to think this.

George Eliot has none of Conrad's dogged use of adjectives, grand manner, or preoccupation with symbol; nor does she share Lawrence's throbbing rhythms and repetitive prose. Her language is often dense but not harsh; it is more precise, less vague and mysterious. Her syntax is often complicated, but on close reading the meaning is revealed, whereas rhetorical passages in *Heart of Darkness* and *Women in Love* often hide the absence of concrete objects and ideas.

George Eliot is the historian of provincial society, of nineteenth-century England:

> Old provincial society had its share of this subtle movement, had not only its striking downfalls, its brillant young professional dandies who ended by living up an entry with a drab and six children for their establishment, but

> also those less marked vicissitudes which are constantly shifting the boundaries of social intercourse and begetting new consciousness of interdependence. Some slipped a little downward, some got higher footing: people denied aspirates, gained wealth, and fastidious gentlemen stood for boroughs; some were caught in political currents, some in ecclesiastical . . . In fact, much the same sort of movement and mixture went on in old England as we find in older Herodotus, who also, in telling what had been, thought it well to take a woman's lot for his starting point; though Io, as a maiden apparently beguiled by attractive merchandise, was the reverse of Miss Brooke, and in this respect perhaps bore more resemblance to Rosamond Vincy.

George Eliot is not restless with English landscapes, environment and social classes; she accepts them inevitably as *the* things, places and people to write about. Her imagination is at home in the Midlands. *Middlemarch* moves briefly to Rome—the world of art, Catholicism, passion and myth—but it centers in the Midlands. The scenes in Rome help us put provincial society in perspective. Lawrence, though English to his bones, must and does leave England. The movement of *Women in Love* to central Europe fulfills the book's structural demands; the setting in the Alps heightens the tension, matching the whiteness of the snow with the blackness of the coal mines, the heights with the depths. The change of scene also satisfies Lawrence's vision of society. The novel must explode beyond, not within, the confines of England; Lawrence must go on his savage pilgrimage.

George Eliot is the historian of gradual action, of unexceptional events. She rejects extremes. The title *Middlemarch* is carefully chosen. The town Middlemarch is the chief protagonist in the action. The title also embodies the author's sense of history as a gradual march forward; the ranks move ahead together, there are no stragglers and no pioneers. Eliot looks for the middle of things, the middle classes, but she also has a preference for the middle range in the realms of psychology, aesthetics and language. It is reform rather than revolution, tradition rather than change, the society of the past rather than the contemporary world which interests her. She chose to write about the England of 1832, at the time of the first Reform Bill: behind her decision lies a sense of the continuity of English history, a history without the revolutions, terrors, communes, emperors, barricades and guillotines of France. George Eliot examines ballots, hospital committees, political campaigns, gossiping ladies and dusty clerics.

Is *Middlemarch* the study of provincial society it purports to be? Do we know what happens in England in 1832? *Middlemarch* is less successful than Stendhal's *Le Rouge et le Noir,* which, in a more systematic and rigorous manner, follows the whole scope of France in 1830. Julien Sorel is the sort of character George Eliot never could have created; his social mobility and the range of his emotional life are foreign to her sense of the individual. He moves from the provinces to Paris. The son of a peasant, he mixes with archbishops and lords, makes love to the daughter of a duke and the wife of a mayor. The schoolboy who memorized the Bible and spouted it on demand watches the secret war councils of popes and emperors. The young romantic who stood in the forest and shouted "I am free" is thrown in jail and guillotined. His beloved holds his severed bloody head in her lap.

Among the best parts of *Middlemarch* are those which present Dr. Lydgate and his conflicts with Middlemarch society; his private life intersects with his public life. In *Felix Holt* George Eliot said that "There is no private life which is not determined by the wider public life"; in Lydgate's case she substantiates that idea. Lydgate's work as a doctor, the politics of medicine, his view of women, his marriage to Rosamond—all these are dramatized in a complex and compelling way which neither Lawrence nor Conrad ever matched. George Eliot has the time to follow the rise and fall of Lydgate's marriage. She has the passion of intellect needed to understand his research and the vision of a woman necessary to see Rosamond's dreams and illusions. George Eliot has a belief in marriage which neither Conrad nor Lawrence could accept. In the last chapter of *Middlemarch* she wrote:

> Marriage, which has been the bourne of so many narratives, is still a great beginning, as it was to Adam and Eve, who kept their honeymoon in Eden but had their first little ones among the thorns and thistles of the wilderness. It is still the beginning of the home epic—the gradual conquest or irremediable loss of that complete union which makes the advancing years a climax and age the harvest of sweet memories in common.

Compare this view of marriage with those at the end of *Women in Love, Heart of Darkness* (Marlow's meeting with Kurtz's intended) and *Nostromo,* and the gap between George Eliot on one side and Conrad and Lawrence on the other opens wide. Conrad did not have the mental equipment to analyze the private drama between husband and wife; he was a male chauvinist who would have been cut down by Miss Eliot. Lawrence, with his continual thrusting toward a level of intensity and anguish, missed George Eliot's sense of marriage as a daily growth toward a complete union.

Middlemarch lacks dramatization of the impact of industrialism and political change on individual lives. The railway comes to the town but we are told almost nothing of its impact, and when we finish the novel we know relatively little about how the Reform Bill of 1832 changed the lives of the characters. No character involved with politics and industry is presented in as full a light as is Lydgate in the medical profession. George Eliot is wary of depicting the Middlemarchers in their political and social roles. She is often skeptical of the social status of her characters and their capacity for experiencing profound emotions and thoughts. Wanting to write tragedy and yet feeling that the genre died with the birth of bourgeois society, she believes that her characters do not have the stature necessary to be tragic figures. But she also knows that though they are only provincials they can experience pity, terror, catharsis. She is divided about the possibilities of tragedy in her age; her characters are often seen in complexity and detail in their private lives, but not in their public, social existence.

George Eliot was a determinist. She saw the individual submitting to, rather than overcoming, the power of the community. George Eliot thinks of life as a web, as a living tissue of relations, but she also uses the metaphor of the yoke to describe the individual's lack of freedom and his acceptance of society's rule. The pattern of *Middlemarch* is the taming of the rebel; the nonconformist elements are incorporated into the traditional society. Her community has a great capacity for healing its wounds: the living social tissue continues unbroken, the yoke of the society is not cast off. Bulstrode, who exudes the social values of the mid-nineteenth-century capitalist, dominates Middlemarch for a time, but his values are not triumphant. His wealth, the power of capital, is contained: his money corrupts, but it does not corrupt absolutely. It cannot taint Ladislaw. By contrast with Lawrence's Gerald Crich—the "Napoleon of Industry," whose god is the machine—and Conrad's Charles Gould—who pins his faith on material interests, unconsciously destroying his marriage through his passion for the silver—Eliot's Bulstrode is a less terrifying figure. Charles Gould on horseback in Sulaco, wearing his silver spurs, and Gerald Gould on horseback before the railway train are industrial and financial magnates of great will and energy.

The machine, like wealth, is a much more awesome force in *Women in Love* and *Nostromo*. In *Middlemarch* the railway is swallowed up by the landscape; in *Nostromo*, it dominates the scene. Conrad thinks of it in terms of war and violence:

> The rumble of wheels under the sonorous arch was traversed by a strange, piercing shriek, and Decoud, from his back seat, had a view of the people behind the carriage trudging along the road outside, all turning their heads, in *sombreros* and *rebozos,* to look at a locomotive which rolled quickly out of sight behind Giorgio Viola's house, under a white trail of steam that seemed to vanish in the breathless, hysterically prolonged scream of warlike triumph.

The prose itself is breathless and hysterical. Lawrence's attitude toward the railway in *Women in Love* parallels Conrad's:

> The locomotive, as if wanting to see what could be done, put on the brakes, and back came the trucks rebounding on the iron buffers, striking like horrible cymbals, clashing nearer and nearer in frightful strident concussions. The mare opened her mouth and rose slowly, as if lifted up on a wind of terror. Then suddenly her fore-feet struck out, as she convulsed herself utterly away from the horror . . . as strong as the pressure of his compulsion was the repulsion of her utter terror, throwing her back away from the railway, so that she spun round and round on two legs, as if she were in the centre of some whirl-wind. It made Gudrun faint with poignant dizziness, which seemed to penetrate to her heart.

George Eliot takes a much cooler look at the railway. She assesses, studies, makes witty remarks; Conrad and Lawrence participate emotionally and ask the reader to join in the hysteria and convulsions. Eliot writes that in the town of Middlemarch:

> . . . railways were as exciting a topic as the Reform Bill or the imminent horrors of cholera, and those who held the most decided views on the subject were women and landholders. Women both old and young regarded travelling by steam as presumptuous and dangerous and argued against it by saying that nothing should induce them to get into a railway carrage; while proprietors, differing from each other in their arguments as much as Mr. Solomon Featherstone differed from Lord Medlicote, were yet unanimous in the opinion that in selling land, whether to the enemy of mankind or to a company obliged to purchase, these pernicious agencies must be made to pay a very high price to landowners for permission to injure mankind.

She speaks of exciting topics and imminent horrors, but her tone, her style, her vision express calm and quiet.

Because of this sense of the power of wealth and of the machine over man, Lawrence and Conrad have a much stronger awareness of evil, of hostile and alien forces; their characters experience isolation and estrangement. In *Middlemarch* there are moments of "midnight darkness," of the "dark-winged flight of evil," but evil is put firmly back into its box. There are no moments which match the scenes in the darkness of the gulf in *Nostromo* or in the whiteness of the mountains in *Women in Love*. Lawrence and Conrad also have a sense of the inextricable connection between good and evil, and it is not surprising that Baudelaire's metaphor *"les fleurs du mal"* plays a central part in both novels. Costaguana is like the other nations of South America, for they all come "into the world like evil flowers on a hotbed of rotten institutions." General Barrios is "like a strange precious flower unexpectedly blooming on the hotbed of corrupt revolutions." Lawrence describes the snow crystals in the mountains as cold, hard, lifeless flowers of beauty and evil.

Symbolism plays a far more important role in *Nostromo* than it does in Eliot's work. The yoke and the web are important metaphors in *Middlemarch,* but they do not dominate the novel as does the darkness of the gulf, or the whiteness of the mountains in *Women in Love*. We know precisely what the yoke and the web are, but Conrad's darkness and Lawrence's whiteness, though they are concrete, express no one single idea, feeling or emotion. They discharge a complex range of images and ideas which tangle with reality. That is not to say that Conrad is a symbolist. He separated himself from the "Symbolist School of poets or prose writers" and claimed that he was concerned "with something much larger." The more nearly a novel approaches art, he felt, "the more it acquires a symbolic character." His idea was that a novel was symbolic in being "very seldom limited to one exclusive meaning and not necessarily tending to a definite conclusion." It was symbolic inasmuch as it made "a triple appeal covering the whole field of life." The symbolic novel, as he saw it, was not esoteric; it did not create mysteries or subtle correspondences, but sought wholeness and contradiction in complexity and totality.

Where George Eliot is often weak Conrad is especially strong. *Nostromo* presents public lives; the private life recedes into the background and forces and movements come into the foreground. *Middlemarch* opens with a description of Dorothea: "Miss Brooke had that kind of beauty which seems to be thrown into relief by poor dress." *Nostromo* begins with a description of Sulaco, its history and economics: "In the time of Spanish rule, and for many years afterwards, the town of Sulaco—the luxuriant beauty of the orange gardens bears witness to its antiquity—had never been commercially anything more important than a coasting port with a fairly large local trade in ox-hides and indigo."

Conrad is confident about writing tragedy. *Nostromo,* with its epigraph from Shakespeare's *King John* ("so foul a sky clears not without a storm"), takes us quickly into a drama of tragic intensity, of pity and terror, suffering and catharsis. *Middlemarch* maintains its wide range to the end; *Nostromo* begins with broad social conflicts and narrows to the point of Nostromo's own drama, his confession to Mrs. Gould, his release from guilt and his subsequent death. While Nostromo is a worker, he is also the King of the Workers, and in Conrad's eyes he is as proper a subject for tragedy as a Renaissance prince. He sees men shaping history. Nostromo almost single-handedly saves the state. The finality of his death, combined with his moral discovery about wealth, exploitation and poverty, has tragic intensity.

Conrad's theme is revolution—the breakup and the reordering of society—but *Nostromo* is more tightly organized by image and idea than *Middlemarch*. *Nostromo* moves in outward, unending circles; *Middlemarch* moves in a linear progression and it stops at a point. *Middlemarch* ends, as do many Victorian novels, with a synopsis of future events. Although George Eliot wrote in the "Finale" to the novel that "Every limit is a beginning as well as an ending," *Middlemarch* is a closed novel. It does not open out at the end; it resolves the conflicts.

Nostromo and *Middlemarch* are the products of two different societies, of two very different minds. To say they are part of the same tradition is absurd. There is no Great Tradition, as defined by F. R. Leavis, of the English novel. There is no unbroken chain of British novelists stretching from the late nineteenth to the middle of the twentieth century. The history of the English novel is the history of cultural revolution. It is the history of anti-novelists. Emily Brontë, Charles Dickens, George Eliot, Joseph Conrad, D. H. Lawrence—these are the arch rebels. What they have in common is their insurrectionary activity. To argue, as Leavis does, that Austen, Eliot, James, Conrad and Lawrence are alike because they are all preoccupied with morality and all exhibit technical originality is to deny cultural warfare—the tension between art and reality. And Leavis neglected the revolution in society and culture between 1850 and 1930. By placing Eliot and Conrad together and by accepting *Middlemarch* as his model, Leavis denies the dynamics of *Nostromo*. He notes that it has "something hollow about it; with the colour and life there is a suggestion of a certain emptiness."

Raymond Williams's tradition—which stretches from Dickens to Eliot, through Hardy to Lawrence—gives rightful praise to Dickens and Hardy. But it neglects Conrad and James, and does not solve the problem of tradition or take into account the revolution in culture and society. Nor is it necessary, as Professor Kermode has done, to make George Eliot like D. H. Lawrence. By comparison with *Women in Love* and *Nostromo, Middlemarch* is not "a novel about a modern crisis." It is not "concerned with the end of the world," as Professor Kermode asserts. We are preoccupied today with crisis, with nuclear destruction, with revolution, but that does not mean that we cannot appreciate an artist who is not concerned with them. And that does not make George Eliot simply a figure of dry historical interest. She is of her time, but she goes beyond it too. She is not as relevant as Conrad is for the late twentieth century, but she enables us to see the continuities in history, the slow, unexceptional developments in society. She asks us to move away from our myths of crisis and apocalyptic symbols. The beginnings, turning points and endings of her novels, organized by character and incident rather than by symbolic places and things, can satisfy our sense of time, our need for unhysterical moments of thought and action.

11

Russians and Revolutions

In Conrad's novels bombs explode, guns are fired, buildings are destroyed, men are murdered. The innocent and the uninvolved become guilty accomplices or dead victims. In this world everyone is carried along by the historical currents. Eventually you open your eyes and see what is around you. In the end you act to defend yourself. In *The Secret Agent* (1906) the revolutionaries plan to destroy Greenwich Tower. All the circles around the globe—meridians, imaginary circles—that give order, latitudes and longitudes, fixed points in time. Exactitude, measurement. The destruction of the zero meridian will be a symbolic attack on universal order, a cry for international anarchy. The anarchist bombers are a sad lot—misshapen, overweight, grotesque, bloodthirsty, lame; misanthropes who are spied upon and incited by agent provocateurs, infiltrated by opportunists. It is Stevie, a kid who is literally mad, who sits at home all day long drawing circles, moving his hand around and around, who carries the bomb to its destination. He trips and falls, setting off the mechanism. The bomb explodes but the target is left standing. Stevie is dead. British secret intelligence is on the trail of the revolutionaries.

The Secret Agent was not a popular novel. It certainly did not offer a flattering portrait of national English types or the national character. The wealthy society patron of the anarchists, the liberal-left M.P.s, the policemen and the government officials are all buffoons. The novel did not—nor was it intended to—have the effect of making the English feel secure on their tidy little island. For Conrad says that a specter is haunting England, the specter of international anarchist terrorists. Your houses, your offices, your island will be blown up.

He published his next novel, *Under Western Eyes,* four years later. During those four years, however, Conrad published *A Set of Six,* a collection of short stories about politics. The characters in these stories are odd combinations: the anarchist who is a slave, the revolutionary who is a police agent, the republican who is a royalist. In *Under Western Eyes* Conrad takes up this material again. The novel is set at a distance, in Russia, where the English know that bizarre things happen. Moscow is not London, St. Petersburg is not Manchester. When the extraordinary characters who populate *The Secret Agent* are shipped to Russia they become more believable. Throughout the narrative the storyteller says that his hero is not English, because no Englishman could ever undergo his experiences. He repeats it so often that we begin to doubt him. In fact, he seems to be saying just the opposite—that it can happen in England, that Razumov, his Russian hero, is English.

Under Western Eyes is about Russia and England. It is about East and West. It is "a Russian story for Western ears." The first part of the tale is set in Russia, the second part in Switzerland. But England's presence is always felt in the background. Switzerland becomes a surrogate for England, for all those nations (and those places of the mind) inhabited by secure couples sitting in cafés, protected from cradle to grave, living boring, monotonous lives. Here Monday is like Tuesday, Tuesday like Wednesday, one week exactly like the next. No shocks anywhere. Russia exists everywhere, in the hearts of all men, in all nations. Russia is revolution. Russia is tyranny. The novel moves back and forth, as if on a seesaw, from East to West, with Geneva at the center. It is also like a tug of war, a rope being pulled from both ends. Conrad's Russia is the land of contradictions, of extremes, of polarities. For Russians the normal pattern is the exceptional. Along with each mouthful of black bread, the peasant also swallows the facts of assassination, bombs, mystical, fanatic priests, hangmen.

At the top of Russia there is the Czar, all powerful, all tyrannical. At the bottom there is the anarchist. At one end there is the bomb-thrower, at the other end the executioner. In 1920 Conrad wrote a preface to *Under Western Eyes.* It is off-center, beside the point, since the Czar and Kerensky were out of power, and Lenin and the Soviets had seized state control. He wrote:

> The ferocity and imbecility of an autocratic rule rejecting all legality and in fact basing itself upon complete moral anarchism provokes the no less imbecile and atrocious answer of a purely Utopian revolutionism encompassing destruction by the first means to hand, in the strange conviction that a fundamental change of hearts must follow the downfall of any given human institutions.

Conrad's sense of extremes, in this case, blinded him to what had happened in Russia. The common denominator between revolutionaries and Czars is not lawlessness. The ferocious, imbecile, autocratic rule did not provoke a purely utopian revolution. There were, it is true, Russian revolutionaries who believed that human nature would have to change before there could be a change in institutions. And there were Russian revolutionaries who turned to bombs. But they were not the only or the most important revolutionaries. In Conrad's scheme there is no room for a Lenin. There is no place for a revolutionary who combines thought and action, who is neither a terrorist nor a utopian, but who wants to see the destruction of the imperial society, an end to all the old institutions and a rebirth of man. At one point in *Under Western Eyes* the hero writes five lines which define his political vision:

History not Theory.
Patriotism not Internationalism.
Evolution not Revolution.
Direction not Destruction.
Unity not Disruption.

Conrad's sense of conflict, of polarities, prevents him from seeing that direction comes through destruction, that unity follows disruption and disruption follows unity, that history and theory are dialectically connected. Conrad wants us to choose. Either/or, he says. He knows we cannot have a little piece of this, and a little piece of that, a loose pudding of a life. But his either/or becomes too abstract. It does not allow for the revolutionary's daily tacking back and forth, in which he moves in six directions at once till he reaches the docks of insurrection, and then begins again a new course of tacking back and forth. In Conrad's world there is no place for the revolutionary party which combines armed struggle and mass work.

Under Western Eyes is the story of Razumov. He is an average student, not brilliant, not a political activist. He attends classes regularly, avoids discussions, expects his degree, prizes, and later, success in the world. But Mr. Haldin, a revolutionary, walks into Razumov's room and destroys everything—all his past, all his future. Mr. Haldin has just killed a minister of the government, a man who, each day, exiles, imprisons and hangs revolutionaries of all sizes and shapes, of all ages and occupations. This head of the secret police is punctual, efficient, tireless. Only a bomb can stop him. On a snowy night, a night of pure whiteness, in which all sound is muffled by the falling snow, Haldin throws a bomb at this flesh-and-blood state terror machine. The machine falls dead. Haldin leaps into Razumov's life, asks for protection, for help in escaping. He needs Razumov to reach the underground. But Razumov betrays him to the secret police. He turns informer and becomes a secret agent, privy to imperial secrets. In Switzerland he uses his unique position to make friends with Haldin's mother and his sister Natalie, and to gain entrance into the revolutionary circles. The tension becomes too great. He cannot serve as a spy and continue to pose as a revolutionary. So, in the end, he confesses to everyone, reveals the imperial secrets. Razumov makes his peace with mankind and returns to Russia.

Razumov's is a tale of isolation, isolation in the Conradian sense. Razumov has no family, no friends, no connections, no traditions. He is "as lonely in the world as a man swimming in the deep sea." Yet in a flash he becomes part of the family of man. In one night he becomes the brother of Haldin, the terrorist, and the brother of the Czar. His sea is Russia; he is at its center, and it surrounds him. In a dark tavern at night he beats a peasant. With each stroke he delivers to the peasant's body, he feels closer and closer to him. His soul and his heart pass down through his arm, through the stick, into the body of the peasant. The two men are brothers. Here Conrad is at his most snide and cynical. *Under Western Eyes* describes the social contract, the rottenness of the ties between men. Razumov attempts to extricate himself from existing relationships and create a new social contract. The solitary man falls into captivity, bound in chains to all Russia, to every Russian. He must free himself. Razumov is part of everything, yet he has no identity. His name is only a label. He is caught in a vise, with two sides closing in on him. His own individuality is destroyed, reduced to nothing. On one side of him is Haldin, the student terrorist, on the other side is Ziemianitch, the peasant:

> Between the two he was done for. Between the drunkenness of the peasant incapable of action and the dream-intoxication of the idealist incapable of perceiving the reason of things, and the true character of men.

The peasant digs in the black earth; the idealist's thoughts rocket into the pure sky. For Conrad, the two men are forever separated. The revolutionary speaks one language, the peasant another.

Razumov becomes the prototype of the Russian. Russia is a land of snow, of whiteness. The snow covers the endless country, "obliterating the landmarks . . . levelling everything under its uniform whiteness, like a monstrous blank page awaiting the record of an inconceivable history. It covered the passive land with its lives of countless people like Ziemianitch and its handful of agitators like this Haldin—murdering foolishly." The vast Russian space pervades the novel. Countless numbers, countless miles. There is a feeling of oppression, of doom, of pessimism. It does not matter who or what you are; you are leveled down. The passive peasant and the agitated students are all together. "His existence," Conrad writes of Razumov, "was a great cold blank, something like the enormous plain of the whole of Russia levelled with snow and fading gradually on all sides into shadows and mists."

Under Western Eyes is filled with little stories which are eddies in the great sea of the novel, but which move with the rush and flow of the full tides of action. There is the story of Peter Ivanovitch, a prisoner in a Siberian jail, who breaks out and makes a trek across the frozen tundra to freedom. He, too, is a typical Russian. He is helped in his escape by a young man and woman, and reaches Asian Russia. Then he leaves for Switzerland. The fugitives reach Switzerland—the end of the road. They settle down in "petite Russie," in Geneva. In Ivanovitch, as he is escaping, Conrad sees

> two human beings indissolubly joined . . . The civilized man, the enthusiast of advanced humanitarian ideals thirsting for the triumph of spiritual love and political liberty; and the stealthy, primeval savage, pitilessly cunning in the preservation of his freedom from day to day, like a tracked wild beast.

That is man—the beast who holds humanitarian ideals. The polarities meet.

Under Western Eyes follows a crime and its punishment. The crime is betrayal, the punishment, loss of self. But the criminal receives a reprieve. The novel is a parody of Dostoevsky's *Crime and Punishment.* It is about Russian culture and politics, the soul of Russia. In all this Dostoevsky figures largely. Officially, he detested Dostoevsky. But he takes Dostoevsky's tale and juggles it around. Turgenev was Conrad's avowed hero. In his essay on Turgenev Conrad plays him against Dostoevsky. "What should make Turgenev sympathetic and welcome to the English-speaking world," Conrad wrote, "is his essential humanity. All his creations, fortunate and unfortunate, oppressed and oppressors, are human beings, not strange beasts in a menagerie or damned souls knocking themselves to pieces in the stuffy darkness of mystical contradictions." A put-down of Dostoevsky. Turgenev's characters are everything Dostoevsky's are not. Conrad concludes the essay with a sneer at "the convulsed terror-haunted Dostoevsky." After reading the Constance Garnett translation of *The Brothers Karamazov,* he wrote:

> I don't know what Dostoevsky stands for or reveals, but I do know that he is too Russian for me. It sounds to me like some fierce mouthings from prehistoric ages.

Most English readers in Conrad's day found Dostoevsky unacceptable. No manners, no art, no ideas whatsoever. Just a madman, a case for a mental institution. His books were out of print for much of the late nineteenth and early twentieth centuries, and while they were in print, most people felt they had no place in the fiction section of the library. Prince Kropotkin, the Russian, spoke for many readers of the time when he wrote of the "obsolete forms" of Dostoevsky's novels, "the disorder of their construction" and their "atmosphere of the lunatic asylum."

Conrad sees in Turgenev a reflection of himself. When he describes Turgenev at work he simultaneously paints a portrait of himself. He wrote:

> Turgenev's Russia is but a canvas on which the incomparable artist of humanity lays his colours and his forms in the great light and the free air of the world. Had he invented them all and also every stick and stone, brook and hill and field in which they move, his personages would have been just as true and as poignant in their perplexed lives. They are his own and also universal.

Turgenev's Russia is a mirror of Conrad's Costaguana. Conrad sees himself in Turgenev, for Turgenev was a Russian who was welcomed in England; he was the most popular of Russian writers in the West. Conrad the Pole wants in. Turgenev fit in socially in the London literary world. As George Moore said of him, he "knew the serf as the gentleman knows the serf: he knew the gentleman as the gentleman knows the gentleman." Turgenev's class consciousness was pleasing to the British upper classes, for they saw themselves in him. It is Conrad the would-be English gentleman who looks up to Turgenev the man at ease grouse-hunting in Scotland and at weekend gatherings in Sussex country houses.

Under Western Eyes was published in 1911, about the time that the English discovered modern Russian literature. The preoccupation with Russian culture coincided with a deep concern about Russian politics. The events of 1905 and 1917 fed the English appetite for news and novels about Russia. In 1912 the first biographical study of Dostoevsky appeared in English. Constance Garnett's translation of *The Brothers Karamazov* was published in 1912, *The Idiot* in 1913 and *Crime and Punishment* in 1914. In 1910 *Crime and Punishment* was adapted for the English stage and presented under the title "The Unwritten Law." In this butchered version Sonia becomes an innocent girl threatened by a lecherous landlord. The landlord becomes Raskolnikov's victim. *Crime and Punishment* is transformed into Victorian melodrama. In writing *Under Western Eyes* Conrad was aware of the perverse English distortion of Russian literature and culture. He saw how the English pushed the Russian experience away from their own. George Gissing, in his study of Dickens published in 1898, argued that Dickens "might well have written *Crime and Punishment*." But, for the most part, he pointed to the Russian experience as anathema to the English. He felt that Sonia's character was "inconceivable in English fiction," that the "magnificent scene in which Raskolnikov makes confession to Sonia, is beyond Dickens." The logic of Raskolnikov's crime, he argued, was inconceivable to middle-class Englishmen. Conrad takes all this into consideration, and uses a narrator—the Western eyes which bring Russian life into focus—the teacher of languages, the linguist, who understands the tongues of East and West. His Western eyes are lenses which filter the light of the East. His Western tongue smoothes over the roughness of Eastern speech.

It is the whole question of the confession which fascinates Conrad. Everyone is continually confessing in *Under Western Eyes:* confessing political secrets to the police, confessing sins to priests. A whole nation on its knees at confession. Razumov sits under a statue of Jean-Jacques Rousseau, author of the *Confessions,* in his birthplace, Geneva, and writes his confessions. Later we find out that they are his reports to Russian secret intelligence. His confessions are betrayals; every time he confesses he sentences a fellow-man, a revolutionary, to death, exile, or jail. When Razumov confesses to the police the first time, Haldin is hanged. Men are continually confessing to women. Conrad parodies the scene in which Raskolnikov confesses to Sonia. He satirizes the idea of the woman, corrupted through her body but pure in her soul, the virginal prostitute who saves the sinning man. But ironically Razumov also confesses to a woman, to Haldin's sister, and is cared for by another woman, named Tekla, after his ears are pierced; he will never be able to eavesdrop again. But Razumov's confession is not like Raskolnikov's. It is neither religious, sacred, nor holy. It brings no redemption in the Christian sense. No analogy to Christ is made here; Razumov is not a crucified man with a crown of thorns. There is no resurrection.

Conrad was born a Catholic, but lived and died an atheist. He did not believe in God or gods. In 1891 and 1892 he explained to his aunt, Madam Poradowska, what it was about Christianity that he opposed. He told her that the "doctrine (or theory) of expiation through suffering" was a "product of superior but savage minds" and that it was "quite simply an infamous abomination when preached by civilized people." Now, it is this idea of expiation through suffering which is fundamental to Dostoevsky and which Conrad cannot accept. He does not like the idea of people being miserable; he does not justify suffering. Conrad came close to the existentialist position when he said "there is no expiation. Each act of life is final and inevitably produces its consequences in spite of all the weeping and gnashing of teeth." "An Outpost of Progress," a stepping stone to *Heart of Darkness,* is a tale about two lone colonialists in the godless Congo. In their trading post is the grave of their predecessor, marked by a cross which casts a shadow over the earth. The two men are unable to exist together in peace. Kayerts kills his comrade Carlier. In one short afternoon he plumbs "the depths of horror and despair." Just before he dies we hear him cry aloud his last words on earth: *"Help . . . My God!"* The only reply is the screech of the horn from the company boat steaming up the river. The machine is god. There is no other in the industrial age. Before the director lands, Kayerts commits suicide. He is found hanging by a leather strap from a cross, his tongue sticking out irreverently.

Conrad also rejected the Christian concept of turning the

other cheek, of doing unto others as you would have them do unto you. If you are hit, you strike back. "To return good for evil," he said, "is not only profoundly immoral but dangerous, in that it sharpens the appetite for evil in the malevolent and develops (perhaps unconsciously) that latent tendency towards hypocrisy." Not to defend oneself, not to strike back, is to humiliate oneself, to further subject oneself. It only prolongs slavery and encourages the oppressor. It destroys the self; all the time that you are turning the other cheek you really want to strike back.

Finally, in 1914, he told Edward Garnett why he was suspicious of Tolstoi's work. "The base from which he starts —Christianity—" he wrote, "is distasteful to me. I am not blind to its services but the absurd oriental fable from which it starts irritates me. Great, improving, softening, compassionate it may be but it has lent itself with amazing facility to cruel distortion and is the only religion which, with its impossible standards, has brought an infinity of anguish to innumerable souls—on this earth." The priests he knew took confessions from Black men and then stood by while white traders sold them into slavery or beat them to death; they took confessions from revolutionaries and then betrayed them to the secret police, who jailed them, exiled them, hanged them.

Conrad Anglicizes and de-Christianizes Dostoevsky. He politicizes him. The crime Raskolnikov commits is not a political crime. Haldin's crime is political. In a sense, all crime is political. The Russian peasant in jail for stealing a loaf of bread was as much a political prisoner as the Russian revolutionary in jail for passing out leaflets at a factory. Yet Raskolnikov's crime—the murder of an old woman—is unique. It is a crime of the will. It is an existential crime. Razumov's betrayal of Haldin is the central act in the drama of terrorists and police. His is a crime against the revolution.

Under Western Eyes is a melodrama. Conrad presents it

on that stage to suit the English. "All ideas of political plots and conspiracies," Conrad writes, are seen by Western Europeans as "childish, crude inventions for the theater or a novel." By presenting Russian politics as melodrama, he makes it crude. It is a campy novel. The narrator asks us to see the whole affair as "something theatrical and morbidly affected." Conrad had what he himself defined as a "theatrical imagination." He thought in terms of the stage: a scene, an action, characters, an opening curtain, a climax, a closing curtain. He saw his characters as protagonists and antagonists. He claimed that the novelist was "like an actor who raises his voice on the stage above the pitch of natural conversation." Conrad takes all the parts. He changes costumes, voice, impersonates all the actors on the stage. He shouts, gesticulates wildly. "In order to move others deeply," he wrote, "we must deliberately allow ourselves to be carried away beyond the bounds of our normal sensibility." Many of the scenes in *Under Western Eyes* are enacted in the Place du Théâtre. Switzerland itself becomes a stage, a plateau slightly above the rest of Europe, the stage toward which Russians and Englishmen all look to see the outcome of the dramatic and historic conflict. In Switzerland the key scenes are in the Gothic Château Borel, a setting familiar to Eugene O'Neill's audiences, who watched his dramas of family decadence, decline and ghastly horrors.

Conrad's theatrical imagination took many forms: *Almayer's Folly* and *The Rescue* are like Verdi operas; *Nostromo* is a Shakespearean tragedy; *Under Western Eyes* is a melodrama. Of course the dividing line between them is narrow; they slide into one another. And there is little point in making hard and fast definitions. Conrad felt that in the theater the "climax of the action" must have a "supreme moment." In *Under Western Eyes* it is Razumov's confession to Miss Haldin. Miss Haldin is wearing a veil; Razumov is holding his book, the record of his life, his true confession. Each one recognizes his need for the other.

Razumov confronts the "old Father of lies—our national patron." He confesses, he tells the truth. Miss Haldin lifts her veil; it falls to the floor, Razumov picks it up and wraps it around his notebook. He reveals all. He seems "to be listening to a strain of music rather than to articulated speech." Razumov leaves the Haldin's house and rushes outside. Conrad marshals all the forces of nature as Razumov is washed clean in the downpour which descends on Geneva. The storm of revolution hangs over all of Europe:

> Razumov walked straight home on the wet, glistening pavement. A heavy shower passed over him; distant lightening played faintly against the fronts of the dumb houses with the shuttered shops all along the Rue de Carouge; and now and then, after the faint flash, there was a faint, sleepy rumble; but the main forces of the thunderstorm remained massed down the Rhone valley as if loath to attack the respectable and passionless abode of democratic liberty, the serious-minded town of dreary hotels, tendering the same indifferent hospitality to tourists of all nations and to international conspirators of every shade.

Conrad felt that it was no crime for the novelist, like the actor, to raise "his voice on the stage above the pitch of natural conversation." But there was a danger in the "writer becoming the victim of his own exaggeration, losing the exact notion of sincerity, and in the end coming to despise truth itself." He noted that "from laughter and tears the descent is easy to snivelling and giggles."

When Conrad deals with revolutionaries, he manipulates our emotions. He wants us to respond with fear and terror. One of the little stories within *Under Western Eyes* is about Tekla. She is a hanger-on about revolutionary circles. Although she is dedicated and hard-working, she is used by men and never treated with respect or as an equal. Her father is a minor clerk in the Ministry of Finances. "I ran away from my parents," she tells us, "directly I began to think by myself." An old apple-woman opens Tekla's eyes "to the horrors from which innocent people are made to suffer in this world, only in order that governments might exist. After I [Tekla] once understood the crime of the upper classes, I could not go on living with my parents." She is a runaway, a dropout, in late nineteenth-century Russia. She feels physically uncomfortable, morally dishonest, living on her father's government salary when thousands of peasants are hungry. She goes to live in cellars with the proletariat, to suffer with them, to help them. But she finds that as a simple humanitarian there is very little that she can do to better their living conditions. Next, Tekla aids a young man imprisoned for distributing temperance tracts. On his release she takes him into a garret, steals bread so that he can eat, finds clothes to cover his naked flesh. He dies.

A group of revolutionaries get Tekla a job with a Jewish family as a governess to their children. She carries across the frontier a packet of secret documents, which she holds near her heart. In Germany she delivers them to the revolutionaries. Tekla is tireless. She performs one task after the other without complaining. The greatest joy of her life is Mr. Haldin's assassination of the Minister of the Secret Police. She ends her days caring for Razumov. Her story is a novel in itself—the tale of a girl from a *petit bourgeois* family who rejects the simple comforts she is born into in order to join the revolution. She is courageous, pitiful, long-suffering, full of love for mankind and desire to fight for oppressed people. But Conrad does not give her her due. She cannot be a heroine in his drama. She provokes no deep emotions in the reader—no laughter, no tears. Instead, we feel sorry for her, and even have a few jokes at her expense. The true, honest emotions we want to feel for Tekla are distorted, perverted. And this is because Conrad's own emotions are warped when he describes revolutionaries, because he hates the revolutionaries as much as he hates the autocrats. He did not recognize the liberating or creative power of rebellion. He felt that the revolution would only breed its own extremes, perversions, atrocities. He sees no way out. Razumov cannot become a revolutionary. He can only confess his past sins to Left and Right, make his peace with both sides and then retire to live a peaceful life. "The oppressors and the oppressed are all Russians together," Conrad wrote, "and the world is brought once more face to face with the truth of the saying that the tiger cannot change his stripes nor the leopard his spots."

After *Under Western Eyes* the fires of Conrad's energy burned out. They flared again briefly in *Chance* (1913), but most of the late novels recapitulate earlier material. The sharp-edged contradictions are dulled. The clear outline of things, men and forces is dimmed. Conrad mimics himself. His late characters are pygmies when compared with the giants in *Lord Jim, Heart of Darkness* and *Nostromo. Chance* is his last assault on the English citadel; after it Conrad was tired of fighting. He resolved the issues without testing them to the utmost.

Conrad had the courage to disrupt the traditional. He had a ruthlessness which enabled him to probe and provoke; he never blindly accepted the weapons placed in his hands. Conrad was a fighter, a combatant. He knew it was better to burn than to rot, better to crash through the clear glass than to suffocate in a plastic box. He is desperate, and he survives to fight again. He is a corrupted, fallen man who knows his crimes and limitations, but pushes ahead. Man is a conquering animal, Conrad assumes. In his essay on Henry James, he offers up for our thoughts a vision of the end of the world. The earth is dying; no blades of grass cover the soil; the last airplane has fallen to the ground. A group of men are watching the feeble glow of the setting sun against a black sky. They are the last survivors "in the stilled workshop of the earth." Among them is an artist, a man "gifted with a power of expression and courageous enough to interpret the ultimate experience of mankind." His indomitable listeners resist the misery and pain which settles about them like falling nuclear dust. What does this last artist say? "I am inclined to think," Conrad writes, "that the last utterance will formulate, strange as it may appear, some hope now to us utterly inconceivable." Conrad's men refuse death's calling card. They reach out, fists clenched, calculating victory. Their guns are never holstered, their presses never stilled. The battle is never over. Their hope, their vigor, their ache for struggle is never diminished. When he died in 1924 he was in the midst of a novel, *Suspense*. Although unfinished and showing signs of his fatigue and age, it radiates the spirit of contradiction and rebellion which glowed hot in *Heart of Darkness* and *Nostromo*.

12

Forster and Cary: Old and New

E. M. Forster was a child of the nineteenth century. Joyce Cary was a son of the twentieth century. Forster was a creature of old Europe. Cary was a product of the new society. Forster was born in 1879, the year of Kipling's fourteenth birthday, Conrad's twenty-second. He was thirty-five in 1914, ninety-one when he died in 1970. Cary was born only nine years later, in 1888; Disraeli had been buried for seven years, Darwin for six, Marx for five. He was twenty-six in 1914, and seventy-one when he died in 1959. One went to Cambridge, the other, to Oxford. Both Forster and Cary are liberals. They belong to the middle class. They wrote about the colonial world. At first glance they look very much alike, but they are very different men.

Take the Great War, World War I. By 1914 Forster was already an old man. The world war finished him off, even though he continued to haunt Bloomsbury and Cambridge for over half a century. Cary was a young soldier in Africa during the war. He came to maturity long after the cataclysm; Cary's finest work was done during World War II. The Great War was an explosion in both writers' lives. It leveled Forster's house, and he was unable to build a new one. But it cleared a space for Cary to move. He built a foundation and put a roof over his head. Forster felt the earth tremble, the sky darken, his own heart quicken and jump. He ran for cover. He cried out for shelter. Forster is the weather vane of the storm cloud. His observation from the watchtower was:

> . . . even when they are not directly about a war—like the works of Lytton Strachey or Joyce or Virginia Woolf —they still display unrest or disillusionment or anxiety, they are still the products of a civilization which feels itself insecure.

English prose, he concluded, "is the product of people who have war on their mind." Forster was fixated with the war; he never comes to terms with it in his work. Cary is not traumatized by the war; he glides over its horror and destruction.

For Forster, World War I destroyed a splendid civilization he had loved and identified with. "I belong," he wrote, "to the fag-end of Victorian liberalism." He looked back at the nineteenth century through rose-colored glasses. In "The Challenge of Our Time" (1946) he wrote of the Victorian era:

> . . . it was an admirable age. It practised benevolence and philanthropy, was humane and intellectually curious, upheld free speech, had little colour-prejudice, believed that individuals are and should be different, and entertained a sincere faith in the progress of society. The world was to become better and better, chiefly through the spread of parliamentary institutions. The education I received in those far-off and fantastic days made me soft and I am glad it did . . . But though the education was humane it was imperfect, inasmuch as we none of us realised our economic position. In came the nice fat dividends, up rose the lofty thoughts, and we did not realise that all the time we were exploiting the poor of our own country and the backward races abroad, and getting bigger profits from our investments than we should.

Forster wants adjustments to be made. But a smash-up, no, not that. He wants smaller profits, not the end of all profits. He wants men to become conscious of their fat dividends, not to fight for a society in which there will be an end to classes and class conflict.

Forster hugs Victorian bric-a-brac to his breast. Cary is nostalgic about Victorian things but he does not collect them. Forster is an old maid. He is like his aunt Marianne Thornton; her eighteenth-century world is the one he worships. It is the world of big houses, the comfortable bourgeois life, of philanthropic families who have made their fortunes from colonial trade. In *Marianne Thornton* Forster describes his aunt's world. Battersea Rise, the house, is its center. It was, Forster wrote, "a blend of feudal loyalty and eighteenth-century enlightment." It antedates the world of monopoly capitalism. Henry Thornton, the founder, was both chairman of the Sierra Leone Company, and president of the Sunday School Society. Forster calls him a "typical Thornton, pious, benevolent, industrious, wealthy, shrewd." He admires the family's sense of reason, their "loyalty of soul," which, he argues, is so unlike modern love. Forster accepts the Thornton heritage. He admits that it gave him his "slant upon society and history," and claims that that perspective "has been corrected by contact with friends who have never had a home in the Thornton sense, and do not want one." Forster stands inside the house; he invites different people in to supplement the Thornton fare. He does not give up Battersea Rise. He thanks his aunt for leaving him eight thousand pounds—"the financial salvation of my life," he calls it. "She and no one else," he concludes, "made my career as a writer possible, and her love in a most tangible sense followed me beyond the grave." Forster believes that art rests on material ease, that the artist needs leisure and wealth. He recognizes his privileged position but he does nothing to change it. "Talking with Communists," he said, "makes me realise the weakness of my own position and the badness of the twentieth-century society in which I live. I contribute to the badness without wanting to. My investments increase the general misery." He holds onto the investments because they give him the independence needed for writing.

Forster's own reaction to World War I emerges from his description of the impact of the war on G. Lowes Dickinson, the Cambridge professor, and Forster's friend and companion. In both Dickinson and Forster there is a flabbiness, an avoidance of rigorous struggle. Forster wrote: "It is impossible to convey to a younger generation what 1914 felt like. It was such a surprise. That word is a feeble one, yet I can think of none more appropriate." He said of Dickinson, "In 1914 civilization broke its promise to him, and he never felt sure of it again." Forster defends Dickinson against the men and women who, "with a sneer," say that he "was only a sheltered don who went through no physical hardships and lost no dear friends. This is true, and he realized it, but it is also true that he was in Shelley's words:

> a nerve o'er which do creep
> the else unfelt oppression of this earth,

and that if his suffering is rejected as meaningless, we can ignore the account of Jesus Christ weeping over the fate of mankind." But there is an important qualitative difference between the oppression felt by the sensitive souls of Cambridge and Bloomsbury and the oppression felt by the Chinese peasant and the exploited African. Dickinson offers reason to the peoples of the earth. But reason could not satisfy the Russian soldier at the Eastern front in 1917. It could not satisfy the Vietnamese peasant jailed by the French authorities.

Forster, Dickinson and their circle did not reckon with the conditions faced by the majority of the world's population: poverty, illiteracy, unemployment, lack of housing, starvation, sickness and disease. They were limited by their upper-class backgrounds, by the elite education offered at Cambridge. Forster's own role is extremely limited. In his novels he acts as a tutor to the English middle class. He refines young ladies, encourages them to listen to Beethoven symphonies and to visit medieval cathedrals. But he does not awaken them, as he should, to the injustice and oppression in their world.

Forster's myth of the English past is a denial of conflict, a plea for compromise and a whitewash of British atrocities and injustices. That myth is sharpest in the essay "Notes on the English Character." Forster's primary assumption is that "the character of the English is essentially middle-class." He introduces himself as the typical Englishman. Forster's middle class has done everything. They have made the industrial revolution, evolved parliamentary democracy and constructed the British Empire. There he stands—John Bull. He wears a top hat, his stomach is bulging, his clothes are well-tailored, and every Friday he deposits his money in the bank. Forster's typical Englishman. There are other classes —the aristocracy and the poor (Forster avoids the phrases "the proletariat," "the working class")—but in his estimation they have not propelled the English ship of state. John Bull is practical, calm, empirical, slow to anger—the opposite of the fanatical, instinctive, terror-haunted Frenchman. The character of the average Englishman, Forster writes, which "prevents his rising to certain heights, also prevents him from sinking to . . . depths." He has a mediocre, uneventful existence.

Not all Bloomsbury and Cambridge reacted as did Forster. Leonard Woolf leapt over the walls of Cambridge which contained Forster. Woolf changed and created changes; he was a rebel. He looks back to the same era Forster did, but his observations differ from Forster's:

> Our youth, the years of my generation at Cambridge, coincided with the end and the beginning of a century

> which was also the end of one era and the beginning of another. When in the grim, grey, rainy January days of 1901 Queen Victoria lay dying, we already felt that we were living in an era of incipient revolt . . . against a social system . . . bourgeois Victorianism.

Woolf, like Forster, began as a Cambridge product. He went to Ceylon and served as both a police magistrate and a district judge. The Ceylonese society he lived in was, in his own words, "Kiplingesque"; he says, "I could never make up my mind whether Kipling had moulded his characters accurately in the image of Anglo-Indian society or whether we were moulding our characters accurately in the image of a Kipling story." Woolf did act as a character in a Kipling story. He was an imperialist, as he himself confesses. From 1905 to 1911 in Ceylon he was reborn an anti-imperialist. He jumped over the barricades to the side of the revolution.

Woolf was uninterested in Forster's average Englishman. In 1912 in London he was secretary to Roger Fry's Second Post-Impressionistic Exhibition, the series of art shows which rocked the world of painting. "I used to think as I sat there," Woolf wrote, "how much nicer were the Tamil or Singalese villagers who crowded into the veranda of my Ceylon kachcheri than these smug, well-dressed, ill-mannered, well-to-do-Londoners." These are the Englishmen and Englishwomen Forster coddles. Woolf does not argue that the poor worker and the peasant are more real than the aristocrat and the society lady. He feels that there is just as much reality in Bloomsbury or Cambridge as there is in the Congo or down in a coal mine. But he believes that men who till the earth or dig coal, laborers who are unemployed, peasants who eke out a meager existence in the jungle, are more attractive, more admirable human beings than the rich and the elite. Woolf had no particular stake in the established order. He had no desire to be a duke, a knight or a celebrity. When he looked into the past he saw beginnings and endings, one era halting, a new era starting. Forster acknowledges the terminating points, not the launching pads. Woolf called for violent revolution to change the old order. Forster wanted no abrupt changes. In *Beginning Again,* the third volume of his autobiography, Woolf wrote:

> If I could return to 1917 possessing the knowledge and experience of 1963 I would again welcome the Russian Revolution and for the same reasons for which I originally welcomed it. Like the French Revolution, it destroyed an ancient, malignant growth in European society, and this was essential for the future of European civilization.

Forster overlooked the malignancy. He did not see what Woolf saw—that nineteenth-century European society was "belligerent, crusading, conquering, exploiting."

Cary, even more than Woolf, and far more than Forster, concentrates on the new, on the beginnings. *Castle Corner* (1938) is his clearest view of the end of Victorian England —"the bag end of things." For the most part the novel takes place in the 1890s. There is Victoria's death, the Irish struggles, the "end of British imperialism." There is also an end to the world mood which pervades the book. Cary's interests are eschatological. His characters talk about the coming of the anti-Christ, death, the Last Judgment, Heaven and Hell. The novel opens with the death of John Corner and his old world. Corner believes that God is the Father in Heaven, that the king of England is the father of his people, that he, Corner, is the father of his English and Irish tenants. With his death falls the old, patriarchal, religious and hierarchical society.

But the main thrust of the novel is accumulation of the new. Cary gobbles up the present and the future with a passion. There is a new breed of millionaires who have made their money in South Africa; new artists, new styles, new ideologies, new political causes. The novel is a stream of inventions, innovations, new talent—the young.

In the 1920s and 1930s there was a new political order and new combatants to assess. The rise of fascism. The growth of communist Russia. Cary and Forster looked across the Channel. Where Napoleon once stood they saw Hitler and Stalin. England, the empire and democracy threatened, the free world under siege. Cary will shoot and then ask questions. Forster interviews his opponents, then invites them to join in a dialogue. For Cary, Hitler and Stalin are identical twins—both dictators, equally totalitarian. They rely on terror, purges, concentration camps. Cary broadcasts the voice of liberal anticommunism. He wants to see Stalin's Russia destroyed. He will not rest till communism is wiped off the face of the earth. He does not believe in coexistence. In his eyes the communist is his enemy; enemies must be jailed or killed. He goes into the fray armed with propaganda to defeat totalitarians.

Cary swallows whole the big lie about communism. He believes that a socialist society is not free. He sticks by the Western democracies. For Forster, there is a difference between Hitler and Stalin. The Nazi uses evil means for evil ends, he says. But the communist uses evil means for good ends. Forster presses for a popular front, a united front. He is the liberal who joins up with communists at a few intersections on the road. He is an anti-fascist, but he will let others do the brunt of the fighting. When he does fight, his weapons are archaic. Liberty, variety, tolerance and sympathy—these are the remedies Forster offers to stop the fascist boot. For Forster, the arch anti-fascist of all time is Voltaire. His ammunition against twentieth-century fascism comes from an eighteenth-century Enlightenment philosopher. He loads his pistol with wit and skepticism. Forster wants to preserve human life. He identifies with the Jews when anti-Semitism stalks the land. He sees a defeat for all humanity when Jewish men and women are exterminated in the gas ovens. The Nazi kills and destroys. Forster would rather put up with the enemy than be forced to jail or execute him.

The colonial world stretches the imagination of both Forster and Cary. The war between Europe and the colonial world, between white and Black, busts wide open the tidy, well-swept rooms of their mind. For both of them the heart of darkness is in the Third World. "The attraction of Africa," Cary wrote, "is that it shows . . . the powerful often subconscious motives . . . which in Europe hide themselves under all sorts of decorous scientific or theological or political uniforms." In Africa they are "seen naked in bold and dramatic action." The African setting demanded "violence and coarseness of detail . . . a fabulous treatment." What Cary tapped in Africa, he felt, was the perpetual situation of the whole world—"confusion, conflict, the destruction of old values before the new are established." Doris Lessing, who grew up in Southern Rhodesia and who has written extensively about Africa, looks at the continent from a similar vantage point. "Writers brought up in Africa," she says, "have many advantages—being at the centre of a modern battlefield; part of a society in rapid, dramatic change." Man is man in Africa. For Cary, life is constant turmoil and transformation; Africa is the place of swiftest change. There primitive tribesmen learn to drive Mack trucks and to read Marx in Swahili in their lunch breaks.

In India, Forster sees a land which "knows of the whole world's trouble, to its uttermost depth." India is the saddest, most tragic land. In "The Nine Gems of Ujjain" (1914) Forster describes a visit to an ancient Indian city. From the train station he travels by horse and wagon over the fields. There are no tracks, no road. "There was no place for anything, and nothing was in its place," he writes. "There was no time either . . . nothing remained certain but the dome of the sky and the disk of the sun." India expresses most clearly what he feels about modern life: nothing fixed or definite, a clock without hands, a field without fences. The landscape expresses disintegration, confusion and chaos. India challenges and upsets the cart of normality, the values of the Mediterranean world. It injects the abnormal, the extraordinary and the monstrous. The West is balance, the East is polarity. England is finite, India is infinite. England is boxed in, but India is unfettered. To write about the colonial world is to write about the irreconcilables. But even Forster's colonial world has a musty odor about it. Young ladies sit down to drink tea. They are thinking about impending marriages. Young men are plotting their careers. You would think you were back in the early nineteenth century. It is almost Jane Austen shipped to the East. Cary's Africa is modern. It exemplifies the new, the most recent.

The dichotomy between Forster and Cary is also sharply defined through their reactions to the mass media. Before them they see millions of men and women moved by actors on the screen, by the headlines in the daily press, by words on the lips of broadcasters. The radio and, later, the television dominate the living rooms of Forster's and Cary's suburbanites. They are conscious of televisions and radios turned on in millions of houses all over the world.

The generation of writers who preceded them were gently swayed by the gusts of modern communication, but they were not uprooted. Conrad was curious about and receptive to the film and the radio. In 1923 he gave a lecture in which he argued that the "imaginative literary art" was "based fundamentally on scenic motion, like a cinema." Looking back to the late 1890s, when he collaborated with Stephen Crane on a play, Conrad claimed that the two of them "must have been unconsciously penetrated by a prophetic sense of the technique and the very spirit of film-plays." But he was also quick to point to the differences between film making and the craft of fiction. He felt that the writer was "a much more subtle and complicated machine than a camera, and with a wider range, if in the visual effects less precise." In 1920 he made a film scenario of his short story "Gaspar Ruiz," which he entitled "The Strong Man."

In 1923 Conrad explained the process of his own imagination by describing the workings of the wireless. He noted that his craftsmanship consists in his "unconventional grouping and perspective." But the important point he makes is that he is a transmitter. He receives messages and sends them out to his listeners. The matter, of course, is primary; without it nothing would be real "any more than Marconi's electric waves could be made evident without the sending-out and receiving instruments." He concludes, "without mankind my art, an infinitesimal thing, could not exist." But by 1923 Conrad's writing days were nearly over. He lived only another year. His writing was not penetrated by the impact of the film or the radio.

Kipling quickly picked up on the cinema and the wireless. He immediately connected these modern machines with magical powers and ancient mysteries. In the wireless he indulged his fantasy life. It became an instrument for communicating with the "mainstream of subconscious thought common to all mankind." He also found a mysterious force in the film. He accepted literally the concept of Hollywood as a dream factory. Because he wanted power over large audiences he was thrilled with the ability of film makers to set styles, encourage patterns of thought and create cultural heroes. Like everyone else, he was a Charlie Chaplin fan. In packed theaters he laughed at the antics of the Keystone Cops. He found in films a quality of unreality, the destruction of cause-and-effect relationships. In his study of the Irish Guards in the Great War, the best way he found for describing the quality of trench warfare, the mud, the craters, the exploding shells, the dead horses and the human corpses was to write that "the impression of unreality was as strong as in a cinema-show."

Forster feels threatened by radios, televisions and movies. He sees them coming alive—robots taking over the world. At the end of *Aspects of the Novel* he asks of the novel, "Will it be killed by the cinema?" He is afraid that an older species will be supplanted by younger ones. He felt that the genre of Fielding, Austen and Scott was on its way out, and he wanted to preserve it. He wanted to halt the reels, turn off the dials, sit people down in easy chairs and give them novels to read. "It is a mistake to assume that books have come to stay," he wrote sadly in 1932. "There is not only the microphone, there is the cinema. Between them are they not turning us from readers into listeners and lookers, and causing us to depend less and less on books? I think they are and I am sorry." Forster is frightened by movies. He does not trust them. He feels that they can "indicate, but they cannot rub anything in." Only books can do that. He defends the novel, piles books around him in a circle, like a fortress against the encroaching armies of film makers and radio broadcasters. It is Forster's feeling that with the invasion of radio and cinema intimacy is no longer possible —the disappearance of a culture. With the retreat of the novel he senses a world eroding, the world of Jane Austen, Dickens, Meredith, the world that is comfortable and familiar to him. Village gossips in pubs, English lawyers in the courts, newspapermen on Fleet Street, eligible daughters waiting in gardens for their suitors. With the disappearance of the novel, all that, too, will vanish.

For Cary, the important thing about the radio, the cinema and the press is their power. Power is reality; he respects it, wants to grab hold of it. He is interested in the way newspapers and movies influence politics. They educate masses of people, make more people conscious of events as they occur simultaneously in Pakistan, Japan, Mexico, the United States. Cary believes that newspapers do not merely report or reflect; they actively create world turmoil, a world in upheaval. They are responsible for revolutions. "Never before in history," he wrote in 1958, "has the word, in speech and book, the picture on the cinema or on television, the dogma in some national or commercial slogan, had such power. And they have produced such a confusion of ideologies and militant nationalisms that a great many people despair of civilization." Cary's instinct is to leap into the fray, to offer his own competing broadcasts, his own films. Unlike Forster, he does not want to stop them or put them away. He is not the partisan of the novel that Forster is.

Tick-tock, tick-tock. Joyce Cary's watch has a different sound than Forster's. On Forster's clock it is the alarm we hear. It rouses us, shakes us out of our slumber. We are awakened to a danger. For Forster, moments leap out from the continuum of time. He is far more apocalyptic than Cary. He sees the end coming. The riders on horseback are breathing down his back. Forster is crisis-driven. For Cary, each moment is *chaos* and *telos,* beginning and end. He parachutes us down into the middle of an action. The present is all that counts—each moment, one moment after the other, one second after another. Minute by minute; hour, day, week. Time flowing. Gulley Jimson, the hero of *The Horse's Mouth,* speaking for Cary, says that a real picture "hasn't got corners and middle, but an Essential Being."

Joyce Cary is Proteus. Creation goes on endlessly. Cary is a man of many parts. He has a bag full of disguises. He is a comic, a clown, a ventriloquist who takes on different roles and throws his voice into different characters. He is like a traveling street-corner comedian. Cary bubbles over with energy. He is like the boy in school who is always doodling. He was a prolific writer. Cary wrote sixteen novels, plus books of poetry, political science, literary criticism and autobiography. From 1938 to 1947 he published fourteen books, nearly two a year.

In Cary's world things are atomized. Particles and people float alone in space. Each moment of time is distinct from the others. Cary noted that

> . . . the principal fact of life is the free mind. For good and evil, man is a free, creative spirit. This produces the very queer world we live in, a world in continuous creation and therefore continuous change and insecurity. A perpetually new and lively world, but a dangerous one, full of tragedy and injustice. A world in everlasting conflict between the new idea and the old allegiances, new arts and old inventions against the old establishment.

In his late novels Cary shows us the free mind swimming in the world of continuous creation. He creates a troupe of roving actors and, in turn, plays each of their parts. He looks at the world from all of their distinct points of view. This is the world of alienated men and women, isolation and fragmentation. He tells us that Wittgenstein taught him that "everyone has his own world . . . men are together in feeling, in sympathy, but alone in mind."

Cary becomes Sara Monday, Chester Nimmo, Tom Wilcher. Sara Monday is like an exotic, beautiful, Old Testament queen. But she is also a common washerwoman with rough hands, hanging out her starched sheets. She is at the same time a rogue, a common thief and a proper society matron—a twentieth-century Moll Flanders. Cary becomes one with her. He impersonates her. He is Sara. Sara/Cary is flattered by men's advances. She admires her figure in a mirror, douses her body with perfume. Sara is caught between her love for the flesh and her love of God. In church, kneeling to pray, she exhibits her ruddy breasts. Here is Cary looking at her domain, through her eyes:

> So here I am, I thought, mistress of my own world in my own kitchen, and I looked at the shining steel of the range and the china on the dresser glittering like jewels, and the dish covers, hanging in their row from the big venison one on the left to the little chop one on the right, as beautiful as a row of calendar moons, and the kitchen table scrubbed as white as beef fat and the copper on the dark wall throwing out a glow to warm the heart, and the blue

> delft bowls like pots of precious balm . . . I felt bits of myself running out from the grand kitchen into pantry and scullery and larder and beyond into the passage and the stillroom and even to the wood cellar and the boot hole as if I was really a king or queen whose flesh is brought up to be the father of all his countries . . . You would say I was putting out in buds like a shallot with my big kitchen heart in the middle and my little hearts all around in the empire of those good faithful offices, all fitted up as if they were, even the cupboards, in the best of country materials . . . Well, I thought, if you tied a knot of all the roads and railways and pipes and wires in the world it would come to a kitchen in the middle of it.

All Cary's characters create their own empires of things and people, stamped in their own image.

Chester Nimmo is a politician, a radical, a preacher. He comes from a family of poor religious fanatics who live in fear of hell. Cary/Nimmo drinks tea with tin miners, chats with primitive millenarians, debates with Marxists, is captivated by alluring actresses. He flies from material poverty toward a rich spiritual life.

Tom Wilcher is a lawyer, a crotchety old man. He is a man of property. Wilcher is surrounded by his memories; he is overcome with nostalgia. He has a reverence for things of the past. Wilcher/Cary is deeply political. He wants "to be a pilgrim," to go wandering, but he is rooted in traditional ways.

Cary believes there is no one truth; there are only a variety of truths. Of Tolstoi's *Resurrection* and Dostoevsky's *The Brothers Karamazov,* he wrote:

> These great books do not state the case, they weave a spell . . . They state not the case, but a case; they see everything from one angle; they are "true" only for their characters in that situation.

Cary noted that Tolstoi is both Vronsky and Levin, that Dostoevsky is Ivan, Zossuma, and Alyosha. What he finds attractive about the great writers is their ability to play different parts, to see things through another person's eyes. What Sara Monday sees is true, what Tom Wilcher sees is true and what Chester Nimmo sees is equally true.

Cary wrote that "tensions make the artist and the writer." Dickens's novels are complex, he argued, because of the "contradictions in Dickens's personality." Cary analyzed his own work in a similar way. He said that since he was an Anglo-Irishman, he "lived between two worlds so different that they could not be reconciled." In Cary's *oeuvre* there is a repeating pattern of conflict. Cary is both the lawyer and the artist, the judge and the criminal. He drafts the constitution and then violates it. His characters want to live by the commandments, and also to sin. They want to obey the law, but they steal. They want to be monogamous, but they commit adultery. Cary's characters are both the captive and the free, they are both prisoners and fugitives.

But the conflict is often submerged deep in the sand. In his late trilogies, especially, there is an absence of rigorous conflict. Cary neglects qualitative changes. He says that a revolution is going on all the time. He is not concerned with the swift and decisive transformations which take place in a short timespan. With Cary, all changes have equal significance. Cary's actors shadowbox with themselves, in separate rooms. They never get together to spar in the ring. Cary renders the world from a number of different perspectives—Sara's, Nimmo's, Gulley Jimson's, Wilcher's. But he sacrifices dramatic conflicts. Cary's sense of continuous creation means that the crossroads of time are not reached. He skirts the moments of crisis—just the opposite of Forster, who aims directly at the heart of the crisis. Cary had no dialectical sense of change. "The dialectic," he wrote, "is artificial and abstract. It does not square with the facts of history or psychology." He argued that "Marx's dialectic, like Hegel's, denies real liberty to man." Engels, the dialectician, began with the idea that "Freedom is the recognition of necessity."

Cary, the idealist, started with a belief in the uniqueness of the free mind.

Forster and Cary both look back in awe and with puzzled glances to Kipling and Conrad. They are children of the decline. End-of-empire artists. Before them were the giants. They live in an age of mortals. Forster and Cary marched through the territory Conrad and Kipling had colonized. *A Passage to India* is a rebuttal of Kipling; Cary's *Mister Johnson* is an annex to Conrad's African writings.

Forster reviewed Conrad's *The Rescue* in 1920. He noted that "Conrad believes as uncompromisingly as Kipling in Duty and Action." He did not disentangle them. But he began to grapple with Conrad when he wrote that he plays "contradictory roles," that he is "moralist and magician," that he possesses sternness and enchantment. Forster's longer piece on Conrad, which is reprinted in *Abinger Harvest,* also originally published in 1920, is flat. Because here, instead of dealing with Conrad's contradictions, he decides that Conrad is elusive, that he is unclear. He is quick to affirm that Conrad is a "noble artist," but essentially he is frightened by Conrad. Instead of analyzing the contradictions, he talks of "constant discrepancies" in his work. His view is that Conrad

> . . . is misty in the middle as well as at the edges, that the secret casket of his genius contains a vapour—rather than a jewel; and that we need not try to write him down philosophically, because there is, in this particular direction, nothing to write. No creeds, in fact. Only opinions, and the right to throw them overboard when facts make them look absurd. Opinions held under the semblance of eternity, girt with the sea, crowned with the stars, and therefore easily mistaken for a creed.

Forster went looking for a truth, a simple, neat formula. But Conrad is complex. Forster makes him an eel rather than a whale. Because he has a sense of intimacy, of the private life, that is fundamentally different from Conrad's, he is disappointed with Conrad's autobiography. Conrad, unlike Forster, connects his personal, private life with history. On the question of Conrad's Polish background and his exile in England, Forster loses his footing. He does not see the Conrad who lurks in the dark, alien streets of London, the man who is lost in the labyrinths of offices, who scowls at civil servants and their tea ceremonies. He sees a Conrad who salutes an England connected with a "rural and aristocratic and adventurous past." He makes Conrad more comfortable in his England than Conrad ever was.

Forster was quicker in grasping one of the central flaws in Kipling's work—his inability to synthesize, his difficulty in coordinating. But he excuses Kipling's political crimes. He sees Kipling as a child, a case of "arrested development." Here is a writer, Forster says, "of great genius whose equipment has never developed." Kipling is like Kim in Forster's eyes: the "very spirit of growth—mischievous and irreverent." Since he feels that Englishmen are not consciously evil but only muddle-headed, he does not confront Kipling's racism. One can "enjoy his works without bothering over his Imperialism," Forster says. That idea pops out of his little boxes, which separated imperialism, capitalism, racism and communism from people, love, hate and personal relations.

Cary consistently distinguished Conrad and Kipling. But he also tried to reconcile them in his novel *Cock Jarvis,* an unpublished book set in Nigeria. He wrote that Cock Jarvis, the hero, was "a Conrad character in a Kipling role." He is a Kipling imperialist who endures the mental dilemmas of the Conradian hero. Cary wrote that Jarvis "believed in the Empire, in fact, as the only hope of liberal civilization in the world, and he would say that the fall of the Roman Empire before the tribes of nationalist barbarians had wrecked civilization for a thousand years and would do it again if they could smash the British Empire."

Cary saw Kipling as a man trapped in his age, Conrad as

a creature of it, and at the same time, standing outside its limits. He explained that Conrad, in his stories of the Far East, "belongs profoundly to Europe of 1900," but that he also jumps out of the year 1900. "Hardy in *Tess* or *Jude* was no less of his time than Kipling in *Plain Tales* or *Kim*," Cary writes. "But we do not read Hardy or Conrad as we do Kipling and Wells for a light on their period . . . George Eliot, Hardy, Conrad, the greater writers, though they were planted so firmly in their time, were bigger than their time. They stand out of it like towers from a fog, and their minds belong in general ideas, in fundamental judgment to a universal sky." What makes Conrad and Hardy and Eliot more than period novelists is their "deeper sense of fate, of the evil will."

Cary imitated Conrad in his early novels. But the similarity between the two is more than a question of influence. They are in the same camp; Cary is a lesser light, Conrad the pivotal star. Cary had read Conrad while he was stationed in Africa. In his *Borgu Diary* for 1918 he made two important observations about Conrad. The first was: "for what is it in Conrad which touches you to the bone . . . the sympathy of feeling, life recognizing itself." The second was: "Meredith has a peep-show, Hardy a view, our sympathies are engaged with their people, but at a little distance. With Conrad's people we rub shoulders." In his library he had Conrad's *Arrow of Gold, Nostromo, The Shadow-Line, Tales of Unrest, Twixt Land and Sea* and *A Personal Record*. Like Forster and Leonard Woolf, Cary knows the Kipling types. He has met them in Africa; he knows the retired Army officers on their pensions in the south of England. He recommended Kipling's stories of India as "well worth study," though he felt that Kipling was greater as a poet than as a novelist or a short-story writer. Forster resented Kipling's "cult of the job," since he had no respect for work or craftsmanship. He scoffed at Kipling's cockney soldiers because he was an upper-class intellectual. But Cary cheers Kipling for the day's work; he admires "the great poet of the common soldier."

Cary and Forster set out on their voyages with Kipling and Conrad as guides, as crutches, showing them the way, holding them up, but they were also wary of scouts leading them down false paths, into dangerous places. Within the New World discovered by Conrad and Kipling they made their own original tracks.

13

Disconnections

I. LITTLE YEOMAN AND THE IMPERIALS

Howards End is a house, not a home. The House of Wilcox Limited. An old house, Forster's ideal, constructed on the plan of Battersea Rise, the Forster family establishment. The house is England, Forster's England. The Wilcoxes are not the sole possessors; they are joined by two other families, Schlegels and Basts. All these people getting together in one house. Harmony is the note sounded. "Only connect," Forster pleads. Outside the house—you can see it from the window—is a wych-elm, an English tree.

> It was neither warrior, nor lover, nor god; in none of these roles do the English excel. It was a comrade, bending over the house, strength and adventure in its roots, but in its utmost fingers tenderness, and the girth, that a dozen men could not have spanned, became in the end evanescent, till pale bud clusters seemed to float in the air.

It is a sappy tree; a sappy, sentimental book, too. Forster wants us to go away feeling all warm and soft and mushy inside. When he uses the word "comrade" he does not expect to hear the "Internationale," to talk of armed struggle or to listen to the sound of gunfire. His comrade is a friend, steadfast in times of trouble.

Look at the characters. There are the Schlegels. Two

aggressive sisters, Margaret and Helen, and a passive, effeminate brother who goes to Oxford. The Schlegels are supposed to be the embodiment of the spirit of femininity; they are wealthy, living off their foreign investments. Their father is German, but not a Prussian in military uniform, nor a fat Bavarian in shorts. He is a philosopher; his imperialism is "the imperialism of the air." He is interested in expanding his thoughts, creating an empire of the intellect. He reads Hegel's *Phenomenology of Mind* and Kant's *Critique of Pure Reason*. He thinks about the dialectic, about the ideal. He is a peace-loving man, opposed to all empires, except the empire of the mind, the dominion of thought. He is dead set against naval powers, colonial possessions, commercial interests. He leaves Germany, settles in England and becomes a British subject. All very logical to Forster, in a novel published in 1910, four years before the Great War. England is not an imperial state, not like the Germany of 1910, Mr. Schlegel and Mr. Forster believe. All anti-imperialists should move to England. Forster was like all those internationalists who before 1914 shouted for universal fellowship, but after the first guns were sounded, defended their own nation.

The Schlegel sisters are well-bred and well-educated. They have manners. They have been tutored. Sensitive souls. A little bit daring, some spice in their lives, occasionally an exotic cup of tea—and not the usual bland variety. They go to concerts—Beethoven's Fifth is their favorite—and when Helen Schlegel listens to the music, she sees goblins. They give her a feeling of "panic and emptiness." The sisters are imaginative. Not gifted with bold, original imaginations, but playful, ladylike ones. Their imaginations can be trotted out at gatherings. They are a talent, like the talent of the young girl whose mother proudly watches while she plays the piano or sings a little. The Schlegels are enlightened. They are liberals. They believe men and women should be equal; they give to causes. "Temperance and tolerance," they simultaneously murmur. They give their approval and reach into their pockets for a few coins to drop into the collection box. But they do not want anything disturbed. They will criticize the *haute bourgeoisie* in quiet tones, but flirt with those fat bankers. They will be kind to the poor, but shun working-class political parties or rallies. About what is happening in the world they are totally ignorant. They "would at times dismiss," Forster writes, "the whole British Empire with a puzzled, reverent sigh." And he excuses that attitude. It is not their fault that they are not responsible, and there is nothing they can do. Just being themselves is enough. They want public life to mirror private life, they want people to be kinder and more considerate to each other. Old ladies should be helped across streets, litter should be picked up, orphans should be placed with good families, poor widows should receive modest allowances. The two sisters are all for personal relations; if each one of us were nicer, we would have a nicer world. They are sister saints, worshiping the "inner life." Heartwarming. They are the best that we can expect in this life, Forster believes.

Then there are the mean old Wilcoxes. Imperialists. Businessmen. Bank accounts and bonds, offices, mistresses in town. Looking at the stock index first thing in the morning; driving expensive cars. Snobbish. But they, unlike Margaret and Helen, do not like to talk about money. In this respect they are inferior to the two sisters, for Forster wants the rich to be liberated enough to feel comfortable about their money. They should accept their pounds sterling and then do good, think right, express themselves creatively.

But Mrs. Wilcox is unlike the rest of her family. There is something special about her. She is not an intellectual, not a twentieth-century woman. She talks very little. She is graceful, slow-moving. She has "instinctive wisdom," Forster tells us—whatever that is. She is an aristocrat; money has not soiled her. Mostly, Forster bluffs when he describes her.

She is an ideal. Shake her, and the sawdust comes out. Her long dresses come down to the floor, she moves effortlessly. You cannot see her feet. She is like a wound-up old-fashioned doll, like nothing you could find in a modern department store.

Finally, there is Mr. Leonard Bast, Mr. Lower Middle Class. When Forster describes him, all his class prejudices, his snobbery, his elitism, his pretentiousness are made shockingly manifest:

> We are not concerned with the very poor. They are unthinkable, and only to be approached by the statistician or the poet. This story deals with gentlefolk . . . The boy, Leonard Bast, stood at the extreme edge of gentility. He was not in the abyss, but he could see it . . . he was inferior to most rich people, there is not the least doubt of it. He was not as courteous as the average rich man, nor as intelligent, nor as healthy, nor as lovable. His mind and his body had been alike underfed, because he was poor.

Forster kills Bast over all the pages of the book. He makes fun of him. He is incapable of understanding the lower-middle classes. He is frightened of them. He thinks of dirty, smelly passageways, two or three families sharing bathrooms —mournful, sorrowful lives.

The working classes never enter *Howards End*. They are in the abyss which Forster cannot bear to look into, much less leap into. To fall into it means to fall into poverty, out of bourgeois grace into proletarian sin. The abyss of the poor is hell. The novelist cannot even write about the poor. His hands are tied in that respect, Forster believes. Only the poet or the sociologist can deal with them. But Forster, in his own way, wants to be helpful. What he recommends to the Basts of the world is a walk in the country in the night air. Get in direct contact with nature, go back to your roots in the soil. Bast's ancestors were forced off the land by the enclosures, which created an urban working class. Now they should get back to where they once belonged. Leonard Bast is a reader. He wants to learn, to study. Forster tells him that that is all a waste. He will not develop his soul that way, oh no. But he will develop his spirit if he communicates with nature. In essence Forster says to the scholarship boy at Cambridge: "All this learning will get you nowhere. A Cambridge education is a waste. Your father ploughing the fields in Huntingdon was a happier man." Here is bookish Forster, Cambridge-trained Forster, feeling uncomfortable about the lower-middle classes entering his own safe world. Social advancement through education is morally offensive to him. And since he does not advocate that the working classes seize power, he advocates each person standing in his place, each class doing its task. Feudal society is his model.

These are the major characters. They move about in neat formation. About face. Attention. At ease. Helen has an affair with Paul Wilcox. Schlegels meet Bast. Mrs. Wilcox dies. Margaret marries Henry Wilcox. Bast's wife, Jacky, turns out to be Mr. Wilcox's former mistress. Helen and Leonard Bast make love. Leonard dies. Everyone else lives happily ever after.

Howards End is supposed to be about England. The Wilcoxes and the Schlegels are the English. The poor, the working classes, the all-powerful aristocracy and the big bourgeoisie do not count. Forster is not interested in them. They cannot reveal the secret meaning of England, he believes. The Schlegels—imaginative, well-mannered, humane, advocates of the heart and the spirit. The Wilcoxes—practical, efficient businessmen. These families are supposed to, and do, get together. They connect. These two families are supposed to be different. There is supposed to be a conflict between them. But, mostly, they are the same. Lionel Trilling writes that:

> *Howards End* is a novel about England's fate. It is a story of the class war . . . The class struggle is not between classes but within a single class, the middle class.

Marx and Engels are turning in their grave. What a perversion of the theory of the class struggle! "The history of all hitherto existing society is the history of class struggles," Marx wrote in *The Communist Manifesto* (1848). "Freeman and slave, patrician and plebian, lord and serf, guildmaster and journeyman, in a word, oppressor and oppressed stood in constant opposition to one another, carried on an uninterrupted, now hidden, now open fight, a fight that each time ended either in a revolutionary reconstruction of society at large, or in the common ruin of the contending classes." This class struggle is not reflected in *Howards End*. Trilling would have us believe that differences within a single class —not conflicts between the proletariat and the bourgeoisie, oppressor and oppressed—constitute the class struggle. There are temperamental differences, not class conflicts, between Schlegels and Wilcoxes. Forster writes about a family quarrel. The refined, bookish, cultured sisters resent the crudity and ill-breeding of their money-gathering cousins. There is a squabble and a making-up. After all, who are the Schlegels to complain? They are impractical, and the world needs practical-minded, efficient men like the Wilcoxes to get things done. Margaret Schlegel yells angrily at her sister:

> If Wilcoxes hadn't worked and died in England for thousands of years, you and I couldn't sit here without having our throats cut. There would be no trains, no ships to carry us literary people about in, no fields even. Just savagery. No —perhaps not even that. Without their spirit life might never have moved out of protoplasm. More and more do I refuse to draw my income and sneer at those who guarantee it.

If the Schlegels were the true adversaries of the Wilcoxes, they would be radical women fighting for the end of the British Empire, fighting for the end of male chauvinism, fighting with the oppressed against the Wilcox oppressors. Margaret is honest, not hypocritical. She accepts the Wilcox money, for it gives her comfort and ease, time to read books and go to concerts. She doesn't want to want. She sees history as Forster does. The entrepreneur spirit has made civilization. It is the Wilcoxes who have built railways and ships. There are no working people in this scheme of things. Brecht's poem "A Worker Reads History" asks the key questions Forster wants to sweep under the rug:

Who built the seven gates of Thebes?
The books are filled with names of kings.
Was it kings who hauled the craggy blocks of stone?
And Babylon, so many times destroyed,
Who built the city up each time? In which of Lima's houses,
That city glittering with gold, lived those who built it?
In the evening when the Chinese wall was finished
Where did the masons go? Imperial Rome
Is full of arcs of triumph. Who reared them up? Over whom
Did the Caesars triumph? Byzantium lives in song,
Were all her dwellings palaces? And even in Atlantis of the legend
The night the sea rushed in,
The drowning men still bellowed for their slaves.

Young Alexander conquered India.
He alone?
Caesar beat the Gauls.
Was there not even a cook in his army?
Philip of Spain wept as his fleet
Was sunk and destroyed. Were there no other tears?
Frederick the Great triumphed in the Seven Years' War. Who
Triumphed with him?

Each page a victory,
At whose expense the victory ball?
Every ten years a great man,
Who paid the piper?

So many particulars.
So many questions.

Margaret Schlegel, like Forster, sees Schlegel culture inevitably dependent on Wilcox money. "Us literary people," she calls the Schlegel tribe. But they are not even that. They appreciate literature and music, but they certainly do not write symphonies or novels, or engage in cultural debate. They are the fashionable middle-class ladies who read all the in-magazines and go to all the new art exhibits.

At the end of the novel the feud is ended. The Schlegels move into Howards End. It is a Schlegel takeover—a coup d'état. Margaret embraces Henry. Helen's son, too (Leonard Bast's son), moves to the country home. Everyone is together—lower-, upper- and middle-middle class. No more feuds. And Forster offers this as his view of the course of English society. His "only connect" is hardly what the Rolling Stones mean by "Connections," the Beatles by "Come Together" or the Yippies by "Get It Together." Forster is uptight. He is an electrician perfunctorily connecting two wires. There is no orgiastic coming-together of Basts, Wilcoxes and Schlegels. No communal society is created, no tribe of loving, sharing brothers and sisters. Forster is too sexually repressed, too much of a philistine, too much of a bourgeois to "let it all hang out," to "get down with it," to "come together."

He would have us believe that it is something new, this merger between the firms of Wilcox and Schlegel. But, in fact, it is what had existed in England for over one hundred years; it is what the English middle classes have always been. These two families have always existed side by side: liberals, when it didn't disturb their economic position, and empire-builders. The merger is made in rural England, in the countryside, at Howards End. Back to the farm, where there are fields of hay, country bumpkins, old ladies, deference on the part of inferiors to their superiors. No idiocy of country life for Forster. The only hope for an existence where we can "see life steadily and see it whole," connect Wilcoxes and Schlegels, is on English farms. It is the old land that Forster has a feel for, as does Kipling in *Puck of Pook's Hill*. Both

Forster and Kipling have a reverence, an awed respect for the English countryside. "The feudal ownership of land did bring dignity," Forster assures us, "whereas the modern ownership of movables is reducing us again to a nomadic horde." London is Forster's target: people living in hotels, living out of suitcases, having no permanent ties, loosing all contact with the earth. London is vulgar; vulgar commerce, the vulgar lower classes. Forster uses the word as James did. It expresses his class consciousness. When he says the word "vulgar" he turn his nose up, a superior look spreads across his face. He is thinking of dirty little shop assistants. He is upset by the commercialism of the 25th of December. He wants to put Christ back in Christmas.

Forster sees two antithetical types. The first is the imperial type, the destroyer, the overreacher, the cosmopolitan, the dynamo. The second type is the yeoman. The yeoman rises early. His hours are ruled, not by the time clock in an office, but by planting and harvesting, sunrise and sunset. "Half clodhopper, half boardschool prig"—that is Forster's definition of the yeoman. He is "England's hope." The yeoman is, he believes, the true adversary of the imperial type. Only let him breed and the imperial will die out. England will see a new day of glory. He is hoping that Helen's son, the son of Leonard Bast, inheritor of Wilcox money and Schlegel culture, living close to the land, will be the new Englishman of the future. Forster's yeoman is no hippie or yippie. Nor is he a dropout or a cultural revolutionary. He is a working farmer who reads Shelley in the evening.

It is Forster's crippling defect that he is unable to imagine revolutionary alternatives. He cannot define the arch opponent of the imperialist. Because the yeoman is a domestic animal, close to the English soil and local traditions, Forster sees him as the opponent of the imperialist. But the yeoman spirit did not defeat the empire. Kipling's yeoman fought for England in the trenches during World War I. It was not British farm boys who destroyed British imperialism. In *Howards*

End Forster does not recognize that the imperial type is opposed most fiercely by the international type. Forster dislikes the empire. In its place he offers love of England. He does not want to force antagonisms or a confrontation. He wants people to connect, not fight. He does not want to fight the imperial type till death. He tolerates him. Forster accepts, he never protests. The spirit of patriotism rises and bubbles over in this passage:

> If one wanted to show a foreigner England, perhaps the wisest course would be to take him to the final section of the Purbeck Hills, and stand him on the summit . . . How many villages appear in this view! How many castles! . . How many ships, railways, and roads! What incredible variety of men working beneath that lucent sky to what final end! The reason fails, like a wave on the Swanage beach; the imagination swells, spreads and deepens, until it becomes geographic and encircles England.

There's no room for criticism here. It was this English attitude which made Conrad shudder. "An early Victorian . . . sentimentalist, looking out of an upstairs window . . . at a street—perhaps Fleet Street itself—full of people, is reported," Conrad writes, "to have wept for joy at seeing so much life." Forster's vision of "the incredible variety of men working" beneath the English sky brings tears to his eyes. Conrad went on to note that the "arcadian tears, this facile emotion worthy of the golden age comes to us from the past, with solemn approval, after the close of the Napoleonic Wars and before the series of sanguinary surprises held in reserve by the nineteenth century for our hopeful grandfathers." Forster's tears of innocence and joy are embarrassing, for they reveal his historical naïveté. While England and the whole world was in crisis, moving toward World War I, he intuited none of it. He has an incredible blindness to reality. The Wilcoxes are imperialists and are responsible for World War I. But Forster does not see British complicity in the imperial catastrophe of 1914. They escape untouched by any deep, penetrating criticism. D. H. Lawrence was right when in 1922 he told E. M. Forster, "you *did* make a nearly deadly mistake glorifying those *business* people in *Howards End*. Business is no good." Forster's liberalism was barren in 1910 because he was reconciled to the Wilcoxes, to the financial interests that created World War I. The Schlegel sisters, his heroines, accept limitations. The best we can expect, Forster says, is rich people who are imaginative and kind, who respect the personal life, and yet reach out to the infinite. The feminist movement, the struggle for women's rights, had thrown up many brave, intelligent fighting women in the years before World War I, but Forster did not tap that source of political vitality. He tries to co-opt that movement by presenting the Schlegels as his heroines. He thinks he is celebrating women through the Schlegels by making them sensitive, well-educated and imaginative. But he only maintains the same stereotypes women have always been cast in. His men are stereotypes too. He contrasts practical men with impractical women and diminishes the limits of both men and women. "Only connect" is a feeble cry. "Come together" would be more forceful. "Seize the time" is beyond Forster's comprehension.

II. EXPLOSION

Howards End is a throwback, a modern relic. History changes, art stands still, Forster says. That is simply not true. Everything changes, including art. *Howards End* is reactionary, counterrevolutionary in content and form. If we want to tangle with English society, English classes, thought and feeling, we have to go to Lawrence's *Women in Love*. This novel, written during World War I but not published until 1920, rips apart the society and the culture Forster glues together. Lawrence shows us a civilization in crisis, the frenetic existence of bourgeois man and bourgeois woman. Men and women clawing at each other. He takes us on a death trip, and then puts us on the road to life. Forster offers us the Schlegel sisters, the Wilcoxes, Leonard Bast. Lawrence throws down two artistic, intellectual sisters: Ursula and Gudrun; a business family in the Criches, a lower-middle-class man named Loerke and a route to the future in Birkin and Ursula. Lawrence does not see a coming-together here and now. No, he sees a smash-up, a crack-up; life going on, creation unstoppable, but not in this, its present, form. His book is totally revolutionary—a new book for a new age. In *Howards End* we are in the world of Jane Austen. *Women in Love* is futuristic. It has plasticity of form. *Howards End* is a house; the characters go in and out of its doors, look out its windows, sit in its rooms. *Women in Love* surrounds us; we walk about in it; we live in one crisis after another. There is Gerald Crich on horseback as a railway train steams by; Gerald Crich swimming in the lake; Crich and Birkin wrestling; in the morning a group of men walking around the statue of a primitive woman in labor; Birkin making love to Ursula in his car; Birkin throwing stones into a pond at night to shatter the image of the moon; Ursula and Gudrun confronting a bull on an island; Gudrun, Ursula, Birkin and Gerald in the snow-white mountains. From all of these scenes, out of the flatness of the page, the words lying still, there emerges a sense of sculpture, of dimensions. It is not a traditional narrative we read. Isolated pockets of time are strung together; images of eternity are planted in twentieth-century England. Lawrence stabs at the tension, the brutality, the cold hardness of modern life. He penetrates to the heart of power, the warfare in English society. He wants not delicate form, not a series of arabesques, but a rough harshness of unfinished stone, like Michelangelo's bound slaves. Lawrence knows what he is about, working with his hammer and chisel on the stone. He wants to stay close to his raw material, not to transform it beyond recognition, not to create an object of art beyond life. Lawrence tears apart Loerke's theory that art is autotelic. Loerke describes one of his paintings:

> It is a work of art, it is a picture of nothing, of absolutely nothing. It has nothing to do with anything but itself, it has no relation with the everyday world of this and other, there is no connection between them, absolutely none, they are two different and distinct planes of existence, and to translate one into the other is worse than foolish, it is a darkening of all counsel, a making confusion everywhere. Do you see, you *must not* confuse the relative work of action with the absolute work of art. That you *must not do*.

Very much like one of Forster's own pronouncements.

Women in Love presents a battle between Gudrun and Gerald. Gerald, the industrial magnate, explorer in the Amazon, owner of a coal mine, cursed with the mark of Cain, the blood of his own dead brother on his hands. A philistine, hating the primitive, fearing his own body. He is force itself, pushing himself, the coal miners, Gudrun. Gudrun, the artist, the bohemian; a modern woman in her bright-colored stockings, unfettered by social conventions; a cruel, cutting face. Two powers colliding in space. Coexistence is impossible. Emptiness. Sex through domination, domination through sex. Lawrence knows that art does not rest on money, that aesthetic young ladies and practical businessmen are not the basis for the England of the future.

In Forster there is no sex. His men and women do not hunger for each other; nor do they notice each other's bodies, or caress each other's limbs. They do not probe, do not do it in the road. No one has an orgasm. All dusty, no wetness. Lawrence drags in naked bodies. That is his revolution: people making love, touching, kissing, coming. Passion, visceral sensations. Lawrence makes us feel the connection between Gerald's power as a capitalist and his power as a man over women. He exploits the miners and degrades Gudrun; he dehumanizes. But he is overthrown.

Lawrence was a male chauvinist. Man, not woman, is at the center of his universe. The phallus has power. The secret is in man's loins. This is the holy litany he sings, singing the male body electric, the almighty phallus. But in *Women in Love* Lawrence strives to break that; he builds a new arena for man and woman, between Birkin and Ursula. He looks for equality, not the male sun worshiped by the lesser female moon revolving around it. Two separate, equal stars, held fast by each other, neither one dominated by the other.

Gerald Crich's power, political and sexual, is unenviable. Lawrence does not idealize the industrial magnate. Lawrence does not portray him as kind or lovable. Crich is the twentieth-century capitalist. As Lawrence saw him, he is unlike his nineteenth-century ancestor, who exploited his workers but at the same time believed in Christian charity. Crich wants only efficiency, a well-run, impersonal industry with modernized techniques. And the miners admire him; they are less hostile toward him than toward the nineteenth-century capitalist.

Nothing salvageable from this old world—that is Lawrence's view. England dying, the modern world rotting. Crich dies in the Alps—a suicide, but also defeated by Gudrun. She is his murderer. We hear time ticking away in the book, time running out. Lawrence's image of the world is of a time bomb ticking away. *Tick-tock, tick-tock, tick-tock.* Eternal boredom on the face of this old clock. An explosion at hand. Loerke and Gudrun "dream of the destruction of the world by a ridiculous catastrophe of man's invention: a man invented such a perfect explosive that it blew the earth in two, and the two halves set off in different directions through space." The world does end, the world Forster knew, the England of the nineteenth century. There is no linking of hands in joy and family peace in *Women in Love.* Yet it is fundamentally a more optimistic book than *Howards End.*

Because we cannot swallow the optimism of *Howards End*. It is too sugary. It is not the future we want. Lawrence's optimism rests in a world Forster never entered. Lawrence feels that the creative energy will never stop. If man destroys himself, destroys civilization, that is the end of man, but it is not the end of life or creation. Lawrence is confident that there will be a new species, new races. It is a courageous ending. A brave leap into the future. Lawrence is ready to lose everything, throw it all away if it is rotten and start anew. Forster accepted the old Victorian world, the old form of the Victorian novel. He dusts an old house, puts on a new coat of paint, dresses up a troupe of old actors. We can see the wrinkles beneath the make-up, the cracks beneath the shiny paint. Lawrence's earth is cracking, splitting down the middle. Cities topple. The industrial magnates fall into the deep crevices of the earth, never to rise again. There is tragedy here—men cannot be brothers in this world, Lawrence says to us, but men and women can be lovers, can wander on the plains of the earth to create a new civilization.

Women in Love discards old plots, old characters, old settings. When the world is ending, Lawrence believed, you must reject the old forms. After you close *Women in Love* you feel you are looking at one of Michelangelo's bound slaves. There is the figure of a man not yet alive, but struggling to be born, to emerge from the lifeless stone, to speak as no man has ever spoken before and to lead us into places no man has yet been. New men on a new earth. A lot better than Helen Schlegel's son sitting in a hayfield.

14

↑ ↑ ↑ ↑ ↑ ↑ ↑

Trips East

I. A PASSAGE TO INDIA

E. M. Forster went East three times: to Egypt during World War I and to India twice, in 1912 and 1921. His East is neither sensuous nor exotic; it is not beauty in evil. Nor is it the colonial world of Pierre Loti or Flaubert, of dark-skinned courtesans in ornate, silk-curtained boudoirs. There are no aphrodisiacs here, no opium dens, no hashish. Pleasure in all its decadent trappings is absent from Forster's India. No cities like Lawrence Durrell's Alexandria; we are never chased by eleven-year-old prostitutes; there is no Eastern woman whose haunting beauty snares us, holds us, drives us mad with lust and love. Forster's East drives him away from his body. The physical becomes more repulsive.

There are no gurus, no wise men. He did not go East to get his head together, purify his soul or strip away the over-refinements of the West. It is not a magical mystery tour. No, there is no simplicity in Forster's India, no escape from civilized mess. This is not the East of Hermann Hesse; we will find no sacred parables in Forster's passage. This passage is not a pilgrimage. We do not go with Siddhartha on his trek. There is no religious truth or spiritual essence to be picked up on the roads of Forster's India. India only scrambles his brains.

Forster's East is not Red. In modern fiction and legend China has always figured as the seat of revolution: Malraux's terrorists in *Man's Fate* and Brecht's communists in *The Measures Taken.* There is no Indian Mao, no Indian long march, no Indian proletarian cultural revolution. But India, too, has had its mutinies, insurrections, dictators and wars. Forster does not travel from Europe to India to find politics. There are colonial civil servants, the club, all of Kipling's characters and settings, but they are peripheral. He is not concerned with the mind of the colonial administrator, the sahib's job. And Forster sees few possibilities for art in the Gandhi resistance movement. He does not want to write about colonial liberation struggles in the East. Forster's India is something else.

Forster's India is an enigma. A hundred Indians, a million Indias. Diversity. Puzzling. Forster is uncertain what to make of this subcontinent. It is chaotic, confusing, irritating. Nothing ruled out in clear lines, with sharp boundaries. Instead, everything sliding off into everything else. Hindus, Muslims, Buddhists, Jains, Christians, Brahmans, Untouchables. The catalog of Indian castes, religions and sects would stretch around the globe; like a list from a rummage sale. The passage to India is a passage to the unmeasured, to the infinite. India is flat—a vast, flat land, a wasteland, where nothing seems more significant than anything else. Everything except the extraordinary Marabar Caves. They stick up, stick out, higher than the rest; especially important. Mostly, life slumbers. It is like being in the larval stage of a cocoon forever, or like waiting for sunrise, for the glorious sun to appear on a summer morning. But in India when the cocoon bursts an ugly crawling creature emerges. When the sun rises there is no glory, just unbearable heat, glare, dryness, lifelessness. The sun king is mercilessly cruel. India always promising, always hinting, always failing to fulfill the promise or reveal the secret.

This is Forster's own vision, and also the vision of his close friend G. Lowes Dickinson. Dickinson "came to feel that the main cleavage in civilization lies not between East and West but between India and the rest of the world." In 1912 Dickinson wrote of his reaction to India:

> The barrier on both sides of incomprehension is almost impassable . . . Indian art, Indian religion, Indian society, is alien and unsympathetic to me. I have no sense of superiority about it, but one of estrangement. What indeed is there or can there be in common between the tradition of Greece and that of India?

Dickinson's ideas are wedged into the novel. He found in *A Passage to India* what he had long whispered into Forster's ears, and in 1926 he wrote to tell him:

> The theme—the incompatability of Indians and English—is done as perhaps only you could do it—with the power of understanding both sides.

A Passage to India is divided into three sections entitled "Mosque," "Cave," "Temple." The mosque is unexceptional, unextraordinary. "It embodies no crisis," Forster wrote of it in his essay "The Mosque" (1920). It is indeterminate, vague. It is the place where East meets West, a place of duality. The sky arching over the mosque is not threatening, alien or intimidating. The mosque is the world of Islam. The cave is the world before man, before any religion. The Buddha did not stop here, nor did Allah or Christ. In the caves you come face-to-face with the oldest thing in the world; you meet something you can meet nowhere else. It is nothing you can see, feel or touch. In the caves there is nothingness; it is Forster's equivalent of W. B. Yeats's "rough beast" emerging in the second coming. Unity is impossible in the cave. Opposites remain separate, distinct, irreconcilable. The cave is extraordinary, and the extraordinary events of the cave outweigh everything else. It is evil. On his first trip to India Forster visited caves. He felt they were the palace of the devil. "They are Satan's masterpieces to terrify others," he wrote. East and West do not connect—they move apart to opposite ends of the earth. It is a blowup between the races. Adela Quested, a white English girl, thinks she has been sexually molested by a Brown-skinned man. Mrs. Moore, Forster's sibyl, a wise old lady, passes through the cave and emerges with the "horror of the universe and its smallness" stamped on her consciousness.

In *Howards End* when the Schlegel sisters listen to Beethoven's Fifth Symphony they see goblins. And the goblins suggest to them "panic and emptiness"; the goblins make you feel "that there was no such thing as splendour or heroism in the world." But Forster notes that the Fifth Symphony ends with "gusts of splendour, the heroism, the youth, the magnificence of life and of death . . . amid the vast roarings of a superhuman joy." There are brief moments of panic and emptiness in *Howards End,* but they are submerged in the orchestral sounds of joy and laughter. We do not close the book with the feeling that emptiness and panic will meet us around the next corner. We feel that we have left the goblins far behind us at the last intersection. But in *A Passage to India* we always return to the cave. We know that the disillusionment and nothingness of the cave will return to us, that they are always there. In the cave there is an echo. Anything and everything you say is bounced back to you, and no matter what you say, the answer is always the same. The sounds of love, of joy, of farting, the squeaking of new shoes—all return the identical, monotonous noise—*bou-oum*. Echoes of despair and disillusionment always come back to you; you cannot stop the echo. Man is powerless to halt the sounds of zero. Traditionally, in literature, an echo suggests man's affinity with nature. In Forster's early novels and short stories his heroes, sheltered in dells in the pastoral woods, cry out and are answered by the friendly spirits of nature. But in *A Passage to India* the echo says that man is alone in the universe. There is no kindred spirit to reply.

Forster wants a universe with heaven and hell, God and the devil, zones of good and evil; he wants to look up into the night sky and recognize the constellations of the lion, the goat, the scorpion, the fish. This is the universe of the Greeks, the universe of the ancient world of classicism, of order and category. But in India you look up into the sky and there is only sky; there are no friendly forms or faces. Here you are not at home in the universe. The sky does not reflect the images in your head or the things about you. It is not familiar. Forever and ever there is the dome of the sky: blue, deep blue, arch over arch over arch, extending backward, upward infinitely. No limits to the universe. You never reach the last arch, the final courtyard, the wall at the end of the road.

In many ways Forster's cave is like Conrad's gulf. In the cave and the gulf man is estranged from his fellow-man; he is alienated from the world of nature. The cave is nightmare. It is the world Forster lives in after the muddy trenches of Verdun, the echoing guns in Belgium, the shock of Indian horror. It is the despair after the collapse of the civilization he was confident and optimistic about in *Howards End*. The cave shatters Howards End; the house is not left standing on the face of the earth. Conrad handles terror and despair with less panic than Forster. It is part of his everyday world. Alienation, the clash of polar extremities, are there in Costaguana twenty-four hours a day. Conrad's extraordinary is contained in the ordinary. For Forster the extraordinary comes from outside, like a monster from the deep lagoon. It is a quirk of nature which can not be explained. *Nostromo* begins and ends with descriptions of the gulf; the dark gulf is at the center of the novel. "Except for the Marabar Caves —and they are twenty miles off—the city of Chandrapore presents nothing extraordinary": this is the first sentence in *A Passage to India*. The caves are there from the start. The word extraordinary bobs up everywhere on the surface of the novel. But the extraordinary caves are dropped on us from a great height. We feel Forster pushing his characters toward and into the caves, like a guide on a tour hurrying a crowd through a museum to get to the main exhibit. And then he wants to get them out the exit as soon as possible. The bus will carry them away, on to the next tourist attraction. Just before they go out the back door he reminds them of the highlights of their visit. The gulf is a gulf is a gulf. The cave is an idea, an idea about man and man, man and the universe. It is not that there are no ideas in *Nostromo;* there are complex ideas. *Nostromo* is a moral tale, but the ideas and the morals are embodied in the dramatic conflicts. Forster brings his tourists to the cave and then gives them a lecture. He wants to tell us he is pessimistic, disillusioned, in order to articulate and thereby release the burden he carries. But it gets the better of him. We know precisely what happens in the dark gulf with Nostromo and Decoud. But we never know precisely what happens in the cave with Aziz and Miss Quested. The one thing which upset G. Lowes Dickinson about the novel was Forster's evasion of the events in the cave. He teases the reader, plays a game.

Within the cave, illusion reigns. Mrs. Moore smells an odd odor, hears a weird echo, feels the touch of something strange. She believes that while "everything exists, nothing has value." From every source the report is the same; man's senses carry back no pleasure, only the same monotonous, dulled, nowhere news. It is the modern condition as Forster sees it.

For British writers, the discovery of alienation was parallel to the discovery of the colonial world. British writers sailed into the Third World and struck the rock of alienation. Isolation meant the isolation of white men among Brown men and Black men. It meant disbarment from civilization, Christianity, capitalism. The Englishman was divided from everything he had been and had been educated to be. His white skin was an encumbrance. Imperialism's bright shield, its cover of romanticism, had cracked and dissolved. The myth of the romantic East, the sacred Orient, mystical India, was worm-infested, rotten at its core. The seed of romanticism was planted along with the first colonial outposts, with the seeds of empire, and the vines of romanticism wrapped around the columns of imperial exploitation—like one of the old white Southern colonial mansions built on slave labor but smoothed over by marble, ivory, silks and satins.

The title for Forster's novel comes from Walt Whitman's poem "Passage to India." Whitman's is a voyage in fact, a celebration of the material world of machines, and also a spiritual passage, a passage to infinity. Whitman links the passage on the steamship with the passage of the mind. But Forster's passage does not soar that high. Forster sinks Whitman's optimism, unity and joy in the Indian Ocean. *A Passage to India* is a death elegy to nineteenth-century romanticism.

The third section of the novel is entitled "Temple." It is the world of Hinduism. In the temple nothing is excluded. It is a muddle of things, but in the muddle there is a mystery. In the confusion there is a reverberation of truth. The third part of the book describes the Krishna festival, the "strangest and strongest Indian experience ever granted me," Forster wrote. The festival celebrates the birth of the god. In a Hindu temple Forster feels that beauty and time are frustrated; the viewer is not pleased by its shape. But Forster noted that when we "care . . . for truth alone then the Indian temple exerts its power." In 1915 he had written that Hinduism "stripped of its local trappings, of its hundred-handed gods, and monkeys and bulls and snakes, and twice-born . . . preaches the doctrine of unity." Krishna's true disciples shout both, I am different from everybody else, and I am the same as everybody else. Forster makes Hinduism the religion for alienated man. It is unlike Christianity or Buddhism or Islamism in that it does not ask man "to meet his god congregationally." Each individual man in isolation, surrounded by muddle, can meet his own individual god, can participate in the mystery. Forster's Hinduism is a metaphor for the universe. Hinduism enables him to survive in a chaotic universe. We eat of the cake of chaos and swallow the wafer of unity. In the temple there is a mystical coming-together of East and West. Professor Godbole, the Brahman, communicates with the dead Mrs. Moore.

Godbole is a comic mystic. He is an amusing sight, with his turban that looks like purple macaroni and his socks with clocks. "The clocks matched the turban, and his whole appearance suggested harmony—as if he had reconciled the products of East and West, mental as well as physical, and could never be discomposed." Godbole is never defeated, never cynical. He is a rock. He never tires of singing, of calling for Krishna to "come, come, come." Krishna, God the Friend, never comes; man is alone, but he does not despair. He continues to say, "come, come, come." God the Friend is not present. Man is not together with his fellow-man. But the failure of anything or anyone to be present does not imply its absence, or mean that solitude is man's eternal sentence. It is the only comfort Forster can honestly salvage from a shipwrecked civilization.

India made Forster more concerned with philosophical questions, with *being* and *nothingness*. But his social consciousness was also intensified. *A Passage to India* is about the amity and enmity between Dr. Aziz, the Muslim, and Mr. Fielding, the English schoolmaster. Dr. Aziz is the first Indian to figure as a major character in an English novel. He is not like one of Wilkie Collins's Indians on the quest for a stolen moonstone, nor is he like one of Thackeray's rajahs making a tour of England. They are incidental figures. Aziz is a new man in the cast of characters; an Adam on the Indian stage. Aziz is based on Forster's Indian friend Syed Ross Masood. *A Passage to India* is dedicated to Masood "and to the seventeen years of our friendship." Aziz is a poet, a doctor, a romantic; he is suspicious, hospitable, charming. Fielding is like Forster himself, an Englishman flung out on the shores of India. He is an intellectual who believes in good will, culture, the virtues of private conversation, dialogues between men of different races and creeds. Fielding is colder and more rational than the warm, passionate Aziz. Their friendship builds under crisis. When Aziz is charged with sexually molesting Adela Quested in the cave, Fielding is forced to take sides. He turns his back on Anglo-India and defends Aziz. To the Anglo-Indians he is a traitor. To the Indians he is a true friend. "If I had to choose between betraying my country and betraying my friend," Forster once wrote, "I hope I should have the guts to betray my country." Of all his statements this is the most frequently quoted by Indians. To them it meant standing fast with Indians and cutting ties with England. Fielding does just that. He has a choice of betraying the empire or of betraying Aziz, and he refuses to let Aziz hang.

Forster's belief in personal relations, the private conversation, is broken by India. All private relations in India are public. Aziz is always a Muslim, Godbole a Hindu, Fielding an Englishman. When one individual relates to another he relates as an Easterner to a Westerner, a Christian to a Muslim, or a Muslim to a Hindu. Take this scene: Aziz is at Fielding's home, and Fielding is dressing for the tea they are both to share with Mrs. Moore, Miss Quested and Professor Godbole. Fielding breaks his last collar stud, and Aziz, telling Fielding that he has an extra one, takes off his own and offers it to him. Forster's personal relations at work. But he expands the scene so that we have a larger, more complex view of the two men. Here is a conversation between Aziz and Fielding which brings out the politics of colonialism, the conflicts between the Indian and the Englishman, and reveals Aziz's joy, spontaneity and honesty:

> "Why in hell does one wear collars at all?" grumbled Fielding as he bent his neck.
> "We wear them to pass the Police."
> "What's that?"
> "If I'm biking in English dress-starch collar, hat with ditch —they take no notice. When I wear a fez, they cry, 'Your camp's out!' Lord Curzon did not consider this when he urged natives of India to retain their picturesque costumes . . . Sometimes I shut my eyes and dream I have splendid clothes again and am riding into battle behind Alamgir. Mr. Fielding, must not India have been beautiful then, with the Mogul Empire at its height and Alamgir reigning at Delhi upon the Peacock throne?'

Personal relations alone are incapable of resolving the conflicts between England and India. Early in the novel Forster says of Mrs. Moore's son, a latter-day version of a Kipling colonial administrator, "one touch of regret—not the canny substitute but the true regret from the heart—would have made him a different man, and the British Empire a different institution." In a tiny corner of his heart Forster believes that idea, but the book does not communicate this feeling to us. In 1922, two years before *A Passage to India* was published, Forster wrote in his essay "Reflections in India":

> . . . though friendship between individuals will continue and courtesies between high officials increase, there is little hope of spontaneous intercourse between the two races.

Forster distinguishes between his own seventeen-year friendship with Syed Ross Masood and the drying-up of the friendship between Aziz and Fielding. Aziz and Fielding cannot be friends because there is a British Empire. An Indian and an Englishman cannot be brothers while the English control India. For Indians, this has been the most important thrust of *A Passage to India.* Mulk Raj Anand, the Indian novelist, addressing Forster, wrote of *A Passage to India:*

> You wished to say one important thing: that there could be no friendship between Indians and Englishmen until Indians were free.

At the end of the novel Fielding and Aziz are "friends again, yet aware that they could meet no more." They have been polarized. Aziz is a nationalist. He is determined to drive the English out of India, to free Indians from imperial rule. "Down with the English," he shouts. Fielding has retreated to defend British rule; India without the English, he says, will be a muddled land. Indians are children. In the thick of the political fight to accord Aziz justice, the Indian and the Englishman are comrades. But when the fight is over and Aziz is free, Fielding is not ready to renounce England for the colonial people, and when it becomes clear that he is not ready to join Aziz in the nationalist movement, their friendship cools. Suspicion sets in. At the trial Aziz's acquittal is ambiguous. It is a political victory for the Indians, a defeat for the English, but it is not a political battle—a "Free Aziz" campaign—which brings justice. No, it is Mrs. Moore who does it. It is a victory for mysticism. The supernatural influence of Mrs. Moore recalls to Adela what actually happened in the cave. She remembers that Aziz never touched her, and she tells the judge just that. It is unbelievable. Brown men charged with molesting white women were, in Forster's day, castrated or hanged. That is what happens in Faulkner's South. The acquittal of Aziz is a fairy-tale ending. Mrs. Moore is the good fairy.

The ending of *A Passage to India* is flat. The rhetorical flourishes do not ring true. Aziz and Fielding have their parting shots at each other. Aziz says, "We shall drive every blasted Englishman into the sea . . ." He half-kisses Fielding, and concludes:

> "You and I shall be friends."
> "Why can't we be friends now?" said the other, holding him affectionately.
> "It's what I want. It's what you want."
> But the horses didn't want it—they swerved apart; the earth didn't want it, sending up rocks through which riders must pass single file; the temples, the tank, the jail, the palace, the birds, the carrion, the Guest House, that came into view as they issued from the gap and saw Mau beneath: they didn't want it, they said in their hundred voices, "No, not yet," and the sky said, "No, not there."

Forster writes well of the extremes in a world without man, of the gap between earth and sky. His images are all carefully chosen to gather up the main threads of the novel. We have a last glimpse of India, of the India of a hundred voices, a final catalog of the land of muddle. There can be no friendship, no unity of couples, because man is alone, forced to pass in single file. But the whole passage makes it seem that it is in the nature of things that Aziz and Fielding can not be friends. In this concluding passage Forster mentions temple, jail and palace—the social institutions. They prevent the coming-together of East and West. Organized society has seen to it that the Englishman and the Indian cannot be comrades. But the weight of the conclusion, of the entire book, is that earth and sky have a weightier voice in this matter. Man's efforts are futile in the context of the infinite Indian universe.

The middle section of the novel, "Caves," shows man alone in the universe—in the caves—and also man in society, in the courtroom. Forster pours all of his energy into the scene in the cave. The scene in the court is disappointing. Forster is much more excited by the image of man in the cave, representing a vision of the human condition, than the social conditions, the conflicts between the colonizers and the colonized. Caves rather than courts hold Forster's imagination. So *A Passage to India* misleads us when Forster suggests that the sky and the earth say no to the coming-together of a white man and a Brown man. It is a social system, colonialism, which says no, not now, not here. But Forster does not believe that imperialism as a system, that the British Empire, is evil and must be abolished. He wants India to be independent, but he is not an advocate of national liberation struggles, of revolutionary violence to achieve independence. No, he advocates the action of individual men to improve things. But he does have the humane intelligence to understand that under imperialism a friendship between colonized and colonizers cannot be a relationship between equals.

Forster's message has been articulated by radical Americans in the 1960s. National liberation for Blacks, equality between Blacks and whites, must be achieved before white men and Black men can be friends. Amerika spoke of friendship, but exploited and oppressed her Black population. It is necessary to end the exploitation and oppression in order to make friendship a reality.

In *A Passage to India* Forster is in an odd position. His creed of personal relations is tattered. He knows that individual efforts, the "one touch of regret," will not really change the empire for the better. Yet he has not become a partisan of revolution. Forster sees the inadequacy of his own liberalism, but is not ready to espouse communism. Under these circumstances there is an insubstantiality about his social position. He is thrown into a ring of philosophical and metaphysical speculation. He is fixated on the gap between man and the sky. He wants to reach an accommodation with infinity, to come to terms with the universe, but the universe says no. The only thing that can help is a mystical old lady named Mrs. Moore.

A Passage to India is Forster's finest novel. But it is a sad work. A sense of disappointment pervades its pages. A brief conversation between Fielding and Miss Quested and a description by Fielding crystallize this sentiment:

> Adela: "All these personal relations we try to live by are temporary."
> Fielding: "We are subdued to what we work in . . . I want to go on living a bit."
> Adela: "So do I."
> Forster: A friendliness, as of dwarfs shaking hands, was in the air. Both man and woman were at the height of their powers—sensible, honest, even subtle. They spoke the same language, and held the same opinions, and the variety of age and sex did not divide them. Yet they were dissatisfied.

India is the mirror of Forster's mind; his image of the modern world, a world of not here and not now. Forster does not say never, but he says not today. No heroism, no coming-together of white and Brown, no harmony with the universe. *A Passage to India* is a reflection of the changes World War I and the conflicts of the Third World wrought in Forster. *A Passage to India* is the product of a world and a mind unlike that which brought *Howards End* into existence. In place of the harmonies and reconciliations of *Howards End* are the harsh echoes, the infinite fissures of *A Passage to India.* At the end of *Howards End* the English middle class is solidified, England is bound together, the liberal aesthetes join the conservative businessmen. At the end of *A Passage to India* the differences between races and civilizations continue, unreconciled. Man is still out of harmony with his world, still alienated from his own self. But there is the possibility of a future coming-together. *Howards End* is the world before the discovery of India. *A Passage to India* marks the return from the journey to the East.

Forster's passage has been the trip of most liberal intellectuals. After a glimpse of Third World, life in the imperial nation is not the same for him. *A Passage to India* is a triumph. It got written. Forster had to struggle for a long time to bring it into existence. The encouragement of his old Bloomsbury friend Leonard Woolf was decisive. But after *A Passage to India* Forster published no other novels. He tried, but nothing clicked. World War I and India cleared a whole new space, but it also destroyed Forster. *A Passage to India* is the last statement of the last of a vanishing breed. The world which he had known and loved, the world in which his imagination thrived, no longer existed. He found the world foreign, unmalleable. The currency of the world had changed. Forster was unable to cash his old imperial coins in for the coins of the new century.

II. THE NEAR AND THE FAR

A Passage to India has been overrated. What is needed now is a rediscovery of L. H. Myers's *The Near and the Far*. In the 1930s and 1940s Myers and Forster were frequently placed side by side, compared and contrasted. Myers came from an aristocratic family, attended Eton and Cambridge, passed through Bloomsbury, went to Ceylon, knew Forster and the Woolfs, dabbled in mysticism. But Myers was a rebel from Bloomsbury. In the Camp in *The Near and the Far* he condemns London's aesthetes. He rejects the humanism of G. Lowes Dickinson and Forster. In his novel, in the character of Smith, he cuts up Dickinson and takes a few swipes at Forster, too. Myers scorns their admiration for ancient Greece. As he sees them, they unwittingly find themselves in the same boat with the arch criminals. Myers's novel is set in India, but it is unlike any India found in Forster's or Kipling's works.

In 1935 Q. D. Leavis wrote that Myers's novel "makes even so mature and thoughtful a work as *A Passage to India* look provincial." For a time Q. D. Leavis and F. R. Leavis praised Myers. But they quickly dropped him. He was too thoroughgoing a revolutionary in art and politics for them. Their failure to sustain their initial appreciation of Myers, their withdrawal of support, is the clearest and most decisive example of the severe limitations of *Scrutiny*. Myers was the finest English novelist of the 1930s and 1940s. After Lawrence it is he who breaks with the old and remakes the house of fiction. In turning their backs on Myers, F. R. and Q. D. Leavis helped to bury the single most important creative genius of their day. It is time he was brought back to life.

L. H. Myers's *The Near and the Far* is set in sixteenth-century India. It is a journey in time, a voyage through space, from here to there, from this time to that time, from the world there and then to the world here and now. The route is from near to far, the inner to the outer, the past to the present, and back again on all three tracks. *The Near and the Far,* Myers wrote, is "not a historical novel . . . I have done what I liked with history and geography, as well as with manners and customs." And he goes on to say that

> In choosing sixteenth-century India as a setting, my object was to carry the reader out of our familiar world into one where I could—without doing violence to his sense of reality—give prominence to certain chosen aspects of human life and illustrate their significance. It has certainly not been my intention to set aside the social and ethical problems that force themselves upon us at the present time. On the contrary my hope has been that we might view them better from the distant vantage ground of an imaginary world.

The novel is a voyage into human consciousness. Myers's characters scrutinize their motives, their situations, their values. They are all intensely aware of the contradiction between *seeing* and *being*. In the opening scene we met Jali, the central character, the character closest to Myers himself. Jali's story is Myers's autobiography. Jali is a small boy. It is evening. He is lonely, separated from his parents, unable to sleep, thinking about who he is, who he will become, where he stands in the universe. The young Jali, gazing at the two deserts—the nearer and the farther—identifies with the whole world about him:

> Little Prince Jali stepped on to the balcony and looked down upon the plain in awe. It was true that from the tower of his father's palace at home there was an even wider view; but that view was familiar, this one was full of mystery. The wall of this strange palace went down and down, until it merged into the sweeping side of the fort; the fort itself crowned the summit of a hill; and the bare rock of the hill continued a precipitous descent down into the River Jumna. The red glitter of sunset lay upon the river; across the water shady groves alternated with sun-swept patches of millet and corn; beyond stretched the desert.

Then he watches a kite "balancing in strained immobility," and, with a child's naïveté and inquisitiveness, wonders: "What was the kite thinking about? What held it motionless and intent, in that particular place?" He sees a small plant growing out of a crack in the palace wall. It is bent by a cool breeze. Suddenly he sees a snake gliding along the gutter, and he sympathizes with the snake too. He understands "what the snake was feeling. He entered into its cold, narrow intelligence and shared its angry perplexity. Its movements were cramped, its advance difficult, it was in constant danger of slipping over the edge." The snake lunges at the little plant, and in coiling itself for the strike, loses its balance, falls and is killed.

Myers pulls us into Jali's thoughts. Our mind spins around and around the snake and the plant. "The world, unquestionably, was a place of mystery and terror," Myers writes, following Jali's inner monologue. "This was revealed in the writhing of the crippled snake, in the jaunty waving of the innocent plant in the wind, in the bright-eyed intentness of the hovering kite, in the terrible numerousness of living beings, both animal and human, all separate, all alone, all threatened by evil in ambush." At the conclusion of the novel Jali looks from the same balcony out at the plain and says, "here I stand once again, suspended between the past and the future." He has become a new Jali, with a new vision of things. The world about him has also changed, but he is, now, then and always, intensely conscious of the present moment, the gap between the past and the future, the separation of the near from the far.

Myers's universe vibrates at every point. Any and every object, large or small—a snake, a plant, a kite, an elephant, a whip—can and often does become charged with energy and power. Everything on the horizon, everything in the external world, is surrounded, possessed, dissected and digested by the imagination. Myers is concerned with the "correspondence between outward things and the inner landscape of the mind." He shows us Rajah Amar contemplating his retirement from the world, thinking about purity, sacrifice, the ideals of self-abnegation, but surrounded by perfumed, silk-clad, beautiful young women. The tension between his inner landscape and outer reality is explosive. And we also see Jali:

> . . . leaning back against the wall, with an absent gaze fixed upon the water-lilies, and all at once he found himself looking into a tiny eye that was staring straight into his. At first he thought it was a snake, but suddenly the creature gave a sharp movement which showed it to be a large newt. The scent of the lilies was again sending him into a lethargy, and again he felt as if Time were halting in its course . . . he felt the Present expand, and stagnate, and reflect everlastingness; only there was no foretaste of beatitude in this experience; it was, rather, an initiation into a state of living death. In this standstill of time some-

> thing seemed to be maturing but with a slowness that gave every moment the value of eternity.

Jali is at this moment with a beautiful and sinister young woman named Gunevati, who exists solely for pleasure. He is in love with her. She is ignorant and superstitious, betrays friends and enemies alike. But she has power because she knows that "even Rajahs and Emperors were males, and that as males they were simply complementary to her own lowly self. Great ladies, too, were women and as such had no secrets from her." Gunevati nervously and uncontrollably twitches her foot. She pushes Jali down on the couch, presses her lips against his. Jali's mind is spinning, his reasoning powers are in retreat. Myers moves from the objects in the room to the watcher's mind, and then to a realm where space and time can be smelled, touched and tasted. He captures moments of hallucination; the external world seems to disintegrate, and sounds and lights preside in the consciousness. His characters are often possessed by aphrodisiacs or hallucinogens; they hear, smell and see things of which others are unaware. Some seem to have extrasensory perceptions.

Gokal, an old sage and Jali's teacher, tells Rajah Amar an unusual story:

> . . . something outside the ordinary course of nature took place in the neighbourhood of your house that morning. I was not alone in feeling it . . . It was a morning of the hottest, brightest sunshine, as you know; every ripple on the lake, every leaf upon the trees, was sharp and clear; the face of nature . . . shivered and trembled as might its own reflection upon the surface of the lake. The thinness of the crust of tangible things, the emptiness of matter, the superficiality of appearances suddenly were revealed.

At that moment he and Jali hear the trumpeting of a mad elephant, and they are startled out of their trance. Jali's Uncle Hari is awakened from "dreaming fearful dreams."

Only a handful of people hear the trumpeting of the elephant. When they report what they have heard, no one believes them; they are told that they have had a mystical experience. But an elephant has in fact bellowed; it is close by and real enough to stomp a woman to death. To those who can read the signs of the future, the bellowing of the elephant is an indication of impending disaster. Myers feels that those men who probe the landscape of their own minds will be more attuned to the depths of the external world. They will hear the roar of mad elephants, the sounds of social doom, while others are comforted by the soft sounds of social harmony.

The novel is divided into two main sections. The first part is entitled "The Root and the Flower," the second part "The Pool of Vishnu." The most important scenes in "The Root and the Flower" take place in an artificial, plastic city which is built over a swamp and which is called both the "Pleasance of the Arts" and "The Camp." It is the world of evil and decadence, and it is governed by Prince Daniyal, one of the Emperor Akbar's two sons.

> The whole of the Camp . . . was built on a platform that stood in part over the water and in part over the marshy ground behind. All the gaieties of a popular pleasure-resort were to be found here, but they had all been slightly parodied and, as it were, denatured, to suit a subtler taste. Music was sounding in the air; a bright-looking throng were strolling or sitting about; some, under fantastically decorated awnings, were drinking snow-cooled beverages, some were watching jugglers and mountebanks, many were flocking to an arena where combats between various kinds of wild animals, including even snakes, had been announced. Everyone wore the brightest and most daring costumes.

In the Camp, art is deified, life denigrated. Homosexuality and lesbianism are the normal sexual patterns. Drugs, personal and sexual liberation, the avant-garde—this is the Camp. From a distance it appears attractive. Prince Jali gazes at it from afar as it shines

> . . . palely in a subdued light of its own. Pink and yellow, orange and violet, the paper lanterns made dim dots of colour on a frontage that was otherwise spectrally faint. In the midst of Nature's wilderness the Pleasance of the Arts lay perfect and complete, a little paradise of artifice and art, a small gem-like thought in an unthinking world.

Myers lures us into the pleasures of the Camp. As Jali moves nearer and nearer to its heart he discovers that it is artless, imperfect, incomplete. Paradise becomes hell.

The last scene in "The Root and the Flower" reveals the evil at the core of the Camp, and presents an act of muted defiance against that evil. It takes place on stage. There are four main actors, a group of minor court officials and attendants and a large white purring Persian cat. Daniyal directs the scene. He nervously paces back and forth, leaves the stage, reappears and juggles three colored cork balls. He is extremely tense because his brother Salim's army has attacked the Camp; the realm of art, leisure and affluence is no longer safe. The country is gored with civil war. The Prince has also just discovered that there are spies and saboteurs in his own ranks. The charming salons disappear and the Camp becomes a prison; the libertarian society becomes a fascist regime.

Gunevati sits silently in a corner, occasionally petting the Persian cat, which is curled up in her lap. Rajah Amar, who has favored Daniyal over Salim but has not decided whom he will support as the successor to the throne, waits impatiently to speak to the Prince. Daniyal tells the others a story. He describes how the Princess Lalita, his fiancée, met secretly at the Royal Hunting Ground with Hari, Jali's uncle. Lalita's horse knocks a man down, and as Daniyal explains

> . . . that man, as it happens, was none other than my dear brother Salim! You see, Salim and Gunevati and some other Vamacharis were on their way to a deserted pavilion, where they were going to have a little orgy together. Well! in the confusion of the accident poor dear Lalita dropped her riding whip, and Gunevati picked it up.

Daniyal treats the incident unhysterically. He acts silly even when describing incidents of crucial importance. More than a simple orgy was to have taken place at the Royal Hunting Ground. The Vamacharis, to whom Daniyal refers, are a religious sect. Salim is a Vamachari, and since it is an outlawed underground sect, in opposition to the state religion, it is a political crime to belong to it. It is a religious group at the center of a political crisis, celebrating its religious rites through sexual rituals. Gunevati is the Goddess of Passion, worshiped through sexual intercourse.

The incident which Daniyal describes is like the stone thrown into the pool, sending out ripples in all directions. It ties all the main characters together into a complex network. The whole of the novel is an unraveling of this event. Myers first offers us the outline of this mysterious incident, and as the story unfolds he assembles more and more of the pieces in the puzzle. The sapphire-studded riding whip, a token of Daniyal's affluence and brutality, is the most important clue in tracking down the hidden pieces. It passes from one hand to another, from Daniyal to Lalita to Gunevati to Mabun to Hari.

The action of the first part of the novel culminates here on the stage:

> All remained where they were; but the white cat, which had got up from Gunevati's lap, was yawning and stretching itself. It now came running across the floor, and, on reaching Daniyal, rubbed itself against his legs, causing him to miss one of the coloured balls. Then it threw itself down on the ground in front of him, lying on its back, and

> with a mew invited him to play with it. But Daniyal had frowned when the ball dropped, and now lifting the sole of his right foot, he placed it on the cat's head. Then, with a swift and smiling glance at his spectators, he slowly pressed his foot down. One after another the bones in the cat's head could be heard to crack, and, when this sound came, the Prince's eyes glanced for one smiling second into those of Gunevati. The cat's paws were beating the air; its body rose stiffly in an arc and then collapsed in spasms; a little pool of blood spread out upon the floor.

Rajah Amar now knows for sure that Daniyal is sinister, that he wants to make the world "a place of purposeless evil." Daniyal's evil is "pure cruelty." He pursues it for its own sake. Myers does not dignify evil. For him, evil acts are trivial acts. Amar knows that he has been morally tainted by his tacit approval of Daniyal, that he must sever all ties with him. He reaches for his sword, but before he can draw it out of his scabbard, a henchman knocks him unconscious. He has deliberated too long to be able to strike out successfully at the enemy.

In "The Pool of Vishnu" the imperial crisis is at hand; there is open warfare, violence, revolution. The conflict between Salim and Daniyal for control of the empire is intensified. "I have done my best to make the present volume," Myers wrote of "The Pool of Vishnu," "self-sufficient—a whole with its own symmetry." Many of the main characters in the first part appear again in central roles in the second part; others vanish. After Gunevati's tongue is cut out, she is executed. The blind Amar carries out his plans and joins a company of pilgrims, leaving behind his wife, his son, his palace. He is never seen or heard from again. A new group of characters—Móhan, Damayanti, and the guru—appear on the stage. The world they inhabit is very different from the Camp, which has been burnt to the ground. Palaces are under attack, peasants are starving, armies cross the Indian plains and engage in combat. The harshness and strife of this new world is suggested by the opening paragraph of "The Pool of Vishnu":

> There were three pools sunk in the white marble of the terrace; the water in them was black, and the westering sun put a glitter upon their darkness. The terrace itself rose out of the desert in serene and lonely beauty, its whiteness flushed to the pink of a sea-shell. Above, the windless sky was flecked with vultures; they wheeled and slanted, and at times they dropped. Beneath them moved a slow, dark trickle of humanity—a trickle pushing its way from horizon to horizon through the clogging, desert dust.

In "The Pool of Vishnu" the colors are stark blacks and whites. Men are minute figures against a backdrop of sky and earth. The land is parched, peasants are clothed in rags. India is a wasteland.

The few pockets of luxury and opulence are seen in contrast with poverty, oppression, brutality. Atop an elephant Mohan's father, a rajah, returns to his palace from a tiger hunt. The route he travels is "lined with the dying and the dead . . . the dead lay stiff and still; those who were dying raised their arms and filled the air with a thin unending wail." The lavish palace of Mohan's brother Bhoj is surrounded by the "common habitations of men," by the "poor, whose squalid hovels cling, like swallows' nests, to its thick, frowning walls." Jali steps from Bhoj's palace to the squalid hovels.

There are two imaginative and moral centers in the novel. They give it the symmetry Myers sought. The first is the pool of Vishnu itself:

> A large figure of Vishnu, outstretched as if in sleep, lay in the water, the head with its aureole of hooded cobras just rising above the surface. Calm and beautiful was the face of stone that looked up into the evening sky. The place breathed out repose.

The second center is the guru's dell. These two places are quiet and untroubled; both are removed from peasants' hovels and prison cells, but they are very different from Bhoj's palace. No wealthy ladies, no celebrities, gather beside the pool of Vishnu or in the dell. Mohan and Damayanti, who live beside the pool of Vishnu, leave their palace to struggle with the peasants against the rajahs. The guru rejects affluence and fame to teach the necessity of social change and moral regeneration. "The Pool of Vishnu" describes the new values and institutions which men seek in the midst of war and revolution. Myers's heroes strive to be revolutionaries, to cast off the corruptions of the Camp. They struggle to create the new world, continually comparing their inner and farthest vision with the outer, nearer reality. From the isolation of the guru's dell and the pool of Vishnu they move toward social action. The novel alternates back and forth between stillness and strife; the comradeship and equality at the pool and in the dell are contrasted with the oppression and inequality of Bhoj's palace.

Bhoj "thinks that for all time there should be a very few wise and rich and cultured men (like himself) at the top of society, and progressively less wisdom and less wealth and less culture as you go down the social scale. He would not have society arranged different for anything in the world." While Jali looks at Bhoj's palace, his thoughts

> . . . turned to an ancient ant-hill on a piece of waste land behind the stables at home. That ant-hill was, indeed, a noble pile. Many hundreds of years old, towered and turreted, spacious and intricate, it bore witness to the well-ordered diligence of countless generations. There was certainly no palace in all India that could vie with it as a monument testifying to social stability and traditions faithfully upheld. Perhaps, Jali now reflected, that was why, as a child, he used to take an irreverent pleasure in poking at it with a stick.

Jali becomes a revolutionary. He, the guru, Mohan and Damayanti want society to be arranged on the basis of social and economic equality. They are utopian communists. They start as well-meaning aristocrats playing at revolution, but they become disciplined rebels. At first they are benevolent despots. Later they help create a democratic commune. Myers defines the dilemma of the wealthy, intellectual revolutionary who confronts the poor, unintellectual peasant. He also describes how the aristocracy seeks the destruction of the commune. Once Mohan and Damayanti become revolutionaries, the members of their own class define them as traitors, turn the peasants against them and seek their defeat.

The guru is the prophet of the revolution; Mohan and Damayanti are the practical revolutionaries. The guru is unlike the ordinary wandering sage because his thoughts are meant to stir men to action. "India has always been full of holy men preaching the religion of freedom and equality, but without producing any practical results," Damayanti tells Jali. "It was not until we moved here and began putting the Guru's ideas properly into practice that Bhoj . . . came to understand that those ideas were different and dangerous." Damayanti knows that Indian philosophers previously have sought to interpret the world; the guru tries to change it. He demands of men that they transform their lives, that they engage in struggle.

Myers changed in important ways from the late 1920s to the late 1930s. Like many writers of that era, he moved from bohemianism to radicalism, from the aesthetes' Camp to the revolutionary's commune. Myers is unusual because in becoming a communist he did not become a social realist, he did not reject his remote settings and exotic characters. The novelist L. P. Hartley, for a time one of Myers's friends, writes that in the "troubled years of the 'thirties Myers's political ideas . . . underwent a fundamental change. At the outset he was a patron and amateur of the arts . . . he emerged to all intents and purposes a Communist." Hartley felt that the Myers who wrote "The Root and the Flower" was a visionary and a mystic, and that the Myers who wrote "The Pool of Vishnu" was a revolutionary and a humanist. But there is no sharp dichotomy in Myers's work. In "The Root and the Flower" he reveals the corruptions of the imperial society and he implies the need for radical change. In "The Pool of Vishnu" he is still a visionary. Myers was both a visionary and a revolutionary. In his later work the problem of being and seeing, of inner and outer landscapes, is related to revolution. Hartley assumed that visionaries make better artists than revolutionaries, that as Myers became a revolutionary the quality of his art declined. Yet, when Myers became a revolutionary he developed a more complex vision of society, his range of characters broadened and his understanding of the political and the philosophical mind deepened.

All his life Myers was a student of aristocracies. It was from Myers that George Orwell derived much of his understanding of the British ruling class. Orwell recorded in his war diary in 1940 that Myers had told him:

> . . . with exceptions like Churchill the entire British aristocracy is utterly corrupt and lacking in the most ordinary patriotism, caring . . . for nothing except preserving their own standards of life. He says that they are also intensely class conscious and recognize clearly the community of their own interests with those of rich people elsewhere.

Myers was a rebel from his own class. Long before he became a communist, he was very much concerned with the social movements of his time. In a fuzzy way he dealt with them in his early novels. "Diaz in Mexico, Lenin in Russia, Mussolini in Italy," mutters one of the characters in *The "Clio"* (1925), a short novel which describes a group of British aristocrats traveling by yacht to and up the Amazon River. There is no indication from the Myers of 1925 that he sees the differences between Mussolini and Lenin. They are both viewed as extremists. The "Clio" is the yacht which takes Myers's aristocrats on their pleasure cruise; it is his microcosm of the great world. Like the rich in Mexico and Russia, the wealthy Englishmen on the "Clio" are threatened by violence. A revolution takes place in Brazil; at the same time the boat crashes into a bank of the Amazon and the wild, irrational forces of the jungle invade the comfortable, affluent, orderly little world aboard the yacht. In *The "Clio"* Myers tried, but was unable, to write about the people and the issues in a revolution. Instead, he offers a parable: the boat is order and civilization, the jungle is chaos and revolution. He was unsure of the world beyond the drawing room or the luxury yacht, and he presented a distorted view of it.

By the time he wrote *The Near and the Far* he understood the social and political movements of his time. And he joined with the communists in the fight against fascism. In his last novel he explores an entire country, follows the paths of rich and poor, rajahs and peasants, soldiers and statesmen, rather than, as in *The "Clio"*, a limited group of aristocrats. There is a crisis in his India, but it is not represented by an encroaching jungle. There are peasants and gurus, wars and insurrections. Society is a network of individuals and institutions in conflict and change. Myers sheds the aristocratic bias; he no longer regards peasants and revolutionaries as archetypal figures of fear and terror. They are the heroes of the twentieth century.

Myers the visionary and Myers the revolutionary merge into Myers the novelist. In *The Near and the Far* he probes intense states of consciousness, he shows men absorbed in their own thoughts. And he also depicts men joined together in political action. He sees institutions and social forces. Myers seeks both pleasure and the revolution; he likes the elegance of a Persian carpet, but he wants the end of luxury for an elite while peasants are exploited. Myers was an aristocrat, an aesthete, a moralist, a mystic, a revolutionary. In

The Near and the Far he explored his different selves and created a whole world. But he never resolved the contradictions in his life. He ended them by committing suicide in 1944, three years after Virginia Woolf, his old friend from Bloomsbury, took her own life as she agonized about the war. Myers was divided; attached to the old world but longing for a new order, he was caught between the near and the far in his own mind and in the world about him. But his novel speaks for cultural revolution in the West, for the transformation of oppressors and oppressed, powerful and powerless, exploited and exploiters into the Jalis, the Mohans, the Damayantis, and the gurus of the future.

15

School Lessons: History and Geometry

Aspects of the Novel (1927) and *A Passage to India* (1924) are closely connected. It is not simply that three short years separate publication. The work of criticism is a gloss on the novel and the novel is a gloss on the criticism. The critical and creative energies tangle with similar problems. The 1920s was a decade of extraordinary literary and critical production. *Women in Love* appeared in 1920, *The Waste Land* in 1922, *Ulysses* in 1922, *The Sacred Wood* in 1920 and *Studies in Classic American Literature* in 1922. Between Eliot's poetry and criticism and Lawrence's fiction and criticism there is a mutually sustaining relationship. This is equally true for Forster's last novel and his one major critical study.

Aspects of the Novel is utopian criticism. After the actual world of India, Forster creates an ideal world. Criticism provides protection against muddle and chaos. Forster's literary criticism is his therapy, his medicine. *Aspects of the Novel* is his fix: it enables him to escape from painful history. Give me life, life, he cries, but we always find pattern, pattern, pattern in his books. Forster gives us a little pill to swallow at the start of his book. It induces a vision. He asks us to see all the English novelists "seated together in a room, a circular room, a sort of British Museum reading-room—all writing their novels simultaneously." He scraps history, throws it on the rubble heap. There is Sterne and Woolf, Richardson and James, Dickens and Wells—three charming couples, their pens all scratching on their pads at the same time, nobody influencing anybody else. They are floating like balloons in the air, under the dome of the British Museum, with no roots in the real world. They never change; they are never affected by wars or revolution, sunshine or rain, cold or heat, poverty or affluence. The British Museum reading room, where James, Dickens and Sterne are all writing their novels simultaneously, is a place in which Forster feels unthreatened. It is at the center of Bloomsbury. It is full of books—a quiet place where, in the heart of London, you can be undisturbed, lost in thought, in writing or research. It is not the British Museum of Marx or Lenin, where the point of research is to change the world.

"All through history," Forster tells us, "writers while writing have felt more or less the same." In a tone which mocks all public events, he says, "Empires fall, votes are accorded, but to those people writing in the circular room it is the feel of the pen between their fingers that matters most." Now, this concept is a half-truth, because while writers throughout history have shared a common identity, they have always felt very differently. To invest his criticism of the novel with dignity and authority Forster quotes from T. S. Eliot's *The Sacred Wood:*

> It is part of his [the critic's] business to see literature steadily and to see it whole; and this is eminently to see it *not* as consecrated by time, but to see it beyond time.

Eliot has many things to say about literature and criticism. His position is complex. He contradicts himself. If Forster had wanted a more representative, more complex statement of Eliot's position, he would have done well to read a little further on in *The Sacred Wood.* In "Tradition and the Individual Talent" Eliot says that tradition involves

> . . . the historical sense . . . and the historical sense involves a perception not only of the pastness of the past, but of its presence; the historical sense compels a man to write not merely with his own generation in his bones, but with a feeling that the whole of the literature of Europe from Homer and within it the whole of the literature of his own country has a simultaneous existence and composes a simultaneous order. This historical sense, which is a sense of the timeless as well as of the temporal and of the timeless and of the temporal together, is what makes a writer traditional. And it is at the same time what makes a writer most acutely conscious of his place in time, of his contemporaneity.

Forster covers his hook with the wrong bait and the fish do not bite. He pulls up his rod and goes home empty-handed. The wholeness of Eliot's statement—that literature is both temporal and timeless, that the writer is sogged with the waters of his own time and dried with the sands of the timeless—brings out the complexity and the joy of literature. Forster does not want to negotiate with time; he refuses to sit down at the conference table for even preliminary discussion. Forster's sense of the writer's imagination is mechanical. His metaphor for the mind is a mirror, a reflecting surface. He notes that the mirror of the mind does not change when "an historical pageant passes in front of it . . . It only develops when it . . . acquires new sensitiveness." Forster's writers are all in cellophane bags, in a vacuum, wrapped up, untouched by history. The mind of his man is unchanged by history.

Forster articulated in the fullest way his view of the relationship between culture and society nearly a quarter of a century later in the essay "Art for Art's Sake" (1949). Forster is on a tower looking over the plains of history. He sees disorder, a mess, a muddle, confusion. Everything torn, scattered. Napoleon, Babeuf, Jefferson, Julius Caesar, Roosevelt, Cleopatra, Attila, Mao—all thrown together in the same bag. Feudalism, slavery, capitalism, socialism—all these societies jumbled up together in a tangled ball. Forster's tower is art: order, pattern, significance. The great world is in total disarray and disruption. Brick by brick, art builds a little world of harmony. Forster flees from life as if it were the plague. He is afraid of the plains of history. Books are sanctuaries for him. He can open the covers, turn the pages and lodge himself in a world where the artist controls everything, even the unexpected. Forster tells us that

> Ancient Athens made a mess—but the *Antigone* stands up. Renaissance Rome made a mess—but the ceiling of the Sistine got painted. James I made a mess—but there was *Macbeth*. Louis XIV—but there was *Phèdre*. Art for art's sake? I should just think so, and more so than ever at the present time. It is the one orderly product which our muddling race has produced.

Forster believes that art brings human salvation. Before World War I he had thought of Victorian England as a glorious society; he believed that things would get better and better each day in every way. Then the war made him feel that he had been betrayed by history. Like a spoiled child, he turns his back on history. Once he thought society was orderly. Now it is all disorder. But both are equally distorted. He never saw that history is conflict and change, the clash of opposing forces. For him, history is garbage; art is the flower. Forster sees no necessity for men to dedicate their lives to the struggle for freedom and equality because he believes every era makes a mess. He does not celebrate the human will and spirit of the Renaissance, of the French Revolution, of World War II; he does not recognize man's fight to control his destiny, win his liberation, build a new world. All these historical struggles are not messes, as Forster thinks, but heroic battles to throw off oppression. His dichotomy between disorderly history and orderly art drives a wedge between forces which cannot be and never were separate: culture and society, literature and politics. The point is not to have order, as Forster assumes, in life and art. Society never was, is not, and never will be orderly in the way he wanted it to be. Society is always in conflict. Literature, too, appeals to us not simply or only because of its form. All literature has form, but literature brings to the surface the antagonisms in reality. When Forster says that we read novels because of our need for permanence, he is again only half right, and thereby again misleading, for we read to explore both permanence and change.

Aspects of the Novel is also fun, if we survive the poisonous pill. Forster tries to envision the form of novels. He has a sense of their movement. He sees Henry James's *The Ambassadors* in the shape of an hourglass on its side, like this:

The two men in the novel, Chad Newsome and Lambert Strether, exchange positions. They flow back and forth like the sand in the hourglass. Paris is at the center of the novel: everything passes through it, is shaped by it. Forster was not the first or the only artist or critic to describe the form and movement of a novel by using shapes and lines. Long ago, in the mid-eighteenth century, Laurence Sterne drew the plots of the five volumes of *Tristram Shandy*. The fourth volume looked like this to him:

Harriet Weaver once told James Joyce that *Finnegan's Wake* looked like a square inside a circle:

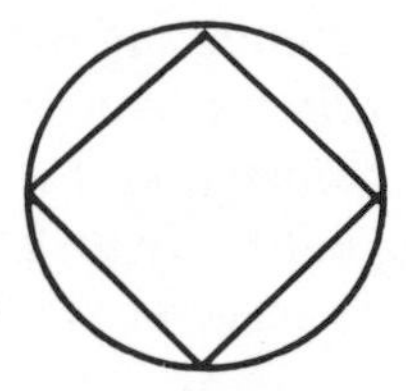

One might divide all novels into two groups—those which suggest geometrical forms, like *The Ambassadors* and *Finnegan's Wake,* and those which suggest squiggly lines, like *Tristram Shandy*. D. H. Lawrence's *Women in Love* looks like this:

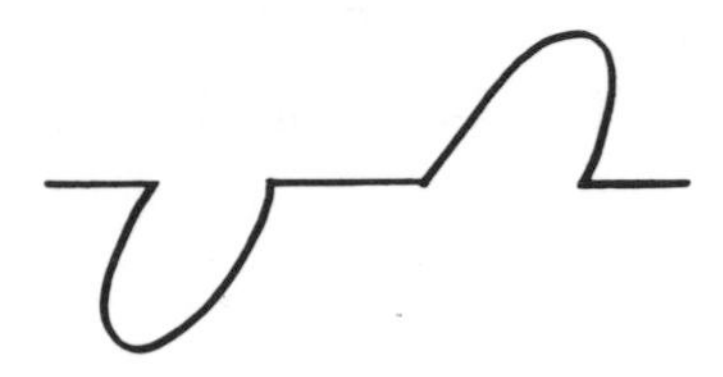

This is the way the novel moves. There are the depths of the mine, the darkness of the coal pit, then the long, flat midlands of England, and finally the heights of Europe, the mountains of Switzerland. The depths and the heights illustrate Lawrence's constant probing—moving away from the flat midlands to penetrate into society, into the human consciousness. Thrusts outward, above and below the ordinary. The abstract shape which the novel suggests also captures the sexuality of the work: male and female genitals.

A Passage to India also has its abstract form, its rhythm. It looks like this:

Mosque, cave and temple. Each one distinct and different from the others, but all alike in that they are moments which gather up experience into a bundle of significance. "There seems something else in life besides time," Forster writes in

Aspects of the Novel, "something which may conveniently be called 'value,' something which is measured not by minutes or hours but by intensity, so that when we look at our past it does not stretch back evenly but piles up into a few notable pinnacles." That is what we have in cave, temple, mosque—places in time where things heave up, places of significance, moments of intensity. When Forster says that India is "country, fields, fields, then hills, jungle, hills, and more," he means that the hills are mounds—natural, like the caves, or man-made, like the temple—where time pours in, brings a rush of intensity, then eddies out and moves on, until it reaches the next mound. History is a series of disorders, but art gives form to the muddle. There is an artistic rhythm to the series of disorders:

The novels of Virginia Woolf were largely responsible for Forster's sense of the rhythm in fiction. In the essay "The Early Novels of Virginia Woolf" (1925) he considers the question of form. He writes that "*Jacob's Room* suggests a spiral whirling down to a point, Mrs. Dalloway a cathedral." Forster always thought of himself as applying the rhythms of music to the novel. He wanted fiction to aspire to the condition of music. But the art that he is actually closest to is architecture. His novels do not suggest symphonies, as he wanted them to do, but buildings. It is the house which dominates *Howards End.* It is mosque, temple, and cave which hold sway in *A Passage to India.* Buildings set the wheels of Forster's imagination going—London train stations, St. Peter's in Rome, Indian temples. Forster is much more literal-minded, much less abstract than he thinks he is. *The Ambassadors* comes across as an hourglass—a specific thing, an emblem. Mrs. Dalloway is a cathedral. This, too, is precise. Novels do not appear to him in the shape of an abstract painting or sculpture. Forster talks on and on about abstract form, pattern, rhythm. In fact, his novels are pedantic, moralistic. He is a schoolteacher, always lecturing his readers; he tries hard to get away from that role, which only makes things worse.

Poor pious E. M. Forster. He always settled for less. He never tried for the big things in life or art. He wanted limitations. He wounded himself. His criticism avoids the complex relationships between literature and society. Compared with other critical works of the 1920's—*The Sacred Wood* and *Studies in Classic American Literature*—*Aspects of the Novel* is shallow. Lawrence's study of American literature is brave; it takes hold of all of American history and culture, of the American mind. *Studies in Classic American Literature* is a critique of American culture as well as a criticism of its finer writers. Forster's categories are limited. He introduces us to flat characters and round characters. Flat characters are unchanging; they are only one thing and they are second-rate. Round characters are more complex; they change. But in practice the distinction is not meaningful, for, as Forster applies the rule, it means that Dickens's characters are second-rate and Jane Austen's characters are first-rate.

Forster craves for something else, something beyond. The man was tormented, unhappy. Yet he was unable to define what he was seeking. At the heart of Forster's writing there is something hollow, an emptiness; not a jewel, but a vapor.

16

Mister Johnson: *On the Road*

Mister Johnson is the Black artist, out of Africa. The poet of life and death, the Shakespeare of the dark continent, the Balzac of Nigeria. Johnson is the supreme singer, the hero of his society, the poet-legislator Shelley waited for, celebrating his people, leading them, recording their history. He is Black Orpheus. The imagination is his to control. Johnson is not a Black man in baggy trousers, plunking away on a banjo to amuse white men at the side show of a carnival or a circus. No, Johnson is the primitive artist, the original singer, the poet of the future. But there are a few cheap gimmicks in Cary's bag. Sometimes he laughs at Johnson the Black clown, the funny man. Sometimes Johnson is the child, the Black man as infant, who needs to be cared for by Europeans. That is Cary's mean side, coming from the corner of his mind covered with cobwebs. Cary can be paternalistic and parade about with a sense of the superiority of white men to Black men, of European civilization to African. He can be a racist. This passage—which was added in one of the later drafts of the manuscript, and which seems like an afterthought, but actually was included for emphasis—describes the town in which much of the action in the novel occurs:

> Fada is the ordinary native town of the Western Sudan. It has no beauty, convenience or health. It is a dwelling-place at one stage from the rabbit warren or the badger burrow;

> and not so cleanly kept as the latter. It is a pioneer settlement five or six hundred years old, built on its own rubbish heaps, without charm even of antiquity. Its squalor and its stinks are all new. Its oldest compounds, except the Emir's mud box, is not twenty years old. The sun and the rain destroy all its antiquity, even of smell. But neither has it the freshness of the new. All its mud walls are eaten as if by smallpox; half of the mats in any compound are always rotten. Poverty and ignorance, the absolute government of jealous savages, conservative as only the savage can be, have kept it at the first frontier of civilization. Its people would not know the change if time jumped back fifty thousand years. They live like mice or rats in a palace floor; all the magnificence and variety of the arts, the ideas, the learning and the battles of civilization go on over their heads and they do not even imagine them.
>
> Fada has not been able to achieve its own native arts or the characteristic beauty of its country. There are no flowering trees or irrigated gardens; no painted or molded courtyard walls.
>
> The young boys, full of curiosity and enterprise, grow quickly into old, anxious men, content with mere existence. Peace has been brought to them, but no glory of living; some elementary court-justice, but no liberty of mind. An English child in Fada . . . would be terrified by the dirt, the stinks, the great sores on naked bodies, the twisted limbs, the babies with enormous swollen stomachs and their hernias; the whole place, flattened upon the earth like the scab of a wound, would strike it as something between a prison and a hospital.

Here is Cary giving us a lecture, an indoctrination session. We resent it and squirm in our seats, waiting for him to finish, waiting for the bell to ring so that we can leave the classroom. The description is hateful. He wants us to believe that African towns are disgusting, repulsive, that Africans are stupid, slow-moving, diseased, closer to the animal than to the human world. He wants us to assume that sickness and disease are innate in Africans, that it is only natural for them to have rotten towns. Not a word about the Europeans who brought sickness, garbage and poisoned doctrines to the shores of Africa. The unwritten assumption is that European and American cities are superior. But in fact, it is New York, London and Paris—with their police, their regulations and laws, their cold, lifeless plastic, concrete and steel—which strike us as a cross between a prison and a hospital. To say all this about the African town and not to mention the ancient civilizations, the elaborate art and rituals, the religions, the complexity of totem and taboo, of tools and masks, or the skill of African hunters and herdsmen—this is to offer a lie about the land and its people. It is also a shocking passage because of what the first sentence of the book has led us to expect:

> The young women of Fada, in Nigeria, are well known for beauty. They have small, neat features and their backs are not too hollow.

Beautiful and elegant—these are the women of Fada. Cary detested the concept of the noble savage. He was outraged by Europeans who idealized the free life of the African. So, to defeat his opponents' arguments, he often took the position that African tribal life was universal misery. He believed in material progress and its inevitability, that it brought men out of disease and starvation. The tribe to him was the totalitarian state in miniature. He believed that through time man became freer. The passage which describes Fada rises out of Cary's sense of guilt and confusion, out of his repressive mentality. It is contradictory to the main thrust of the book.

For Cary is in love with Mister Johnson, and Mister Johnson is freedom and power, imagination and joy, beauty and strength. He is not an ignorant, conservative savage, nor is he a syphilitic Black cripple. He is a dancer, a genius, a rebel. Johnson's poems are for all men; his songs are addressed to listeners the world round. The universal poet, the Black man singing for all men. Not a commercial artist, not an isolated aesthete, not owned by any government, class or elite. A poet of the people. Johnson sings of sex, of work, of death—themes for all time that are ore dug out of the African soil, forged into warrior's spears pointing into the sky. Nigerian songs for Black men and Black women.

Johnson is in love with Bamu; he is happy, and he sings a song to express what he feels:

> I got a lil girl, she roun like de worl'.
> She smoot like de water, she shine like de sky.
> She fat like de corn, she smell like de new grass.
> She dance like de tree, she shake like de leaves.
> She warm like de groun', she deep like de bush.
> How doo, lil girl? I see you dar.
> How doo, lil girl? Why you 'fraid for me?
> I no got nuttin, no stick, no knife.

Courtship is swift. An agreement is soon reached: Johnson is to marry Bamu. There is a festival—drumming, dancing, clapping, singing, eating, drinking. Someone, no one in particular, and no one notices or cares who it is, shouts the line of a wedding song:

> The snake lifts his head,
> The tortoise modestly retires.

Then the women, who are grouped together, sing:

> Oh snake, why do you look at me with your eye?
> What do you want among the maidens?
> I fear this snake, he is dangerous.
> He strikes like the arrow in the darkness.
> He bites like fire. Oh—oh—don't let him near.

Then the bride and the bridegroom enter the drama. First, Johnson:

> Why do you hide, little tortoise,
> Under the leaves of darkness.

Then Bamu:

> I saw a strange creature in the forest.
> A centipede, as big as my arm.

The fearful women must be answered by the men, advancing on them:

> Oh maidens, we sought you in the corn field.
> When we looked it was only the shadow of a cloud.
> We saw you far off and dived into the white water,
> But when we grasped you, it was only the sparkling wave.
> We heard your voices in the air and sprang from the branches,
> But only the bright bird flew between our hands.

Once more the girls sing:

> What do I hear, a lion roaring after his prey?
> What do I feel, an elephant shaking the ground?
> What do I fear, a crocodile lifting his eye from the pool?

At the end, now with increased pitch and intensity, we hear everyone together:

> I fear the snake, he is dangerous to women.
> See, he has struck my poor sister.
> She is all swollen with his bite, she cries out, "Aie, aie!"

It is an elaborate ritual, the celebration of a marriage, by an entire society. A chorus of women questioning and replying to a chorus of men. Bamu singing to Johnson, Johnson to Bamu, the bride and the bridegroom single and separate, at the center of the celebration; but also the one joined with the circle of women, the other with the circle of men. A collective experience, a battle between the sexes, singing the dignity and power of masculinity and femininity, hitching together man and woman—the tribe as one.

Johnson's greatest exploits are on the road. He is a clerk, a government employee, but he is no good in an office, sitting in a chair behind a desk, filling out official questionnaires, adding up a column of figures, filing reports. He is like all modern men in offices: he aches to get out, to be liberated from bosses, from the petty tyranny of paper clips and manila folders. He is like all the clerks, in Africa, Japan, England, who would be poets, who want words of feeling, not form letters.

The road is the project of Rudbeck, the Nigerian district officer. He is one of four English civil servants in the novel, who are all minor characters, satellites of Johnson. Rudbeck is dull, plodding, unimaginative. What he determines to do he does, even if it means butting his head against a wall. Gollup is the most interesting of the white men in Fada. Cary pulls him out of his bag of characters. Cary was a caricaturist. His favorite artist was Hogarth. His character sketches also bring to mind Daumier. The modern cartoonist he resembles the most is R. Crumb. Gollup looks like a character out of a contemporary comic book. He is a soldier, a trader, a drunkard, married to an African woman. While he is a sentimental man of warm heart, he is also a violent and brutal man. A grotesque little man we both fear and laugh at. Cary frequently turns to the grotesque. Distorted faces, spastic movements. There are two responses we make. One is laughter, the other is horror. In African settings the grotesque is usually horrible, as in the following description from *The African Witch* (1936):

> Coker picked up some round object in a bag, and held it at arm's length . . . The object was Schlemm's head.

> Aladai had known for three days that Coker had a great *ju-ju* in the forest . . . He had known perfectly well that Coker's *ju-ju* was Schlemm's head . . . He swayed, and the moans tore him like giant hiccoughs; he couldn't stop them.

The grotesque is demons and devils, severed heads, mumbo-jumbo, strange rites; it is the African witch. In *Castle Corner* there is Porfit, the grotesque radical, poor man, sworn enemy of wealthy landlords. Cary describes how the hero of the book sees Porfit:

> Cleeve looked and saw the small, black figure going up through the meadow. In the long, black coat and the top hat it resembled a beetle with an absurdly small head and one broken leg. The broken leg was the umbrella trailing behind. It had an incongruous look on the bright spring green of the aftermath; like a dung beetle on a flower petal.

In his baggy trousers, floppy hat, pulling along his tattered umbrella, Porfit is ridiculously funny.

Gollup, too, is funny, though there is savage cruelty behind his outlandish appearance. Pacing up and down in his store he wears cotton drawers, a white linen coat, pale blue socks, green suspenders, white canvas shoes. In the afternoon he takes a stroll in purple and green pajamas and wears a special hat. "He refuses to condescend with the African sun. He scorns all topees, terais and sun hats and wears always, if he doesn't go bareheaded, a soft pearl-gray hat with a curled brim . . ." He has had three sunstrokes, and "none of them has quite killed him." Gollup is grotesque walking in public under the noonday sun without a sun hat, wearing purple and green pajamas. "Damn your old sun 'ats," he says. He is audacious; he refuses to be beaten down by the African environment. He will not conform.

Mister Johnson is also grotesque, sitting in a canopy chair in the middle of the jungle, wearing a white helmet, a pair of patent-leather shoes, followed wherever he goes by a small boy who carries the hat and the chair. But he is magnificent. He too, like Gollup, creates dominion wherever he goes. He will not bow down to the sun, be intimidated by the hostile night or be scared away by the dense jungle. When he dresses he defies the elements; he turns his back on the twin dictators, time and space.

On the road, followed by his young servant, Johnson is the master. The road is his turf. He can transform the world of nature, appropriate it and make it the world of man. Through the thick jungle, over surging rivers, a road is built. Where once there was no mark of man, there is the highway of civilization. The road is unending. There is a starting point and a destination, but it is the daily process of building the road, one mile after the other, eating up a little more space each day, which matters. Neither the beginning nor the ending is crucial; it is the journey itself which is important. Roads are for traveling, for movement, not for standing still or waiting. The road is endless creation, and Johnson exists to walk on still another road. The road is the eternal present. The novel itself is written in the present tense, a tense Cary specifically connected with the African experience. "It can give to a reader," he wrote, "that sudden feeling of insecurity (as if the very ground were made only of a deeper kind of darkness) which comes to a traveler who is bushed in unmapped country, when he feels all at once that not only has he utterly lost his way, but also his own identity." The present tense forces the reader's mood to be "not contemplative but agitated." Cary wants us to feel events rushing us along before we can examine, judge, locate or decide why we are agitated. Change, change, change —that is why he chose the present tense. But it also leaves us without a rich, deep feeling about human dilemmas. The present tense is the reflection of a philosophical mood, a historical vision, which dams up the contemplative and analytical waters.

On the road there is a constant flow of energy. Only verbs can describe Johnson's world. For him, even the word "road" is a verb. Wherever he goes there is:

clearing	shouting	exhorting	imagining
marking	swinging	yelling	tumbling
beating	stripping	drumming	crawling
striking	swearing	itching	pressing
yelling	singing	flourishing	hiding
bursting	improvising	hunting	working

Here there is unalienated labor; work is play. Work is for control over nature. Men working together as a collective. Working on the road takes African men out of their provincial tribal life and funnels them into modern, heterogeneous cities. It breaks up, transforms, wipes out. The road is the revolution; change every day. Johnson's songs on the road are work songs, songs which enable men to labor with joy. They combine play with battle. Building the road is an epic struggle. Johnson sings:

> Bow down, you king of cotton trees;
> Put your green heads in the dust;
> Salute the road men of Rudbeck,

and the men, as they wield their weapons like warriors, sing back:

> Out of our way, this is the king road.
> Where he flies, the great trees fall
> The sun and moon are walking on our road.

The lords of the forest are defeated by the lords of youth, work and song. Destruction and creation; leveling the jungle to bring forth a new world. Johnson's songs catch the glory of man's effort to conquer and control his environment. This is the road song he chants in a lordly voice, while pantomiming the chopping down of a tree:

He says to us of the road, go away, you ants, be quiet, you monkey,
I am Rimi the king of the trees, I stand here a hundred years,
The sky is all my palace, that little small sun my fire,
That little moon hangs in the roof, for my lamp,
The thunder comes to war, he tries to frighten me with his trumpet,
My war horse is the strong earth, he prances through the sky.
He tramples over the thunder and pushes him down with his big chest,
He cannot throw me off, I sit upright.
I hold my head high up, I say nothing.
All the trees in the forest bow down to me and whisper,
Agaisheka, King Rimi, God prolong you,
Go away, you little men,
Or my horse will trample you down.

Get out of my way, King Rimi, the road is coming,
It does not stop for kings, it is little Judge Rudbeck's road,
Get out of my way, King Rimi, here are the road men
To chop you down at the feet, kerplunk,
To chop you to little pieces.
Bow to the road men, King Rimi,
Salute the road men with your whole length.
Put your hands on the ground.
Put your face in the dust.

The road is at last finished. But it is not a climactic moment. It is not like the meeting of two railway lines in the middle of a continent, coming from opposite shores. There is no celebration, no driving of a gold stake. One day a truck goes by. The road is open. That is all. No one has officially opened it; it has opened itself. The men have lived in anticipation of seeing the first vehicles on the hardened earth track, and when the first truck passes by they shout and grin. But the driver of the truck is not aware that he is the first man to ride on the Fada road. It is finished, but no one cares very much. Now there are other chores, other dilemmas. Soon everyone goes home. Cary's picture is sharp. With a few well-selected details he gives a picture of the new beside the old. The road men stand under the shade of the ancient trees, their hoes in their hands, their bodies glistening with sweat. The truck driver is very different. He is a tall Yoruba—a Nigerian from another tribe; he is wearing blue dungarees and he has the butt end of a cigarette in the corner of his mouth, in the style of Humphrey Bogart.

The road brings many things beside dungarees, cigarettes and movies. There is more robbery, extortion, assault, disputes between chiefs and their people, fraud, adulteration. The number of policemen is increased. Business and trade mount. The road takes over. It is a power. It becomes a leading character in the novel. To Johnson, Rudbeck, the road men, the chiefs, to the tribes of Nigeria, the road says:

> I'm smashing up the old Fada—I shall change everything and everybody in it. I am abolishing the old ways, the old ideas, the old law; I am bringing wealth and opportunity for good as well as vice, new powers to men and therefore new conflicts. I am the revolution. I am giving you plenty of trouble already, you governors, and I am going to give you plenty more. I destroy and I make new.

Cary overemphasizes the role of tools and machines in history. He does not relate technological changes to class conflicts and cultural forces.

Cary achieves a difficult task. He makes work seem joyous, glorious. Unalienated labor—something few men believe in, something fewer still have experienced in Western society. Western youth have seen it, have been part of it—in the Third World, in Cuba—have harvested sugar cane side by side with the Cubans in a guerrilla war against underdevelopment. Working to raise the standard of living for all Cubans. Fidel working along with his people. People laboring extra long hours now so that machines can be bought, men and women can be relieved of hard tasks in the field, liberated to conquer other problems. Unalienated labor is the building of a bridge in China, without complicated machines, but with thousands of hands joined together; rocks lifted, carted, dumped, filling up a path through the sea, to span shore to shore. Cary offers a glimpse of what work once was in the past, and what it might again be. His picture is not about work in Africa during his lifetime. Working on the road, as Cary sees it, is not exploitation. Yet building roads through Africa in Cary's time, like building railroads through Africa in Conrad's time, was based on millions and millions of unpaid hours of labor by Black men. By devious means Cary's road workers are enticed to chop trees and clear a way. They are paid subsistence wages. We are never made to feel that imperial European companies are building the road to tap the wealth of colonial Africa. As Cary describes it, the road is the project of a man, not of a government or an economic system.

Tolstoi, above all modern writers, knows what work is like. In *Anna Karenina* (1873–1876) Levin labors in the fields. We feel the differences between mental and manual labor. Levin, who usually drives his mind, must now exert his body. He goes into the fields because he is depressed, because he wants physical exercise. But the peasants must work every day if they are to eat black bread and cabbage soup and have wood for a stove on snowy winter nights. Levin has the freedom to choose when he goes into the field; the peasants do not. Tolstoi describes Levin's sensations: the rhythm of the work, exhaustion, sleeping on cut hay, beginning work early in the morning, the hot sun on his back, going home at night. He looks at the scythe—man and his tools, the scythe swinging back and forth—an extension of Levin's arms. Levin works best when he does not have to think consciously of what he is doing, when everything flows organically. The work that Levin and his peasants do is different from the work done by their fathers. The peasants were once serfs. Now they are freemen. It takes the freemen less time than it did the serfs to do the same amount of work. As freemen, their conception of work is a lot different. Levin owns the fields and their produce; he exploits the peasants. He is the oppressor, they are the oppressed. He is conscious of this and he forsees the day when the land will be owned by all, when one man will not exploit another, when labor will be unalienated. Cary misses most of these feelings, these historical observations, these contradictions between exploiter and exploited, free and slave labor, white and Black workers, man and his tools, mental and manual labor.

Johnson is high. He has a fall. He brings the road; the road brings corruption. Johnson brings graft and is corrupted, caught and found guilty. He kills Gollup. Johnson becomes a murderer. The first time Johnson fights Gollup, he thinks he has killed him—farce. The second time, he succeeds: Gollup is dead. Tragedy. Johnson, who was free, goes to jail—a prisoner of the state. The artist is handcuffed by the law. There are new songs to sing, songs of death and farewell. These, like the others, give this section of the novel its distinctive atmosphere. There is a note of sadness which pervades his days behind bars:

> Good-by, my worl', good-by, my father worl'.
> Carry me on you head, give me a chop.
> When this fool child, hear you breathe in the dark he no more 'fraid
> I smell you like de honey beer in de dark night.
> I see you bress shine in de moon,
> I feel you big muscle hold me up so I no fit to fall.
> Good-by, my father, you do all ting for me, never ask for nutting for youself.
>
> Good-by, my mother sky, stretch you arms all round.
> Watch me all time with you eye, never sleep.

> Put down you bress when I thirsty; never say give me.
> Good-by, my night, my lil wife-night,
> Hold me in you arms ten tousand time.

"I may write the end, the middle, and the beginning, and very often in this order," Cary wrote of his novels. "I decide how and where the book shall end, which is just as important to a book as a play; and then I ask myself where are the most difficult turns in the book." There is a special feeling about the ending of *Mister Johnson*: a hushed tone, controlled after the frenzy on the road; melancholy after the joy. Johnson is to die for the murder of Gollup. He is to be hanged. It is grotesque. Rudbeck must first weigh Johnson before he can hang him. But he does not have a regular scale, so he constructs one. On one side are bags of silver, on the other side Johnson. The two sides are not quite balanced. Rudbeck hands Johnson a tin of flour and three tins of jam to hold. Now they are equal. He computes his weight. Everything is cold, calculated, efficient; the pressure mounts. The regulations say that Johnson must be hanged, but Johnson wants Rudbeck himself to shoot him. It is his final request. Rudbeck cannot refuse. He has always admired Johnson and Johnson reveres him. Johnson is down on his knees.

> Rudbeck leans through the door, aims the carbine at the back of the boy's head and blows his brains out.

Violence casually and matter-of-factly described. Only a Black boy shot. Cary does not pause long over the incident. Only a few seconds, and then he moves on to something else. Rudbeck returns to his office and fills out Form No. 5—a coroner's inquest—in duplicate:

> Protectorate of Nigeria.
> In the court of the coroner of Fada district and inquisition taken at Fada on the _____day of _____ 19 _____ before

> ____ coroner on the body of ____ then and there lying dead; who, having to inquire when and how and by what means the said deceased came to death, finds that the death of the said ____ was caused at Fada on the ____ day of ____ 19 ____ by ____.

Johnson is now only a form on a record. He is filed away in the manila envelopes he once tended. His death is his last victory. He has died according to his own plan, not according to the regulations of the law. It is a death consonant with his imaginative vision of his end. His friend Rudbeck has killed him and fulfilled his dream. All these facts and figures, these forms, this coolness. A murderer and a dead man. A white man has just shot a Black man. A Black man, a worker, a king of his people, a poet and a clerk, the builder of the Fada road, is at last shot by the English colonial district officer—that is how it usually ends. A Black man imprisoned by the state, shot by the white sheriff. The ending is as shocking as the blast from the carbine. The white man is a murderer.

It is Johnson's imagination which is his power. It gives him his dignity and it seals his fate, marks him for Rudbeck's bullet. Johnson's imagination both frees him and fetters him; it enables him to be reborn each day as someone new and it determines his death. He lives with his head in England and his body in Nigeria. He lives in two worlds. He dreams until the world changes. He forces reality to conform to his fantasy. Then reality crashes through, smashes the dream, and Johnson dies. He wants to be civilized, to be English, but he is a Nigerian from the bush. The clash between the territory of his mind and the territory of his body is a clash between England and Nigeria, between Black and white. Johnson is caught between the two worlds and destroyed in the crunch.

Johnson is the stranger. He is a foreigner in Fada, alien to the British government officers. He is neither European nor African. He has no fixed abode; a man without a country, a man of many cultures and diverse civilizations. Johnson is the Black man lifted out of tribal life, unable to return to it, varnished with a coat of English lacquer. He has bought shoes but he does not wear them. The two societies are at war in his own self. On the road he is at home because he is in no one place, because he belongs nowhere, because he is constantly on the move. In that sense he is like the heroes of so much of American fiction—like Faulkner's Joe Christmas—who are walkers, travelers on the road. But Johnson is also the friend as well as the stranger. In each new village he shakes hands all around; he marries the town beauty, becomes the leading poet, organizes the men to work in brigades. Stranger and friend, at home and abroad, Johnson is always on the road.

17

The End: Neo-Colonialism

World War I and World War II were death pits for imperialism. Antagonism breaking out in open hostility. Both wars, which inevitably resulted from the necessity of world capitalism to lurch outward, saw the crippling of the power of capital. During and in the wake of World War I and World War II there were victories for colonized peoples and for communism, and defeats for monopoly capitalism. The Russian Revolution of 1917 burst out while Europe, from one end to the other, was a bloody battlefield. Troops leaving the front, turning their guns around. "Peace, Bread, Land." One sixth of the earth lost to the Czars, millionaires, presidents and generals who had brought death and destruction to the peoples of the world; expropriated from right under their thumbs. After World War II, the Chinese revolution: Mao Tse-tung and the Chinese Communist Party, hundreds of millions of Chinese people breaking the great imperial wall which had contained the sleeping giant of a nation for centuries. No more opium trade, no more foreign-owned railways, no more starvation. China had excommunicated herself from the world of capitalism.

Joyce Cary saw the handwriting on the wall. The signs were clear enough: unemployment, strikes, sit-ins, inflation, a crashing stock market, imbalance of trade payments, fierce competition among imperial rivals, the breakup of once-powerful empires. Revolutionary upsurge all over the world. Black men refusing to be slaves, Yellow men refusing to be serfs, Brown men demanding rice, shelter, peace. Africans refusing to fight in European wars, Chinese expelling foreign companies, Brown men demanding schools, medicine, electricity. A growing consciousness of the causes of injustice, oppression, exploitation, war; a deepening awareness of the solution of the problem—an organized political movement, a revolutionary party. Sabotage, people's war, a guerrilla army, Marxism-Leninism, the general strike. These are the weapons of the Third World. The weapons for the imperial powers: co-optation, prisons, firing lines, counterinsurgency programs; cutting the visible political strings and maintaining economic control; using the big lie, anticommunist propaganda, the myth of the free world. Neo-colonialism, the attempt to reimpose the chains of servitude.

Joyce Cary was a neo-colonialist. After *Mister Johnson,* his political analysis of African politics in *The Case for African Freedom* (1941) is horrendous. It is a weapon against colonial liberation. Cary is paternalistic. He speaks for African freedom, but he is dead set against Black Power. In effect, Cary says: You can't take your freedom in your own hands. We've got to hand it to you, and you've got to thank us. He wants gradualism. He is in favor of cutting the direct ties of empire, for he sees it as the only alternative to violent revolution and communism. He wants to hand over the reins of government to responsible Negro leaders who think of England as home, who will invite Shell Oil and General Motors to develop the nation's resources. *The Case for African Freedom* is a defense of the British Empire; it is a whitewash of imperialism, an attack on African civilization, on Black nationalism. "European conquest, with all its faults," Cary writes, "has brought incomparably more good than harm to Africa." All those typewriters, cars, radios; democracy, liberalism, free enterprise, cricket, the old school tie, the English language. The Africans were their own worst enemies, he says. Cary points an accusing finger at the tribal chief, the Arab slave trader, and says, You were more of an oppressor than we white colonialists. He asks us to agree with him that "Slavery has often been so mild that slaves refuse freedom and domestic slavery has sometimes been benevolent." Not a word about the dehumanization of man in a slave society, the sadistic relationship between man and master, the conscious, willful attempt by Europeans to keep Africans a backward people. Cary's argument against complete, total, immediate liberation is that freedom would mean that things would fall apart in the colony. Ignorant Black men would be unable to govern themselves. Those whites who argue for independence, he says, are romantics. They think men were better off in primitive times. For Cary, national liberation would mean reversion to savagery, brutal head-hunting, cannibalism. In Pontecorvo's film "The Battle of Algiers," the revolutionary leader of the underground guerrilla organization says, "It takes great strength to begin a revolution, additional energy to sustain it, even more to win the revolution, and only then do the real problems begin." That, and not the idea that all dilemmas will miraculously end after the revolution, is and has been the perspective of Mao, Fidel and Ho, the Algerians, the Cubans, the Chinese, the Vietnamese.

George Orwell wrote a foreword to the first edition of *The Case for African Freedom* and promoted the book as the answer to "the left-wing sentimentalist who imagines that the African peoples can be 'set free' by a stroke of the pen and that their troubles will thereupon be ended." Neither Cary nor Orwell envisions white revolutionaries in England, or in the European nations, who fight for immediate and total colonial liberation for Black people. This white revolutionary, whose existence they refuse to recognize, knows that the problem is not merely one of "troubles"; that economic underdevelopment will not be ended immediately; that freedom is not achieved by signing a document. This white mother-country revolutionary perceives that continued rule by the European nations and the United States, continued exploitation by General Motors, Standard Oil, United Fruit and Amerikan armies all over the world, will only ensure the continued oppression and poverty of the Third World. He knows that wars of domination by England and the United States will intensify colonial liberation struggles.

Cary knows very little about the African; it is only a casual relationship he has, no deep friendship. He is naïve, surprised to find that Africans are intelligent and sensitive. He talks about them as if they are creatures from another planet. He had lived beside them for years, but not among them. "The African," he writes, "has an unexpected grasp of a situation which, though apparently unfamiliar to him, is natural to mankind. It appears that the sense of wit and plot, like the sense of beauty, has factors common to all the world." A surprise for Cary that Black men are quick-thinking, have good memories, have deep feelings. His white men in the tropics are perfect scholars and gentlemen. He knows of no Kurtzes, no Charles Goulds, no Gentlemen Browns, no graft or corruption, no beatings of African peasants and workers. "The British colonial service," he writes, "is a picked corps; the flower of the country's quality in brains and the energy which goes with brains." The British, he claims, have always prepared Africans for self-government; it was a major part of the colonial enterprise. He pays tribute to British rule all over the world, and warns of the danger of colonial independence. "We gave India the best government it ever had, the most just, incorruptible, altruistic; and the masses know it," he wrote. "Congress rule would mean disaster for India; a return of all the evils of corruption, jobbery, family influence, and religious wars from which we saved it." But it was the British who instigated conflict between Hindus and Muslims to divide and conquer. They created India and Pakistan. The British destroyed the existing Indian cotton industry and prevented industrialization in India in order to protect and sustain the growth of the English factory system. The Indian masses were kept in ignorance, poverty, ill health. Only six years after Cary offered his analysis of Indian politics, England was forced to grant the nation independence because the Indian masses were in rebellion against British rule. The slave does not love his master, as Cary would have us believe.

He grasps for any and every argument he can to oppose an immediate end to colonialism, to imperial rule. Since one day there will be one world and one government, and all men will be brothers, it is counter-productive and inefficient, Cary argues, to allow independence of each single nation. That only makes it harder to get things back together again. He is opposed to nationalism for the present era because internationalism is the goal for 2001, the twenty-first century.

The Case for African Freedom is pervaded with an anti-revolutionary bias. Cary wants to stop Blacks from picking up guns. In his eyes, Black Power would result in "a sacrifice of freedom, by the masses, for the benefit of a few." He is unwilling to grant them the power to determine their own lives. His view is that men are corrupt, that revolutions are betrayed, that new elites inevitably replace old elites. "Men are born unequal," Cary writes. It is better to recognize inequality and to work from this base, he feels, than to envision the possibility of equality and strive for it.

"The typical revolutionary leader, everywhere in the world," Cary says, "is the mystical fanatic, to whom no reason can appeal because he lives in a world of fantasy; he is indifferent to human values, self-centered, merciless, because for him real men do not exist but only the abstract 'Revolution' . . . The nationalist leader is inhuman, dangerous, an enemy of God, because he has abandoned reason and lives with abstraction." This is a grotesque portrait, a reflection in a mirror which inverts reality. The revolutionary leaders of our time have not been merciless, self-centered, inhuman, mystical fanatics, indifferent to human values. Ho Chi Minh, Fidel Castro, Che Guevara, Mao

Tse-tung—these leaders of the Third World revolution have devoted their lives to ending starvation, ignorance, tyranny, illiteracy, disease, injustice. They have turned to serve their people. Sacrificed for the masses. The realities of daily oppression, not abstractions, are their concerns. In jail they have endured solitude, in exile isolation; all this because they have a vision of a world where there is neither master nor slave, neither rich nor poor, neither exploited nor exploiters.

Joyce Cary was a colonial administrator. Judge, jury, prosecutor. He admits that he was an absolute dictator in Nigeria. It was hostility and fear of the Black man he felt much of the time. He writes of

> . . . the sense of blindness and distrust which took possession of me in those first months of solitude in Borgu. I say took possession—because it was at once like a foreign invader seizing on my mind, and a kind of demon. I would wake up at night and feel as if the dark itself were an immense black brain, meditating, behind its thick, featureless countenance, some deep plan for a new and still more surprising outbreak.

Cary is the white invader, the emissary from a civilization which terrorizes Black men, but he looks at the Blacks as the hostile invaders terrorizing him. Deep down he knows he is guilty, but refuses to recognize his guilt. He transfers all his hate into the heart of the man he hates. He turns reality inside out. It is this terrorism of colonialism which the revolutionaries of this century have exposed and raised their fists to halt. "Under the mask of democracy," Ho Chi Minh writes, "French imperialism has transplanted in the country of Annam the cursed system of the Middle Ages . . . the Annamese peasant is crucified by the bayonet of capitalist civilization at the cross of prostituted Christianity." In the essay "The Glories of French Civilization" he describes the daily injustices and brutalities inflicted on the peasant:

> Colonial custom has it that every native, regardless of rank, age and sex, must humbly bow to a European. In Indo-China, Madagascar and other colonies, the native people are manhandled, beaten and jailed for having overlooked this mark of respect due to the prestige of the civilizers.

Corruption and inequality are drilled deep into the colonial society Ho knows:

> French citizens serve eighteen months in the army while the colonial people are compelled to serve three or four years with the flag under whose folds spirits, opium, corvées, porterage, native status and exploitation are introduced into their countries. While the natives are exiled, deported and jailed on flimsy pretexts, planters and administrators accused of assassination, bribery, dereliction of duty and theft enjoy a brilliant career.

Thousands of miles away in another colonial land—Cuba—Fidel Castro observed economic backwardness, illiteracy and disease bequeathed to the people by Amerikan rule. "What did the Revolution find when it came to power in Cuba?" Fidel asked. He answers:

> The Revolution found that 600,000 able Cubans were unemployed—as many, proportionately, as were unemployed in the United States at the time of the great depression . . . three million out of a population of somewhat over six million did not have electric lights . . . three and a half million out of a total of slightly less than six million lived in huts, shacks, and slums, without the slightest sanitary facilities.

Nowhere in Cary's *The Case for African Freedom* do we listen to an account of the curse of underdevelopment placed on Nigeria, the corruption deposited by England, the tribal factionalism generated by British colonial officials. Cary wants to end ignorance, sickness, poverty, but he believes that the "duty lies still upon the imperial peoples of Britain, of the United States" to see that this is accomplished. He closes his eyes to the work of the revolution in ending poverty, illiteracy and starvation. "The ideal state," he writes, is "the highly complex modern state, like the U.S.A." But to the colonial peoples of the world the United States is not and has not been the ideal state. It has been the monster state. In 1924 in the essay "Lynching" Ho Chi Minh wrote:

> It is well known that the Black race is the most oppressed and most exploited of the human family. It is well known that the spread of capitalism and the discovery of the New World had as an immediate result the rebirth of slavery . . . What everyone does not perhaps know, is that after sixty-five years of so-called emancipation, American Negroes still endure atrocious moral and material sufferings, of which the most cruel and horrible is the custom of lynching.

In the past half-century the Vietnamese have not come around to seeing the United States as an ideal society. Neither have the Congolese, the Bolivians, the Palestinians, the Chinese. The United States is certainly not the ideal state for the Cubans. In "The Second Declaration of Havana" Fidel spoke of the battle that was unfolding between the Cuban revolution and Yankee imperialism:

> Cuba represented the people; the United States represented the monopolies. Cuba spoke for Amerika's exploited masses; the United States for the exploiting, oligarchical and imperialist interests . . . Cuba for the nationalization of foreign enterprises; the United States for the new investments of foreign capital. Cuba for culture; the United States for ignorance. Cuba for creative work; the United States for sabotage and counter-revolutionary terror practiced by its agents . . . Cuba for bread; the United States for hunger. Cuba for equality; the United States for privilege and discrimination. Cuba for the truth; the United States for lies.

> Cuba for liberation; the United States for oppression. Cuba for the bright future of humanity; the United States for the past without hope . . . Cuba for peace among peoples; the United States for aggression and war. Cuba for socialism; the United States for capitalism.

As Amerika invades one country after another, kills Blacks and white students at home, more and more of the peoples of the world, including people in the United States, are seeing this nation as Fidel does. They are choosing Cuba, the road to revolution, colonial liberation, equality, bread and peace. It is this path which Cary did not look down. It is this blindness which makes *The Case for African Freedom* reactionary. Cary did not want a Third World revolution. But it was happening under his own eyes. He chose to fight against the Chinese revolution, the Cuban revolution, the Vietnamese struggle. It is the history of our time which makes Cary's study hollow. The movement of millions of people for liberation from imperialism passed over him. A terrible affliction. Poor Joyce Cary, hating Lenin, Ho, Fidel, Mao, Che—the men most loved by the peoples of the earth, the men who gave their lives in the service of humanity, to give birth to new men and new women, to see the day when no child would be hungry, no family homeless, no woman illiterate. They were fighting in Cary's interests too, but he did not recognize this. He betrayed himself by fighting against African liberation. Cary's sickness is the deadliest of all—to be cut off from the revolution, caught in the heart of a putrefying imperial monster. With his sense of the duty of white nations, he takes us back to Kipling's white man's burden. That is what neo-colonialism is: the white man's burden with a new name.

18

Works of Passion and Imagination

Gulley Jimson, the hero of Cary's novel *The Horse's Mouth,* is an artist and an anarchist. He is a cousin to Mister Johnson; less of a stranger but more of a rebel than Johnson. Jimson is a dropout. He starts out in life as a clerk; he wears a nice bowler, he has a nice home, a nice little wife, a nice, cute baby, a nice, ample bank account. He is a "nice happy respectable young man." But he leaves all that behind, chucks the job, the wife, the home, the bank account. He loses his facile happiness, his respectability, his youth. Jimson becomes a painter. He becomes a hustler, living from hand to mouth, fighting to stay alive, to breathe for another day so he can paint another picture. No nine-to-five job, no regular pat existence. He is the original Yippie, the father of Abbie Hoffman and Jerry Rubin. He is out to get it for free, to steal it. He is an outlaw in the eyes of Britannia. Every time he passes a telephone booth he pushes the coin-return button, hoping for a few coins. He will think nothing of ripping off an old canvas from a junk store if he can use it for a new painting; he will flatter a wealthy old lady to get some of her money so he can buy oil paints. He would steal his own paintings hanging in a gallery or a private collection in order to sell them and, with the money, rent a studio.

Jimson has a hard nose. He has been pushed around a lot

in life, and he pushes back. In doss houses and cheap boarding houses he looks out for himself and his mates, squeezes ahead of others in the line. Jimson gets into trouble; he annoys his rich patron, breaks the law, violates ordinances. Private property is not sacred to him. Your home is the studio where he can work. He has been in and out of jails and hospitals. The state, women, respectable people try to lock him up, tie him down, but he keeps moving, disrupting wherever he goes. Guerrilla theater is Jimson's specialty. "What you want to do with government," he says, "is to put a bomb under it every ten minutes and blow its whiskers off . . . blow off some of the old limbs." He is a terrorist with a sense of humor; not out to do structural damage, just blow off the whiskers.

To paint is his passion. If a fellow human being tries to stop him, he knocks him down. Jimson will not rest until every blank wall is covered, until every image and idea is drained out of his mind and embodied in color and shape before him. Art is subversive to the established order of things—that is Jimson's belief. He is half-serious, half-joking when he says that modern art is "Creeping about everywhere, undermining the Church and the State and the Academy and the Law and Marriage and the Government—smashing up civilization, degenerating the Empire." In order for him to paint, Jimson finds he must evade policemen, leave his wife, kick the official portrait painters in the teeth, scoff at bishops and threaten millionaires and ministers in Parliament. He does battle daily. He is given nothing. For everything he must push ahead diligently, like a lonely traveler walking against a harsh wind on a steep hill. Life is glorious, but life is also continually unsatisfactory. Gulley is unhappy when he is without his paintings, but he is also unhappy when he has them. Without socks on his feet he is cold and damp; with socks on his feet he is cold and damp because they are full of holes and he happens to be walking through torrents of London rain. He starts from scratch, reaching his hands into his empty pockets as he saunters down the Victoria embankment along the Thames. He is Adam the artist, naked before the world.

Gulley is a pub crawler. He knows the city, all its back alleys, its different neighborhoods. He walks down street after street in tattered clothes, using newspapers under his torn trousers to keep out the cold. He is a dirty old man who pinches women on their asses. Master of the word, he juggles sentences, spins off pun after pun, uses all the double entendres in the book. He could be a figure out of James Joyce's Dublin. But he is the artist who is closer to Leopold Bloom than to Stephen Daedalus. Cary's artist is neither isolated nor aloof. He does not live in any ivory tower. The "ineluctable modality of the visible" is no concern of his. He is an old man who is nearing his end, coughing, hobbling along, conscious of his body, his aching feet, his bad stomach. For Cary, the artist-hero is not alienated, living in an attic with his young mistress. Nor does he leave civilization behind and go off to the South Seas, like Gauguin. He stays at home. He is on the fringes of the bourgeois world. The sidewalks and the pubs of London know his gawky figure. He is an urban artist. He is lumpen. The street scene is his turf. Down and out.

We look at the world through Jimson's eyes, through the eyes of a painter. Cary himself was an artist, and he did sketches of Gulley and Sara and Gulley's paintings. *The Horse's Mouth* is the biography of an artist. It describes how the painter paints—his ideas, his techniques, his canvases, his palette, his patrons, his critics, his models, his relationship to artists of the past, his relationship to society. The novel is infused with Gulley's vision. The novel changed a great deal. In an early draft of the novel the story is told by an acquaintance of Jimson, a man who began as a painter, turned to newspaper work and ended up as a hotelkeeper. At first he thinks that Jimson is a faker, an imitator, but he sees a series of his works and is convinced that he is a genius.

The following is an early draft of the beginning of *The Horse's Mouth* which was later rejected:

> Last year two books were published mentioning a man called Jimson, an artist who had some distinction about ten or fifteen years ago but is now forgotten. I knew Jimson thirty years ago. We were in Paris together, the old Paris of the Fauves, of 1910; and afterwards in London. I remember him a noisy, dirty little man, always full of new theories of art and always taking up a new style. One moment he would say Raphael was the only man and paint like an oleolithograph; and the next he would be copying Van Gogh. None of his work was real; I mean it was all derived, mental stuff; we thought Jimson a faker; a chap who thought he could be a great artist simply by taking to a queerer style than anybody else and hitting the public in the eye with the biggest possible brush. He kidded himself, of course, as they all do, that he was a genius who worked in close collaboration with the Holy Spirit and that he hated the bourgeoisie. His game too, as I say, was to make a big noise and to do it by shocking his grandma.

An uninspiring beginning. It is a put-down of Jimson. We are not very interested in him. He is a fraud, an ordinary bum, a hack. The tone is detached; it is all something that has happened in the past and is being dug up for us to consider. Jimson is dead. The opening of the finished novel is entirely different. Now Jimson, the artist just out of prison, tells his own story:

> I was walking by the Thames. Half-past morning on an autumn day. Sun in a mist. Like an orange in a fried fish shop. All bright below. Low tide, dusty water and a crooked bar of straw, chicken-boxes, dirt and oil from mud to mud. Like a viper swimming in skim milk. The old serpent, symbol of nature and love.
>
> *Five windows light the caverned man; through one he breathes the air*

> *Through one hears music of the spheres; through one can look*
> *And see small portions of the eternal world.*
>
> Such as Thames mud turned into a bank of nine carat gold rough from the fire. They say a chap just out of prison runs into the nearest cover; into some dark little room, like a rabbit put up by a stoat. The sky feels too big for him. But I liked it. I swam in it. I couldn't take my eyes off the clouds, the water, the mud. And I must have been hopping up and down Greenbank Hard for half an hour grinning like a gargoyle, until the wind began to get up my trousers and down my back, and to bring me to myself, as they say. Meaning my liver and lights.
>
> And I perceived that I hadn't time to waste on pleasure. A man of my age has to get on with the job.

The narrator is an old man, a jailbird. He is an eccentric. He has an eye for colors and shapes. Distinctive. He puts his own stamp on everything he describes and paints. The detail is rich, the images expansive. Here is grotesque vitality; a man who delights in life. Gulley knows his William Blake. He quotes lines from "Europe: A Prophecy." *The Horse's Mouth* celebrates Blake. Gulley is the modern Billy Blake; he feels Blake in his bones, lives him, recites him all hours of the day. The one book Gulley insists that his son read is his volume of Blake's poetry. He studies Blake, goes to the Tate Gallery to look at his work. He even collects funds for a nonexistent Blake society; Blake is his hustle. Joyce Cary himself was inspired by Blake. Blake is his own teacher and hero. He reveres Blake the rebel, Blake the painter and poet, Blake the engraver and craftsman, Blake the visionary and mythologist. In Blake's poetry Joyce Cary and Gulley Jimson see reflected their own inner world and the world of their time. In 1956 Cary wrote of Blake:

> He is for me the only philosopher, the only great poet, who had a real understanding of the nature of the world

as seen by the artist . . . What every artist needs is both a general idea of the world and a strong sense of the individual . . . Blake . . . had both in the highest intensity. No one conveys more sharply the unique quality of the particular theory or event, no one is more consistently aware of the world character in which all particulars have universal significance and all events relate to final causes. No one more completely despised on one hand the worm's eye view of the materialist, and on the other, more successfully escaped the dazzled myopia of the idealist philosopher or transcendental poet confounding the limitless novelty of concrete living existences in some empty abstraction called spirit or the absolute destitute of form or significant action. For him, the thinghood of reality was as immediate as its energetic soul, its person; he knew them both in their eternal and pungent quality.

Cary's gloss on two lines from Blake's "Milton"

Giving to airy nothing, a name and a habitation
Delightful, with bounds to the infinite

pinpoint Blake's significance for him. He wrote that, for Blake,

. . . every individual character had its own nature, its "particular" shape, rather like a Platonic form. This was its essentiality by which it was eternal and belonged to the realm of the "infinite."

For Cary, Blake was the great reconciler. He recognized that "Hell was as necessary as Heaven to make a world. They had to make a marriage, so in every work of art we find the marriage of form and content, of technique and intuition, of thought and feeling." Gulley explains Blake's work in a similar way. "As Billy says," Gulley tells a friend, "there exist in the eternal world the permanent realities of everything which we see reflected in the vegetable glass of Nature."

Gulley captures the essential, unique quality of things and people. Everything stands out, radiating its own thinghood, its own glory, which distinguishes it from other things and, in turn, illuminates their distinct thinghood. Each individual person has his special way of seeing things, of relating to people, of defining his own experience. On almost every page of *The Horse's Mouth* you find a concern for both the vegetable, perishable world and the world of permanent realities. Here is Gulley's interior monologue—Cary using Joyce's techniques—his vision of London, and a glimpse of him striving to create "works of passion and imagination":

> Yes, I thought, all alivoh. Eve should be a woman of forty with five children and grey hairs coming, trying on a new velvet. Looking at herself in the glass, as if she'd never seen herself before. And the children fighting round in the dustbin in the yard. And Adam smoking his pipe in the local. And telling lies about his spring onions. Works of passion and imagination.
>
> There was a street market on the kerb. Swarms of old women in black cloaks jostling along like bugs in a crack. Stalls covered with blue-silver shining pots, ice-white jugs, heaps of fish, white-silver, white-green, and kipper gold; forests of cabbage; green as the Atlantic, and rucked all over in permanent waves. Works of passion and imagination. Somebody's dream girls. Somebody's dream pots, jugs, fish. Somebody's love supper. Somebody's old girl chasing up a titbit for the old china. The world of imagination is the world of eternity. Old Sara looking at a door knob. Looking at my old ruins. The spiritual life.

Gulley paints everyday people. He sees that everybody is a star. Every man is Adam and every woman is Eve. *The Horse's Mouth* is a novel about the beauty of old age, of bodies which are wrinkled and drying up, of crooked bones. In "The Circus Animals' Desertion" Yeats writes of his old age. Like Gulley's images of beauty, his arise from

> A mound of refuse or the sweepings of a street,
> Old kettles, old bottles, and a broken can,
> Old iron, old bones, old rags, that raving slut
> Who keeps the till. Now that my ladder's gone,
> I must lie down where all the ladders start,
> In the foul rag-and-bone shop of the heart.

The image incorporated in the title of the novel, "the horse's mouth," is meant to capture this feeling. What you get from the horse's mouth is the vision, the truth, an intuitive grasp of eternal reality. All of this out of the common, ordinary mouth of a horse. It is a colloquial, everyday expression Cary uses to express his aesthetics.

Gulley's friends are two old men, Plant and Ollier. They are working-class men, Londoners. Plant, now retired, was a cobbler, living in a world of tacks and heels, toes and worn-down shoes. But truth, beauty and goodness give Plant's life its meaning. An anarchist like Gulley, he is against all churches. He wants never to see, as Blake wanted never to see,

> Priests in black gowns . . . walking their rounds,
> And binding with briars my joys & desires.

Plant is a working-class intellectual. While he is repairing worn shoes and boots, he is thinking of Bunyan, Proudhon, Plato, Ruskin and Marx. He remembers the fate of Sacco and Vanzetti—Italian anarchists, immigrants in Boston and victims of Amerikan injustice. Among Plant, Ollier, Gulley and their friends there is the closeness of a gang: comradeship, loyalty, love.

The Horse's Mouth is also the story of Sara Monday and of Gulley's relationship with her. Here too, Blake's poetry, and especially the poem "The Mental Traveller," shapes our view of Sara and Gulley. Like Gulley, Sara is old, but we see her age contrasted with her youth, the remnants of her beauty still glowing. Gulley painted her in the nude when she was young. The paintings are now widely regarded as masterpieces. He remembers her as she was then, getting out of the bath, powdering herself, her soft skin, her breasts, her thighs. We see young Sara on the canvas beside old Sara in reality. There is an endless struggle between Gulley and Sara. She wants to possess him, to have him perform for her, to domesticate him. He hungers for her flesh, follows her about, panting. But he also wants to paint; when they are in bed making love, he is thinking of his canvas, reds, greens, blues, brushes. Sara both holds Gulley down and inspires him, brings him down to earth and pushes him into the eternal sky.

Sara is Eve. The eternal female. She is a queen. The love of the artist's life. Life with Sara is bittersweet. Sara is sensuality itself. Gulley says this about her:

> And there was something else about the old boa constrictor that I'd forgotten. Till that moment when she squared up to me and threw me her old smile. Herself, Sara. The individual female. The real old virginal fireship. Yes. The old hulk had it. Still. A spark in the ashes.

In the original description the phrases "Herself Sara. The individual female" did not exist. Cary added it during his revision. Again, it is this uniqueness, this herselfness, that Cary wants to capture in his characters. Between Sara and Gulley there is a continually changing relationship. Sometimes they are allies in the same war, fighting the same enemies. Sometimes they are enemies fighting for opposing armies. Gulley says to himself that "you were always yourself and Sara was always herself . . . there was an exchange of powers . . . you gave something and you took something." It is the deepest relationship in Gulley's life. They are lovers; between them there is a thrust toward equality—the toughness and the softness of giving and taking. Sadness and grief is a large part of the picture. Gulley and Sara have both seen their best days.

Gulley is continually frustrated in his attempt to paint. He has a vision of epic paintings, of murals covering vast walls. But the walls get knocked down. The creative energies are sapped, blasted away, enervated. Gulley never wins; there is no final triumph. He fights a never-ending battle. Cary tells us that we must laugh in the face of tragedy. It is our only salvation; the comic sense enables us to survive in a damned world. This is a grim kind of humor. In a prefatory essay to *The Horse's Mouth* Cary wrote:

> Anyone who has served in a war knows the man who is suddenly full of jokes on the night before an attack, even just before going over the top.
>
> Jimson, as an original artist, is always going over the top into No Man's Land, and knows that he will probably get nothing for his pains and enterprise but a bee-swarm of bullets, death in frustration, and an unmarked grave. He makes a joke of life because he dares not take it seriously. He is afraid that if he does not laugh he will lose either his nerves or his temper, that he will want to run away from his duty, or demand with rage, "What is the sense of anything in a world at war?" and either shoot the nearest officer or himself.

Gulley's sense of humor keeps him alive. There is a kind of heroism about this old man fighting to paint his pictures. He is a little man with passion and imagination, an Adam. But Jimson's and Cary's comic view means not perceiving the injustices of the world as Blake saw them and not advocating, as Blake did, the transformation of the world, the end of servitude. Gulley laughs; he has no sense of rage. There is nothing in Gulley's gallery to compare with the compassionate outrage of Blake's "London":

> I wander thro' each charter'd street,
> Near where the charter'd Thames does flow,
> And mark in every face I meet
> Marks of weakness, marks of woe.

In every cry of every Man,
In every Infant's cry of fear,
In every voice, in every ban,
The mind-forg'd manacles I hear.

How the Chimney-sweeper's cry
Every black'ning Church appalls;
And the hapless Soldier's sigh
Runs in blood down Palace walls,

But most thro' midnight streets I hear
How the youthful Harlot's curse
Blasts the new born Infant's tear,
And blights with plagues the Marriage hearse.

Cary neglects this London. It is not part of Gulley's world. *The Horse's Mouth* is set in the late 1930s, in the age of appeasement, during the Depression, the Spanish Civil War, Hitler's invasions. There were cries of hapless soldiers, blood running down palace walls, the mind-forg'd manacles of fascism, the poverty of the East End, but we do not hear these cries or see these sights in Jimson's London. It is run-down, seedy, but not oppressive for working people. Cary does not call us to battle to bring utopia on earth, to return Eden to England, as Blake does in "Jerusalem":

And did those feet in ancient time
Walk upon England's mountain's green?
And was the holy Lamb of God
On England's pleasant pastures seen?

And did the Countenance Divine
Shine forth upon our clouded hills?
And was Jerusalem builded here
Among these dark Satanic Mills?

Bring me my Bow of burning gold:
Bring me my Arrows of desire:

Bring me my Spear: O clouds unfold!
Bring me my Chariot of fire.

I will not cease from Mental Fight,
Nor shall my Sword sleep in my hand
Till we have built Jerusalem
In England's green & pleasant land.

Gulley is an anarchist. He hates institutions. But he is not quite a revolutionary. He does not envision a new world for man. Individualism is the key to his world. Everything he sees is unique, special; it has its thinghood. All his people are eccentric; they look like gargoyles. Cary's people are cut off from revolutionary movements. They conceive of themselves as separate, distinct. They are individualists. They laugh at rather than turn their guns on their oppressors. Cary does not believe that life will ever change for the artist. He will always have to eke out an existence. Things remain mostly the same in *The Horse's Mouth*. Cary calls it change, but it is really only movement. There is little development. Wherever you turn in the novel you find nearly the same things happening; they are merely in a different setting.

Jimson has his tribe. He deserves to be followed part of the way because he is not a dandy, because he is sly, funny, tough. The establishment has not recognized him. He is on the far left fringes of Bohemia, not yet into revolution. He has not broken through to the other side. He is still the petit-bourgeois individualist who has not been proletarianized politically. It is difficult to judge how fine an artist Jimson is, and that affects our view of him. We know him through his voice, his relationship to Sara and Plant, his ideas and his paintings. But we never see his paintings, so we are not able to evaluate them. Basically, we get the impression that Jimson is not a Cézanne or a Van Gogh, that he is not a genius. And in this way his stature is diminished.

We follow Jimson only part of the route because he stops short. He does not go the whole distance. Jimson does not join the political struggle of the thirties. He is not an anti-fascist. He does not go off to fight in Spain. His best works are "The Fall," "The Creation," "The Rise of Lazarus." None of his paintings match Picasso's "Guernica" or Diego Rivera's and Siqueiros's murals of Mexican history. The artists who have led men in this century have been cultural revolutionaries, communists, warriors against empire, men imprisoned for describing exploitation and oppression. Brecht, Neruda, Nazim Hikmet, Mayakovsky—these are the vanguard poets because they stand with the poor against the rich, the colonized against the colonizers, the oppressed against their oppressors.

The myth perpetuated by imperialist culture is that revolutionary artists are poor artists. Cary accepts this myth, and when he offers his portrait of the artist, he makes him a man who does not derive his creativity and originality from a vision of revolution, a sense of the corruption of imperialist society. What we need is more Brechts, more Nerudas, more Richard Wrights, more Sartres, more Mayakovskys, more Diego Riveras and Siqueiros—artists who work in joy for the revolution. Cary's conservatism trips him up. He admires the anarchist, but he feels he must be complemented, balanced off by the conservative, if society is to function. Instead of pursuing the jangling discord of antagonism and contradiction, Cary harmonizes. He balances out things and forces.

To be a writer and a political and cultural revolutionary, to pursue contradictions to the ends of the earth, to stand fast with the Third World against the powers of imperialism —that is to be the artist-hero in the twentieth century. It is to destroy the old order and build the new.

Selected Bibliography

General Social and Literary Criticism

Chase, Richard, *The American Novel and Its Tradition.* Garden City, N.Y.: Doubleday & Company, Inc., 1957.

Eliot, T. S.

Christianity and Culture. New York: Harcourt, Brace & World, Inc., 1949.

On Poetry and Poets. New York: Noonday Press, 1961.

The Sacred Wood, 7th Edition. New York: Barnes and Noble paperback, 1964.

Forster, E. M., *Aspects of the Novel.* New York: Harcourt, Brace & World, Inc., 1954.

Leavis, F. R., *The Great Tradition.* New York: New York University Press, 1963.

Orwell, George, *A Collection of Essays.* Garden City, N.Y.: Doubleday & Company, Inc., 1953.

Trilling, Lionel

The Liberal Imagination. New York: Viking Press, 1950.

The Opposing Self. New York: Viking Press, 1955.

Novels

Cable, George Washington, *The Grandissimes.* New York: Hill & Wang, Inc. (American Century Series), 1957.

Cary, Joyce

The Case for African Freedom. New York: McGraw-Hill Book Company, 1964.

The Horse's Mouth. London: Penguin Books, Ltd., 1961.

Mister Johnson. New York: Berkley Publishing Corporation, 1964.

Conrad, Joseph (All Conrad's works from the Dent Collected Edition, London)

Almayer's Folly and Tales of Unrest, 1947.

The Mirror of the Sea and *A Personal Record,* 1946.

The Nigger of the Narcissus, 1964.

Nostromo, 1964.

Notes on Life and Letters, 1949.

The Secret Agent, 1961.

Under Western Eyes, 1947.

Youth, Heart of Darkness, and The End of the Tether, 1961.

Forster, E. M.

Abinger Harvest. London: Penguin Books, Ltd., 1967.

A Passage to India. New York: Harcourt, Brace & World, Inc., 1952.

Goldsworthy Lowes Dickinson. London: Edwin Arnold Publishers, 1945.

The Hill of Devi. London: Penguin Books, Ltd., 1965.

Howards End. London: Penguin Books, Ltd., 1963.

Two Cheers for Democracy. London: Penguin Books, Ltd., 1965.

Kipling, Rudyard (All of Kipling's works from the London Macmillan Edition)

A Book of Words, 1928.

A Diversity of Creatures, 1952.

Debits and Credits, 1949.

From Sea to Sea, Volumes I and II, 1900.

The Jungle Book, 1901.

Kim, 1963.

Letters of Travel, 1920.

The Light That Failed, 1964.

Limits and Renewals, 1932.
The Naulahka, 1906.
Plain Tales from the Hills, 1896.
Puck of Pook's Hill, 1906.
Rewards and Fairies, 1921.
The Second Jungle Book, 1901.
Something of Myself, 1964.
Stalky & Company, 1899.
Traffics and Discoveries, 1949.
Wee Willie Winkie, Under the Deodars, The Phantom Rickshaw and Other Stories, 1926.

Lawrence, D. H., *Women in Love.* London: Penguin Books, Ltd., 1967.

Myers, L. H., *The Near and the Far.* London: Jonathan Cape Ltd., 1956.

Orwell, George, *Burmese Days.* New York: Popular Library, 1958.

About the Author

JONAH RASKIN was born in New York in 1942. He attended high school on Long Island and Columbia College in the city. He received his M.A. from Columbia University and his Ph.D. from the University of Manchester in England, where he lived for three years from 1964 to 1967. His first teaching job was at Winston-Salem State College in North Carolina. He is currently an Assistant Professor at the State University of New York at Stony Brook, where he teaches in the English Department. The enrollment in his class on contemporary literature in 1971 was 1200 students.

Mr. Raskin has written dozens of articles for the underground press and has also published articles in *New American Review, Scanlan's, University Review,* and the *Journal of Contemporary History*. For several years he was associated with Liberation News Service in New York. Jonah Raskin is the unofficial minister of education for the Youth International Party and was a member of the Yippie delegation to Algiers in 1970. He has just finished a novel about youth culture entitled *Freak Out.*